Accounting and Debt Markets

Accounting and Debt Markets: Four Pieces on the Role of Accounting Information in Debt Markets provides novel and up-to-date evidence on the role of accounting information in debt markets.

Companies and organisations worldwide rely heavily on debt markets for short, medium and long-term financing, and debt markets and financial intermediaries have significant effects on the real economy. Accounting information has various functions in debt markets, including inter alia, informing pricing decisions and credit ratings, determining the allocation of creditor control rights and establishing bank capital adequacy requirements. The chapters in this book provide illustrative discussion, analysis and evidence on the importance of accounting information in credit markets. The first of the four pieces reflects on how a conservative financial reporting system helps firms obtain debt funds and with better conditions, and why this is the case. The second examines the effects of accounting disclosure on credit ratings of private companies and shows that accounting information is useful for credit rating agencies. The two final pieces reflect on how banks should account for credit losses, and how regulators are tackling this issue.

The chapters in this book were originally published as a special issue of *Accounting and Business Research*.

Mark Clatworthy is Professor of Accounting in the Department of Accounting and Finance at University of Bristol, UK.

Juan Manuel García Lara is Professor of Accounting at Universidad Carlos III de Madrid, Spain.

Edward Lee is Professor of Accounting and Finance at the Alliance Manchester Business School, University of Manchester, UK.

Accounting and Debt Markets

Four Pieces on the Role of Accounting Information
in Debt Markets

Edited by
**Mark Clatworthy, Juan Manuel García Lara and
Edward Lee**

Routledge
Taylor & Francis Group

LONDON AND NEW YORK

First published 2021
by Routledge
2 Park Square, Milton Park, Abingdon, Oxon OX14 4RN

and by Routledge
52 Vanderbilt Avenue, New York, NY 10017

Routledge is an imprint of the Taylor & Francis Group, an informa business

British Library Cataloguing in Publication Data
A catalogue record for this book is available from the British Library

ISBN 13: 978-0-367-68889-9 (hbk)
ISBN 13: 978-1-003-13950-8 (ebk)

Typeset in Times New Roman
by Newgen Publishing UK

Publisher's Note
The publisher accepts responsibility for any inconsistencies that may have arisen during the conversion of this book from journal articles to book chapters, namely the inclusion of journal terminology.

Disclaimer
Every effort has been made to contact copyright holders for their permission to reprint material in this book. The publishers would be grateful to hear from any copyright holder who is not here acknowledged and will undertake to rectify any errors or omissions in future editions of this book.

Contents

Citation Information

The chapters in this book were originally published in *Accounting and Business Research*, volume 49, issue 6 (August 2019). When citing this material, please use the original page numbering for each article, as follows:

For any permission-related enquiries please visit:
www.tandfonline.com/page/help/permissions

Notes on Contributors

Mark Clatworthy, Department of Accounting and Finance, University of Bristol, UK.

Juan Manuel García Lara, Universidad Carlos III de Madrid, Spain.

Begoña Giner, Department of Accounting, Faculty of Economics, University of Valencia, Spain.

Noor Hashim, Department of Accounting and Finance, Lancaster University Management School, Lancaster University, UK.

Edward Lee, Alliance Manchester Business School, University of Manchester, UK.

Weijia Li, Department of Accounting and Finance, Lancaster University Management School, Lancaster University, UK.

Araceli Mora, Department of Accounting, Faculty of Economics, University of Valencia, Spain.

John O'Hanlon, Department of Accounting and Finance, Lancaster University Management School, Lancaster University, UK.

Michael J. Peel, Accounting and Finance Section, Cardiff Business School, Cardiff University, UK.

Fernando Peñalva, IESE Business School, University of Navarra, Barcelona, Spain.

Alfred Wagenhofer, Centre for Accounting Research, University of Graz, Austria.

Introduction

Mark Clatworthy, Juan Manuel García Lara and Edward Lee

Although companies and organisations worldwide rely heavily on debt markets for short, medium and long-term financing, the interface between accounting and debt markets remains comparatively under-researched. As the 2007–2008 financial crisis and its aftermath showed, debt markets and financial intermediaries can have significant effects on the real economy. Accounting information has various functions in debt markets, including, inter alia, informing pricing decisions and credit ratings, determining the allocation of creditor control rights and establishing bank capital adequacy requirements. Nevertheless, our understanding about the determinants and consequences of accounting information usage in debt markets is limited in many important respects.

Some of the key themes in this literature include debt contracting (Shivakumar, 2013), bank accounting (Beatty and Liao, 2014), public and private debt financing, and the formation of credit ratings. Interesting research questions include, but are not limited to: How does debt contracting affect the accounting choices of corporate borrowers and vice versa (Franz et al., 2014; Christensen et al., 2016)? How do changes in financial reporting standards (Christensen et al., 2009; Ball et al., 2015) influence the interaction between accounting information and debt markets, and to what extent do standard setters consider the needs of debt contracting parties? What are the determinants (Beatty et al., 2002; O'Hanlon, 2013) and consequences (Ahmed et al., 2006; Beatty and Liao, 2011) of banks' accounting choices? How does the interaction between accounting information and debt markets affect the real activities of corporate borrowers (García Lara et al., 2016)? How do credit ratings (Kraft, 2015; Jung et al., 2016) and auditors (Kanagaretnam et al., 2010) affect the role of accounting information in debt markets? To what extent is the relationship between accounting information and debt markets influenced by the unique institutional environment of emerging economies (Chen et al., 2010) and by socio-political differences around the world (Kanagaretnam et al., 2014)? What is the impact of the financial crisis of 2007–2008 and economic cycles on the financial reporting of banks and corporate borrowers, and vice versa (Laux and Leuz, 2009; Lang and Maffett, 2011)? What roles do debt markets play in influencing the implementation and reporting of socially responsible practices (O'Sullivan and O'Dwyer, 2015)?

This book includes the four articles from the *Accounting and Business Research* special issue on "Accounting and Debt Markets" (2019). In Chapter 1, Peñalva and Wagenhofer provide a review of the theoretical and empirical literature on accounting conservatism when financial reporting information is used for debt contracting purposes. They offer important insights into the key findings, research designs and possible future research directions, concluding that there is overwhelming support for the view that conservative accounting plays a useful role in debt contracting. In Chapter 2, Peel examines the effects of accounting disclosure on the credit ratings of private companies. He provides evidence of an inverse relationship between accounting disclosure and credit scores, suggesting that financial reporting information is relevant for credit rating agencies. Hashim, Li, and O'Hanlon in Chapter 3 offer an overview of the development of proposals and standards from 2009 to 2016 associated with accounting for credit losses. They highlight important issues and challenges facing standard setters such as the Financial Accounting Standards Board (FASB) and the International Accounting Standards Board (IASB), noting that it is unlikely that any *ex-ante* acceptable method of accounting for credit-loss impairment would have significantly mitigated the effects of a shock of the magnitude that occurred in the financial crisis. Finally, in Chapter 4, Giner and Mora complement Hashim et al.'s chapter in this volume by further discussing the implications of the expected loss approach and how they relate to the notions of accounting conservatism and earnings management. We believe that these articles provide excellent reflections of contemporary research on the role of accounting information in debt markets. As such, this book can serve as an important reference for academic researchers, as well as students who are interested in the relevant topic area.

Mark Clatworthy, University of Bristol, UK

Juan Manuel García Lara, Universidad Carlos III,

Spain

Edward Lee, University of Manchester, UK

References

Ahmed, A., Kilic, E., and Lobo, G. 2006. Does recognition versus disclosure matter? Evidence from value-relevance of banks' recognized and disclosed derivative financial instruments. *Accounting Review* 81(3), 567–588.

Ball, R., Li, X., and Shivakumar, L. 2015. Contractibility and transparency of financial statement information prepared under IFRS: Evidence from debt contracts around IFRS adoption. *Journal of Accounting Research* 53(5), 915–963.

Beatty, A., Ke, B., and Petroni, K. 2002. Earnings management to avoid earnings declines across publicly and privately held banks. *Accounting Review* 77(3), 547–570.

Beatty, A. and Liao, S. 2011. Do delays in expected loss recognition affect banks' willingness to lend? *Journal of Accounting and Economics* 52(1), 1–20.

Beatty, A. and Liao, S. 2014. Financial accounting in the banking industry. A review of the empirical literature. *Journal of Accounting and Economics* 58(2–3), 339–383.

Chen, H., Chen, J., Lobo, G., and Wang, Y. 2010. Association between borrower and lender state ownership and accounting conservatism. *Journal of Accounting Research* 48(5), 973–1014.

Christensen, H., Lee, E., and Walker, M. 2009. Do IFRS reconciliations convey information? The effect of debt contracting. *Journal of Accounting Research* 47(5), 1167–1199.

Christensen, H., Nikolaev, V., and Wittenberg-Moerman, R. 2016. Accounting information in financial contracting: The incomplete contract theory perspective. *Journal of Accounting Research* 54(2), 397–435.

Franz, D., Hassabelnaby, H., and Lobo, G. 2014. Impact of proximity to debt covenant violation on earnings management. *Review of Accounting Studies* 19(1), 473–505.

García Lara, J. M., García Osma, B., and Peñalva, F. 2016. Accounting conservatism and firm investment efficiency. *Journal of Accounting and Economics* 61(1), 221–238.

Giner, B. and Mora, A. 2019. Bank loan loss accounting and its contracting effects: The new expected loss models. *Accounting and Business Research* 49(6), 726–752.

Hashim, N., Li, Weija, and O'Hanlon, J. 2019. Reflections on the development of the FASB's and IASB's expected-loss methods for accounting for credit losses. *Accounting and Business Research* 49(6), 682–725.

Jung, B., Sivaramakrishnan, K., and Soderstrom, N. 2016. When do stock analysts find bond rating changes informative? *Accounting and Business Research* 46(1), 3–30.

Kanagaretnam, K., Krishnan, G., and Lobo, G. 2010. An empirical analysis of auditor independence in the banking industry. *Accounting Review* 85(6), 2011–2046.

Kanagaretnam, K., Lim, C., and Lobo, G. 2014. Influence of national culture on accounting conservatism and risk taking in the banking industry. *Accounting Review* 89(3), 1115–1149.

Kraft, P. 2015. Do rating agencies cater? Evidence from rating-based contracts. *Journal of Accounting and Economics* 59(2–3), 264–283.

Lang, M. and Maffett, M. 2011. Transparency and liquidity uncertainty in crisis periods. *Journal of Accounting and Economics* 52(2–3), 101–125.

Laux, C. and Leuz, C. 2009. The crisis of fair-value accounting: Making sense of the recent debate. *Accounting, Organizations and Society* 34(6–7), 826–834.

O'Hanlon, J. 2013. Did loan-loss provisions by UK banks become less timely after implementation of IAS 39? *Accounting and Business Research* 43(3), 225–258.

O'Sullivan, N. and O'Dwyer, B. 2015. The structuration of issue-based fields: Social accountability, social movements, and the Equator Principles issue-based field. *Accounting, Organizations and Society* 43, 33–55.

Peel, M. 2019. The impact of filing micro-entity accounts and the disclosure of reporting accountants on credit scores: An exploratory study. *Accounting and Business Research* 49(6), 648–681.

Peñalva, F. and Wagenhofer, A. 2019. Conservatism in debt contracting: Theory and empirical evidence. *Accounting and Business Research* 49(6), 619–647.

Shivakumar, L. 2013. The role of financial reporting in debt contracting and in stewardship. *Accounting and Business Research* 43(4), 362–383.

Conservatism in debt contracting: theory and empirical evidence[†]

FERNANDO PENALVA ⓘ and ALFRED WAGENHOFER ⓘ

This paper surveys both the theoretical and the empirical archival literature on conservatism when accounting information is used for debt contracting. The theoretical literature shows mixed results whether conservative accounting is desirable, which depends on the underlying agency problem, the information available, and the contracting space. The empirical literature takes a more holistic view in measuring the degree of conservatism. It studies a broad array of possible effects of conservatism in debt financing, but also beyond. The results overwhelmingly support the view that conservatism plays a useful role in debt contracting, although there are also some mixed results. We describe key results and empirical designs, and we provide suggestions for future research.

1. Introduction

Conservatism is one of the most important features of accounting. It has been present well before the advent of legal innovations such as limited liability of equity, widespread litigation, standard setting and regulation, auditing, stock exchanges, public debt and fractional ownership of equity, which are the bases for the other explanations of conservatism: contracting, litigation, taxation and regulation (Watts and Zimmerman, 1986; Basu, 1997; Ball, 2001; Watts 2003a). Among these many explanations for the existence of conservatism, its usefulness in debt contracting is one of the oldest and probably the strongest (Ball, Robin, and Sadka, 2008).[1]

This paper surveys both the theoretical and the empirical archival literature on conservatism when accounting information is used for debt financing. The theoretical literature shows mixed results on whether conservative accounting is desirable, depending on the underlying agency problem, the information available, and the contracting space. The empirical literature

[†]This paper is based on our contributions to the 'Accounting and Business Research Special Issue Symposium: The Role of Accounting Information in Debt Markets' at the Annual Congress 2017 of the European Accounting Association.

overwhelmingly supports the view that conservatism plays a useful role in debt contracting, although there are some mixed results. Theory and empirical results are not always in line because of different research approaches: theory usually singles out a specific economic setting to derive benefits and costs of conservatism, whereas empirical research has to deal with the wide set of possible different effects embedded in the data. Theory work can benefit from the rich settings studied by empirical research and the insights in economically significant effects; and empirical work can benefit from theory in developing more specific predictions, which allows for better empirical research designs.

Prior survey papers on conservative accounting include, among others, Watts (2003a, 2003b), Beatty, Weber, and Yu (2008), Armstrong, Guay, and Weber (2010), Ewert and Wagenhofer (2011), Mora and Walker (2015), Ruch and Taylor (2015), Shivakumar (2013), and Zhong and Li (2017). Some of them discuss potential benefits of conservatism generally, whereas this paper focuses on how conservatism facilitates debt contracting. Most surveys provide little coverage of the analytical literature, but are geared towards reporting results of empirical research. This paper combines these two streams of research because we believe both provide fundamental insights from different angles and can benefit from each other.

The aim of this paper is not to give a comprehensive survey of the large literature related to conservatism in debt contracting, but to focus on what we, in our opinion, view as important findings.

2. Defining accounting conservatism

Conservatism (or prudence) is a key characteristic of accounting systems, going back for centuries. Sterling (1967, p. 110) claims that conservatism is 'the most ancient and probably the most pervasive principle of accounting valuation.' Maltby (2000) traces prudence in accounting back to one of the bourgeois virtues in the Middle Ages. Conservatism reflects the accountants' rule of 'anticipate no profits but anticipate all losses' (Bliss, 1924).

The previous framework of the IASC defined prudence in a similar way: 'Prudence is the inclusion of a degree of caution in the exercise of the judgements needed in making the estimates required under conditions of uncertainty, such that assets or income are not overstated and liabilities or expenses are not understated' (IASC, 1989, para. 37). In an overhaul of their frameworks, the IASB and the FASB decided to eliminate prudence from the qualitative characteristics (IASB, 2010; FASB, 2010). The rationale is that a conservative bias prevents accounting numbers from being neutral and, thus, representationally faithful. Recently, the IASB Conceptual Framework reintroduced prudence in a specific form: 'Prudence is the exercise of caution when making judgements under conditions of uncertainty' (IASB 2018, para. 2.16) and explains that prudence does not imply a need for asymmetry towards downward biased equity, arguing that 'such asymmetry is not a qualitative characteristic of useful financial information' (IASB 2018, para. 2.17). The FASB did not follow that. Nevertheless, current IFRS and US GAAP – as well as the accounting standards of most countries – include conservative asymmetric requirements and there is no sign that they will be abandoned in the near future. Barker (2015) lists the main instances of conservatism in the IFRSs.[2]

Accounting research distinguishes two forms of conservatism: conditional and unconditional conservatism (Beaver and Ryan, 2005; Ball and Shivakumar, 2005). Conditional conservatism involves the timelier recognition in earnings of unrealised losses than of unrealised gains. Recognition is conditional on the receipt of news and the timeliness of recognition is conditional on the content of the news received. When news is sufficiently bad, conditional conservatism requires timely incorporation of this information in earnings, whereas the information in good news is not incorporated in earnings until it is realised. Alternatively, bad news is recorded even if it is still uncertain, whereas recognition of good news requires a higher degree of verification.

Examples of conditional conservatism are goodwill impairment, long-lived assets impairment, measurement of inventory at the lower of cost or market, and recognition of provisions for expected losses but no recognition of expected gains. In other words, under conditionally conservative reporting, contemporaneous earnings incorporate in a timelier manner bad news information about firm value than good news information. Basu (1997) was the first to formalise this construct even though he did not refer to it as conditional conservatism.

Unconditional conservatism involves the predetermined understatement of assets and overstatement of liabilities regardless of the actual value of those assets and liabilities. Examples of unconditional conservatism are the immediate expensing of research and development expenditures, the non-recognition of internally generated intangibles and internally originated goodwill, accelerated depreciation independent of the loss in capacity, and LIFO inventory valuation. This form of conservatism is news-independent and introduces a downward bias of net assets of an unknown amount in the reported accounting numbers. Consequently, it suppresses information about the value of assets or liabilities that arises over time (Ball and Shivakumar, 2005).

Accounting research generally views conditional conservatism as useful and unconditional conservatism as undesirable. The reason is that conditional conservatism provides some new information in a timelier manner, whereas unconditional conservatism is uninformative. It should be noted, though, that conditional conservatism also suppresses information because it asymmetrically conveys only bad, but not good news.[3] Going a step further, full disclosure of news of any kind would seem to be even more desirable (Guay and Verrecchia, 2006). This argument underlies the use of fair value measurement in financial accounting, particularly for financial instruments. However, concerns about misaligned management incentives and other undesirable economic consequences of fair value measurement are considered important enough so as to suppress the recognition of uncertain favourable news.

This is not to claim that unconditional conservatism is strictly non-useful. For example, it can effectively restrict distribution of dividends, facilitate the design of debt contracts or can be used as a commitment device to less disclosure of information if more transparency can trigger unfavourable economic outcomes. However, evidence suggests that unconditional conservatism is unlikely to play a significant role in debt contracting. For example, Ball, Robin, and Sadka (2008) find that neither balance-sheet-based nor income-statement-based measures of unconditional conservatism are related to the importance of debt markets and Sunder, Sunder, and Zhang (2018) find that unconditional conservatism does not improve contracting efficiency. To understand this, consider the case of depreciation. Accelerated depreciation is considered a form of unconditional conservatism, including its extreme form when internally developed assets, such as research and development or advertising, are not capitalised. Lev and Sougiannis (1996) show that capitalised and subsequently amortised research and development is value relevant and associated with current and future stock returns. Sunder et al. (2018) construct measures of unconditional conservatism that take into account research and development and advertising following Penman and Zhang (2002). They find that none of these measures is associated with reduced borrowing costs (spreads), unlike measures of conditional conservatism.[4] This does not imply that firms' use of accelerated depreciation is uninformative or that changes in depreciation rates do not convey information about the use of assets or future capital expenditures. Yet the lack of timeliness of accounting information due to this form of conservatism appears to attenuate its usefulness in efficient debt contracting. That is a possible reason that accounting research to date has been unable to identify a useful role of depreciation (unconditional conservatism) in debt contracting.

Unconditional and conditional conservatism are not independent of each other. Unconditional conservatism can preempt conditional conservatism: assets unconditionally written down (e.g. expensed research and development) cannot be further written down conditional on unfavourable news, so the firm will appear to be less conditionally conservative. This interdependence causes a negative association between conditional conservatism and unconditional conservatism, even though these two types of conservatism are conceptually distinct. Acknowledging this effect is important for empirical studies across jurisdictions that require more or less unconditional conservatism.

While accounting standards include requirements for conservative accounting, management has room for discretion as to what extent it can report more or less conservatively. While conditional conservatism requires judgment, e.g. regarding the existence of a trigger for impairment, unconditional conservatism can require judgment as well, e.g. when accounting standards contain criteria for recognition or full expensing of development costs.

In this paper, we focus on conditional conservatism because it is the type of conservatism with more contracting value (Watts and Zimmerman, 1986; Basu, 1997; Ball, 2001; Watts, 2003a; Ball and Shivakumar, 2005; Ball, Robin, and Sadka, 2008; Sunder, Sunder, and Zhang, 2018, among many others) and, consequently, it has received most attention in the literature. Following the empirical literature, we use the terms conditional conservatism, conservatism, timeliness of loss recognition, asymmetric timely loss recognition, and financial reporting conservatism interchangeably, unless otherwise indicated.

3. Role of conservative accounting in debt contracts

Conservatism is considered an efficient contracting mechanism, particularly in debt settings (Watts and Zimmerman, 1986; Watts, 2003a; Kothari, Ramanna, and Skinner, 2010). The typical argument is that lenders demand timely information about the performance of borrowers. This information must be observable and contractible to the parties. Therefore, lenders are not interested in difficult-to-verify information about future cash inflows; they prefer expected future gains not to be included in reported earnings and asset values until they are realised. In contrast, they prefer earnings and asset values that incorporate difficult-to-verify expected losses because negative information can act as a timely trigger to increase monitoring and even to take control of the borrowing firm in the most serious cases.

The intuition for this asymmetric preference for timely recognition of losses, but not gains, is that lenders have an asymmetric return function: at maturity of the loan, if a borrower's net assets are worth more than the value of the loan, the lender receives just the principal and the interest but nothing more, regardless of how high the value of net assets may be. On the other hand, when the net assets are less than the value of the loan, the firm enjoys protection by limited liability, and the lender receives less than the contracted amount. The shareholders of the firm hold a corresponding call option as they profit when investments are successful, but lose not more than their equity when investments are unsuccessful. This situation creates a classic conflict of interests between shareholders and debtholders. In this survey, we do not touch the more general question of why a firm relies on debt financing in the first place, but take as given that firms want to raise debt capital.

A complementary explanation for the timelier recognition of losses with respect to gains in conservative accounting numbers stems from the strategic disclosure literature (Verrecchia, 1983; 1990). Managers typically have incentives to disclose good news and withhold bad news, if disclosure is costly or it is uncertain whether firms possess news. Empirical evidence confirms this fact (Kothari, Shu, and Wysocki, 2009). Non-disclosure creates uncertainty about firm value. Contracting parties are aware of managers' self-interest and price protect: lenders demand higher interest rates for borrowings and equity investors discount the stock price of the firm. Managers can reduce this discount for uncertainty by committing to recognise bad news in earnings in a timely manner, thus complementing their voluntary disclosure of good news. This results in lower uncertainty and higher firm value (Guay and Verrecchia, 2018).

The main function of debt contracts is to mitigate the conflict of interests between share-holders and debtholders. Typical instruments are monitoring and detailed contracts. Accounting conservatism can be an efficient mechanism that aids monitoring because it advances the recognition of bad news, acting in this way as an early warning signal. In some cases, monitoring and conservatism can act as substitutes (Erkens, Subramanyam, and Zhang, 2014). We discuss this later in the paper.

As a minimum, debt contracts specify the principal amount, the interest rate, and the maturity; most contracts include further requirements, such as warranties, collaterals, default and remedy conditions, and covenants (Tirole, 2006). Debt covenants can also constrain the firm's actions or require the lender's consent before these actions are carried out, and they give lenders specific rights if predefined conditions are violated. Typical consequences of debt covenants violations are the transfer of control of assets or operations to the lender, immediate repayment of the loan, renegotiation of the terms of the loan, or automatic adjustments of interest rates (performance covenants). Many of these covenants are based on accounting numbers.

Christensen and Nikolaev (2012) classify financial covenants in performance and capital categories. Performance covenants are based on income statement numbers (e.g. interest coverage, debt-to-EBITDA) or operating cash flows. These covenants are typically used to monitor the ongoing performance of the borrower by allocating control rights ex post. Capital covenants are based on balance sheet numbers (e.g. net worth, leverage). Capital covenants protect lenders by requiring the borrowers to maintain a safety capital cushion within the firm, thus aligning borrower and lender incentives ex ante (Demerjian, 2017).

An optimal debt contract considers all these features and trades off their benefits and costs, including contracting costs. Public debt tends to use more standardised contracts, whereas private debt is more flexible and can be designed to accommodate the individual situations of the borrower and the lender (Nikolaev, 2010).

Summarising the discussion above, conservatism plays a crucial role in debt contracting for the following reasons.

- Lenders use lower bounds of the current value of the borrower's assets in the loan-granting decision and require an assurance that this asset value will be enough to recover their loans (Watts 2003a; Sunder, Sunder, and Zhang, 2018). Conservatism provides this lower bound. Göx and Wagenhofer (2009) show analytically that conservatism maximises the ex-ante probability of obtaining financing and that it can reduce debt costs.
- Lenders want to be informed about losses as soon as possible to undertake remedial actions. They value timeliness of bad news more highly than more precise news. Conditional conservatism facilitates the monitoring of debt contracts because it accelerates the triggering of debt covenants based on accounting numbers and the transfer of control rights to lenders (Smith and Warner, 1979; Ball and Shivakumar, 2005; Zhang, 2008; Nikolaev, 2010; Christensen and Nikolaev, 2012). Timely covenant violation thus becomes an efficient mechanism for lenders to exercise their contractual rights and restrict decisions by loss-making managers that could further erode debt quality (Ball, Robin, and Sadka, 2008).
- Ex ante, conservatism reduces the likelihood of asset substitution by mitigating firms' incentives to invest in high-risk projects (Kravet, 2014). Ex post, conservatism induces managers to abandon poor performing projects earlier (Francis and Martin, 2010).
- Conservatism limits available opportunities for successful manipulation of the accounting numbers included in debt contracts to expropriate lenders (Ball, 2001; Watts, 2003a; Chen, Hemmer, and Zhang, 2007; Gao, 2013).

A key question that underlies our previous discussions is whether firms can credibly commit to reporting conservatively. There are four arguments in favour of this possibility. First, debt market relationships are multi-period and deviating from conservative reporting is likely to adversely affect firms' and management's reputation (Diamond, 1991; Milgrom and Roberts, 1992; Ahmed, Billings, and Morton, 2002; Zhang, 2008; Nikolaev, 2010). Second, if the firm deviates from conservative reporting, litigation risk increases for its auditor, who will work hard to curtail such behaviour (Nikolaev, 2010; DeFond, Lim, and Zang, 2016; Amir, Guan, and Livne, 2018). Third, under the assumption that stockholders value the board of directors' demand for conservative reporting, the presence of independent directors is also a commitment mechanism to report conservatively (Armstrong, Guay, and Weber, 2010; Garcia Lara, Garcia Osma, and Penalva, 2009). Finally, the centuries-old presence of conservatism in accounting (Sterling, 1967), even without regulation, seems to indicate that firms can credibly commit to conservative reporting. The mechanisms through which firms can commit to conservative accounting include appointing independent directors, hiring high-quality auditors, encouraging monitoring by shareholders and debtholders, and inducing more analyst following (Guay and Verrecchia, 2018).

The role of auditors is particularly important in the monitoring of conservatism as it is predominantly an accounting recognition decision directly under their oversight. Theoretically, auditors tend to favour conservative accounting because that is a rational consequence of anticipating that managers attempt to overstate assets or earnings (Antle and Nalebuff, 1991). Moreover, litigation risk is asymmetric: it is higher if assets or earnings are overstated because investors are more likely to invest in a project that is falsely reported as profitable rather than unprofitable, in which case they do not invest, thus foregoing a case for litigation (Thoman, 1996). DeFond, Lim, and Zang (2016) analyse the relationship between client conservatism and auditor-client contracting. They find that conditionally conservative clients are charged lower audit fees, receive fewer going concern opinions and their auditors resign less frequently. This evidence is consistent with conservative clients imposing less engagement risk on their auditors. DeFond et al. (2016) also find that client conservatism is negatively associated with the incidence of auditors' litigation and clients' restatements. These findings validate auditors' ex ante assessment of the effects of conditional conservatism on their business risk. On the contrary, DeFond et al. (2016) fail to find any effect of unconditional conservatism on auditors' strategic decisions in responding to client engagement risk.[5] They conclude that auditors perceive unconditional conservatism as not affecting their business risk, which contributes to explain why unconditional conservatism has a small effect on debt contracting.

Related work further reinforces the role of auditing in debt contracting. Mansi, Maxwell, and Miller (2004) find that longer auditor tenure is associated with lower cost of debt capital, which may be explained by the positive relation between audit tenure and conservatism reported in Jenkins and Velury (2008). Krishnan (2007), using the collapse of Andersen in 2001 as an exogenous shock to conditional conservatism, finds that former Andersen clients report more conservatively under the new auditor. Amir, Guan, and Livne (2010) report evidence that auditor independence has increased post-SOX and that debt pricing has become more sensitive to auditor independence post-SOX. They also provide a model that links auditor independence to the cost of capital. Baylis, Burnap, Clatworthy, Gad, and Pong (2017) find increased demand for auditor assurance of debt covenants when contracts involve more complex adjustments. Finally, Amir, Guan, and Livne (2018) document that lower conditional conservatism is positively associated with abnormal audit fees post-SOX, which suggests that post-SOX auditors exert more effort when clients are less conservative and confirms the findings of DeFond et al. (2016).

4.   Theory and predictions

4.1.   *Modelling conservatism*

A key requirement of models is that one needs to specify what conservatism really means in terms of the characteristics of an accounting information system. An accounting standard can be modelled as a mapping of an (unobservable) future outcome x to an accounting signal y that is reported to decision makers.[6] Much of the analytical research that studies conservatism uses a binary information system to enhance mathematical tractability. Consider an investment that returns high output x_H with probability q and low output x_L with probability $(1-q)$ in the future. The accounting system provides early, but imprecise, information about the outcome. Let the signals be y_L and y_H. The accounting system can be described by error probabilities α and β, both of which are 'small' to lend an intuitive interpretation to the signals: Observing y_L suggests that it is more likely that x_L will realise, and y_H that x_H will realise. α is the probability of an understatement error and β that of an overstatement error. Figure 1 depicts such a setting.

An accounting system is more conservative the more lenient it is towards an understatement (α) than on an overstatement (β) error.[7] Assume the errors are parameterised by δ, so that the understatement error is $\alpha + \delta$ and the overstatement error is $\beta - \delta$, therefore conservatism increases with δ. In the extreme, it avoids overstatement for certain, so that $\beta = 0$, and accepts a higher understatement error in exchange.

The probabilities that the two signals realise are

$$Pr(y_L) = (1-q) \cdot (1 - \beta + \delta) + q \cdot (\alpha + \delta),$$
$$Pr(y_H) = (1-q) \cdot (\beta - \delta) + q(1 - \alpha - \delta).$$

Note that more conservatism (higher δ) strictly increases the probability of a low signal y_L and strictly reduces the probability of a high signal y_H. At the same time, higher conservatism makes the high signal y_H strictly more informative about the outcome and the low signal y_L strictly less informative. That is, the belief revision about the expected value of the investment from ex ante $E[\tilde{x}] = (1-q) \cdot x_L + qx_H$ will be stronger for a more informative signal. For example, in the extreme case of $\beta = 0$, y_H is a precise signal that x_H will arise, and we have $E[x_H|y_H] = x_H$. These two features, probability and precision of the signals, are important for the economic effects of conservatism that we discuss later.

In a binary signal setting disclosure of accounting information is a moot issue because by disclosing, say, only y_H lets users immediately infer that non-disclosure must be the occurrence of y_L. If there are more than one signals, or if there is a possibility that no signal arises, then conservatism can also be cast as a disclosure choice. For example, the measurement of an asset at cost with impairment can be captured so that if the signal y is less than a threshold, it will be reported

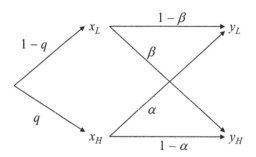

Figure 1.   Accounting system.

through a write-down of the asset; if it exceeds the threshold, the original book value will not be revised, so effectively the signal will not be disclosed. That does not imply that no impairment is uninformative. It is just less informative than an impaired value that let users infer the signal value. The information content of no impairment is that the signal value is greater than the threshold, which leads users to infer that the asset value is greater than the carrying amount.

Of course, the unraveling principle suggests that if disclosure is truthful and is at the discretion of management, then there will be full disclosure (Milgrom, 1981) regardless of the possibility that an accounting standard does not require disclosure as long as there are no further frictions. Accounting standards can be a commitment device for management to avoid disclosure of private information and the effect of the unraveling principle.

Interestingly, the asymmetric timeliness of recognising gains and losses that is inherent in the notion of conservatism, which is prominent in the empirical literature, has not been employed much in the analytical literature. An exception is Gao (2013). A reason may be that it would require a more elaborate timing and information quality structure. Moreover, there are few multi-period models of conservatism. Therefore, we know little about the effects of the catch-up of a conservative bias in subsequent years due to clean surplus. For example, Glover and Lin (2018) study a two-period agency setting and show that conservative accounting can turn out beneficial because it helps fine-tuning interperiod incentives of managers.

4.2. Information before contracting

Accounting information can be useful in debt contracting before writing the contract and during the execution of the debt contract. Most theoretical work studies the latter use in debt covenants. Little research considers how conservatism affect the lending decision in the first place, but simply assumes that the firm and lenders have the same information available at contracting. However, a firm that approaches lenders with an investment project is likely to have superior information about the quality of the project or is better informed about the value of the existing assets in place.

Göx and Wagenhofer (2009) consider a firm that needs a loan to undertake an investment project. The project has a positive net present value only if the manager exerts high effort. Due to moral hazard issues potential lenders will request a minimum collateral. The firm has an asset of uncertain value and the issue is what the optimal measurement rule of the asset is. Their measure of optimality is social welfare, which requires that all projects that are profitable in expectation be financed. Assuming competition among lenders induces them to bid for contract terms that will provide them with zero expected profit. Therefore, optimality reduces to the probability of funding the investment project given the required minimum value of collateral.

Suppose the firm obtains a signal $y \in [\underline{y}, \bar{y}]$ internally that provides information about the asset value of the collateral. Let the value of the asset for simplicity be equal to the signal. The decision rule of potential lenders is that only if y exceeds a specific threshold $\hat{y}$ required by the lender it will provide the funding. Intuitively, one would expect that the firm has an incentive to disclose all $y \geq \hat{y}$ and withhold signals lower than $\hat{y}$. This disclosure rule is a liberal (aggressive) measurement rule in the sense of higher of cost or value. In effect, this disclosure rule results in a probability of $\Pr[y \geq \hat{y}]$ that the firm obtains a loan.

Yet there is a strictly better strategy: Consider the reverse measurement rule, that is, report only small values y and do not report high values. For example, one such rule would be to disclose all $y < \hat{y}$ and withholds signals higher than $\hat{y}$. That rule is conservative because it represents a measurement at cost less impairment, but economically it replicates the liberal rule above: Non-disclosure will guarantee financing whereas disclosure will not. Note that the expected asset value on non-disclosure is $E[y|y \geq \hat{y}] > E[y]$. Now lower the threshold from $\hat{y}$ to a value

$y^N < \hat{y}$ so that $E[y|y \geq y^N] \geq \hat{y}$ still holds. Then the firm still receives the loan for non-disclosure but not for disclosure of low y values. In fact, Göx and Wagenhofer (2009) show that the optimal measurement rule is an impairment rule with an impairment threshold $y* < \hat{y}$ that is implicitly defined by $E[y|y \geq y*] = \hat{y}$. This rule maximises the probability of obtaining funding for the project given the collateral, which is Pr $[y \geq y*]$, and thus social welfare. Given this measurement rule is publicly announced, the firm has no incentive to deviate because it cannot gain but only lose.[8] Moreover, potential lenders hold rational expectations and are price-protected, so they are indifferent as to the measurement rule.

This result is broadly consistent with the argument by Watts (2003a) that lenders use lower bounds of the current value of the borrower's assets in the loan-granting decision and require an assurance that this asset value will be enough to recover their loans.

It should be noted that this impairment rule is not the only optimal rule, but there are others that aggregate low values of y. A special rule that results in the same economic outcome is one with a binary report, y_L, for signals $y \in [\underline{y}, y*)$ and y_H for signals $y \in [y*, \bar{y}]$. That is, the measurement rule collapses to a binary signal. The reason this is feasible lies in the fact that all the lenders want to know whether the expected value of the collateral is greater or less than $\hat{y}$ and their decision is either to provide a loan or not.

Göx and Wagenhofer (2010) consider a similar economic situation with a binary setting of both outcomes and signals. They find that the optimal measurement rule has $\beta = 0$ and $\alpha > 0$ (see Figure 1), which is equivalent to liberal accounting.[9] Intuitively, the optimal rule maximises the probability Pr(y_H) provided the lenders' expectation upon observing the high signal y_H is greater or equal to the threshold $\hat{y}$. This is achieved by making the precision of the low signal y_L maximal. While the economic intuition is the same, the way of modelling the accounting system and the underlying information system lead to different interpretations in terms of conservatism. This suggests that one has to consider the specific signal characteristics when deriving predictions from these models.

Another paper that considers a situation before debt contracting is Nan and Wen (2014) who study project financing through debt or equity. The cost of debt is the bankruptcy cost, that of equity the alternative return of the funds. They find that if the likelihood of good projects is relatively low, a conservative accounting system is preferable because it mitigates investment and financing inefficiency. If the likelihood of good projects is large, a liberal accounting system performs better.

4.3. *Information used in covenants*

Accounting information that arises after contracting but before maturity of the debt can be useful to revise expectations about the firm or its projects. Yet the lender is bound to the contract and can make explicit use of such information only if the contract includes covenants that depend on specific information (Smith and Warner, 1979). Such covenants are mostly about the transfer of control rights, e.g. the lender's right to terminate the loan early or to gain decision rights about the investment project, and the firm's ability to raise external financing. Other covenants are executed automatically, such as a change in the loan conditions, such as performance pricing. Finally, the parties can agree to renegotiate the debt contract, which is more common in private loan contracts than in public debt.

Theoretical work mostly considers covenants that allocate control of the investment project contingent on accounting information. Gigler, Kanodia, Sapra, and Venugopalan (2009) study such a setting, which we simplify to explain the results and the intuition behind them. Consider a simple project with a cost I that yields a positive cash flow X with probability p and nil otherwise in the good state that occurs with probability q. The cash flow is nil in the bad state. The expected cash flow is $qpX > I$ so that ex ante it is beneficial to invest. For simplicity, the firm must finance the investment by a loan. A lender charges a repayment $D > I$, where $D < X$ so that the firm can pay back the loan when the project turns out to be successful. After investment, information about the state arises, and the project can be liquidated at a return L. The option to liquidate generally increases the project value. Assuming $X > D > I > L > pD$, the lender would always prefer to liquidate if it has control. The firm's manager obtains a private non-monetary benefit $B > 0$ from continuing the project; if the project is liquidated, the firm receives nil because $D > L$. Therefore, the firm always wants to continue the project regardless of the information.[10]

Consider a covenant that shifts the control rights of the investment to the lender when an unfavourable accounting signal realises. Assume the accounting system is the same as in Figure 1. Two types of errors can arise. The signal is y_L but the state is good, then the lender obtains control and liquidates the project although it is successful. The expected loss is $-\alpha q(pX + B - L)$. If the signal is y_H but the state is bad, then the firm retains control and does not liquidate. The expected loss is $-\beta(1 - q)(L - B)$. Using the conservatism parameter δ as before, a higher δ increases the understatement error to $\alpha + \delta$ and decreases the overstatement error to $\beta - \delta$. Minimising the sum of the expected losses from the two errors, it is optimal to minimise the understatement error and accept the resulting higher overstatement error because the loss from understatement is greater than that from overstatement. The result is that liberal accounting is optimal from a welfare perspective. Intuitively, because the investment project has a positive net present value ex ante, the project would be continued without interim information. Hence, the unfavourable information, y_L, must be sufficiently precise to turn over this decision and make liquidation preferable. Higher precision goes hand in hand with a lower probability that y_L realises.[11] In terms of asymmetric timeliness the precision – and later recognition – is more important. Essentially, the insights from Gigler et al. (2009) suggest that a common argument for conservatism, that is, lenders get early warning and can take actions to protect their wealth, is incomplete because (i) early information is less precise and (ii) assigning control to the lender leads to over-liquidation. So there is clearly an underlying tradeoff.

Note that after contracting, the lender strictly prefers conservative accounting because it maximises the expected return to the loan (as $L > pD$). This conforms with conventional wisdom. Yet in a competitive lending market, the lender's benefit would be lost ex ante because the repayment amount D would be adjusted downward. Hence, the lender is ex ante indifferent, but the firm benefits from a liberal accounting system.

Jiang and Yang (2016) consider a similar economic setting with a continuous signal y. Rather than adjusting the error rates of the binary signals, they search for an optimal threshold value $\hat{y}$ that separates favourable and unfavourable signals. They find that if the private benefit B is low, the liquidation decision can be implemented, whereas for high B the threshold value $\hat{y}$ is set lower, which incurs an economic loss.[12] Reducing $\hat{y}$ is actually less conservative as we discuss above. Jiang and Yang (2016) also show their results for a more general financing contract, so the results do not depend on specific characteristics of debt financing.

Li (2013) allows for the possibility of renegotiation after receiving the accounting signal in the Gigler et al. (2009) setting. Renegotiation can be beneficial if one contracting party or both parties receive information that cannot be contracted upon in the original debt contract. Li (2013) assumes that the firm privately learns the type of the project but cannot verifiably disclose that information (Aghion and Bolton, 1992). Besides allocating control rights, the accounting information can also be used for renegotiation. Specifically, when an unfavourable signal realises, the lender can make a take-it-or-leave-it offer to the firm to forego liquidation for a higher repayment, which is designed such that only a firm with a good project will accept it. Conversely, when a favourable signal realises, the firm with a bad project can make a take-it-or-leave-it offer to the lender to efficiently liquidate the project. When renegotiation is costless, then its introduction induces efficient liquidation decisions regardless of the characteristics of the accounting system. Costly renegotiation retains inefficiencies but is beneficial so long as the cost is not extremely high (which resembles the Gigler et al. (2009) model). Li (2013) shows that for low renegotiation cost conservative accounting is preferable for projects with a relatively low probability of a high outcome; otherwise, liberal accounting is preferable. The accounting bias changes the expected renegotiation cost, which depends on the error probabilities.

Caskey and Hughes (2012) add another friction to the relationship between the firm and lenders, which is that the firm can select among different projects after obtaining the loan. The asset substitution to a lower net-present-value project benefits the firm at the (higher) cost of the lender ex post. The project selection is assumed to be non-contractible. Thus, the covenant not only induces a specific liquidation decision but should also control the asset substitution problem. Caskey and Hughes (2012) show that there is a trade-off between solving the asset substitution problem and efficient project liquidation. They find that conservative measurement, in the sense of a lower of cost or fair value measure, is preferable.[13] This result is in line with the argument that conservatism reduces the likelihood of asset substitution by mitigating firms' incentives to invest in high risk projects (Kravet, 2014).

Gao and Liang (2018) study costly contract renegotiation and its effect on debt covenants and earnings management incentives. While the covenant can reduce costly renegotiation, it aggravates earnings management; the result of the trade-off depends on accounting quality. Laux (2017) studies a setting in which the manager exerts effort to increase the profitability of an investment project and can manage earnings. While it seems apparent that a debt contract with a covenant to transfer control performs better because it increases efficient liquidation, it also induces earnings management. This possibility reduces the benefit of a covenant, but it still remains beneficial. Once renegotiation is allowed, the covenant can in fact perform worse. It reduces the room for renegotiation because the manager upon issuing a favourable report will not liquidate the asset even if that is efficient, as this implicitly reveals that the accounting signal was manipulated.[14]

Another argument for conservatism is that it limits available opportunities for successful manipulation of the accounting numbers included in debt contracts to expropriate lenders (Ball, 2001; Watts, 2003a). This result is apparent for conservative requirements that constrain upward revaluation. To illustrate, consider fixed assets that are measured at cost less impairment. If the carrying amount is the cost, then any earnings management effort to increase the value is ineffective as the carrying amount cannot be revalued over and above cost. In a binary information setting, the argument is more complicated as a downward bias through conservatism might increase the effort to manage earnings upwards to undo the downward bias. Chen, Hemmer, and Zhang (2007) and Gao (2013) provide models showing moderate conservatism mitigates earnings management because conservatism diminishes the incremental benefit of costly earnings management.

5.   Empirical testing and results

5.1.   *Empirical proxies*

Theoretical work clearly lays out the definition of conservative accounting and the use of accounting information in specific debt contracts. In empirical studies, it is difficult to disentangle the many different sources for conservatism and the potential uses (Christensen, Nikolaev, and Wittenberg-Moerman, 2016). Empirical research therefore takes a more holistic view of conservatism and uses proxies for conservative accounting that are mostly based on general observable features of the reported accounting numbers.

Most empirical studies use the model introduced by Basu (1997) as their proxy for conditional conservatism. Basu focuses on the asymmetric timeliness of the recognition of gains and losses, where conservatism induces an early recognition of expected losses but not of expected gains. Since recognised expected losses may be transitory, they tend to reverse more likely in subsequent periods than gains that are not yet recognised. That difference should lead to a lower precision – and market price reaction – for contemporaneous losses than for gains. To operationalise these ideas, Basu (1997) uses the following piecewise linear regression:

$$\frac{X_{it}}{P_{it-1}} = \alpha_0 + \alpha_1 \cdot D_{it} + \alpha_2 \cdot R_{it} + \alpha_3 \cdot D_{it} \cdot R_{it} + \varepsilon_{it}$$

where X_{it} is the net income of firm i in period t, P_{it} the market price of the firm, R_{it} the (unexpected) stock return, and D_{it} an indicator variable that takes the value of 0 for $R_{it} \geq 0$ and $D_{it} = 1$ for $R_{it} < 0$. If economic losses are recognised earlier than gains, then the coefficient $\alpha_3 > 0$. That is, the contemporaneous association between earnings and returns is stronger for negative returns (i.e. bad news) than for positive returns (i.e. good news) (Figure 2).

This empirical measure attempts to capture asymmetric timeliness and is based on the aggregate of the recognised transactions of firms, whereas analytical models typically consider a single transaction. Nevertheless, a similar piecewise linear concave function arises if one applies the formal definition of conservatism (as shown in Figure 1) and plots the market price reaction to a high or low signal. The reason is that high earnings are more precise and lead to a stronger market price reaction than low earnings. Analogously, if low earnings reflect less verifiable information than high earnings, the information content of low earnings should be less than that for high earnings, producing again a similar figure.[15]

Based on a similar timeliness difference, Basu (1997) and Ball and Shivakumar (2005) develop proxies for conservatism that do not rely on stock returns. These measures can be used for private companies, and they avoid assuming the market price is the benchmark for assessing accounting characteristics because accounting should inform markets rather than the reverse. The first one is a piecewise linear regression of the change in earnings regressed on the change of lagged earnings (Basu, 1997); the second is based on a piecewise linear regression of accruals on the cash flow from operations (Ball and Shivakumar, 2005). Givoly and Hayn (2000) construct two additional proxies of conservatism that are based on accounting numbers: the difference between the skewness of earnings and the skewness of cash flow from operations; and the accumulation over time of non-operating accruals.

Khan and Watts (2009) develop a firm-year measure of conditional conservatism (C_Score). It is based on the Basu (1997) regression and derives a conservatism score as a linear function of firm's financial leverage, size, and the market-to-book equity ratio. Finally, Callen, Segal and Hope (2010) use the return decomposition model of Vuolteenaho (2002) to develop a firm-

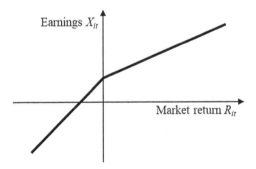

Figure 2.   Association between earnings and returns (Basu, 1997).

year measure of conditional conservatism that shows the proportion of the total shock to current and expected future earnings recognised in current year earnings.

Most empirical studies use Basu (1997) asymmetric timeliness or Khan and Watts (2009) C_Score because these two news-based proxies capture the properties of conditional conservatism (Ryan 2006) better than non-news-based proxies.

There has been a debate about the validity of the Basu (1997) measure of conditional conservatism. Some claim the measure is invalid (e.g. Dietrich, Muller, and Riedl, 2007; Givoly, Hayn, and Natarajan, 2007; Patatoukas and Thomas, 2011 and 2016; Dutta and Patatoukas, 2017), while others, such as Ryan (2006), Ettredge, Huang, and Zhang (2012), Ball, Kothari, and Nikolaev (2013a, 2013b) provide a number of counterarguments. It is beyond the scope of this paper to discuss the merits of each of the arguments in this debate but, in general, the vast majority of empirical studies support the view that accounting is conditionally conservative and that the observed cross-sectional and time-series differences in the level of conservatism are consistent with theory (Ball et al., 2013b). In addition, many of the studies validate their main findings using alternative non-Basu conservatism measures in their robustness tests.

In what follows, we describe empirical papers that investigate the role of conditional conservatism in debt contracting. In Section 5.2, we survey the initial studies that provide evidence on the association between conservatism for debt financing. In Section 5.3, we describe the literature that documents debt-contracting benefits of conservatism. In Section 5.4, we discuss identification issues not fully resolved by the initial group of empirical studies and survey the solutions provided by a second group of papers that provide additional support for the debt-contracting value of conservatism hypothesis. In Section 5.5, we describe some controversial evidence that challenges the accepted view that conservatism accelerates the triggering of debt covenants. Finally, in Section 5.6, we review papers that analyse the impact of fair value on the usefulness of conservatism for debt contracting.

5.2.   *Evidence on the association between debt financing and conservative accounting*

Many studies find a positive association between debt financing and conservative accounting. The reason can be either pre-contract or post-contract or both. More conservative accounting can provide better information about the state of the firm when it raises debt capital, or it can affect the accounting numbers used in covenants.

Ball, Robin, and Sadka (2008) analyse a large international sample of firms in 22 countries during the period 1992–2003 and use the size of debt and equity markets as a proxy for the demand for certain properties of accounting numbers. They find that the size of debt markets, but not of equity markets, is associated with more conservatism and conclude that conservatism exists more for its role in efficient debt contracting than to inform equity markets. By increasing the efficiency of debt contracting, conservatism makes debt a more efficient source of financing and, thus, is associated with larger debt markets. Ball, Robin, and Sadka (2008) research design is an association study, which cannot determine whether conservatism has contributed to the development of debt markets or, on the contrary, debt markets have driven the demand for firms to report more conservatively.

Beatty, Weber, and Yu (2008) provide evidence on the importance of debt in explaining conservatism in financial reports. They investigate lenders' use of conservative debt covenant modifications, usually referred to as income escalators, in the monitoring of debt contracts to understand why lenders cannot just achieve desired conservatism levels by adjusting downwards reported GAAP numbers used in contract calculations. They document that modifications exist but are not ubiquitous and are more likely when agency costs are higher. After controlling for agency costs and non-debt demands for conservatism, they find that lenders use contractual modifications in conjunction with conditional conservatism to meet their demands. These results suggest that lenders do not meet their demands for conservatism entirely through covenant modifications.

Ball, Bushman, and Vasvari (2008) study the pivotal role played by conservative accounting numbers in the optimal design of syndicated loan deals. In this type of debt instrument there is information asymmetry between the lead arranger and the rest of the syndicate members: the leader has more information about the borrower because it performs the due diligence and monitors the borrower's performance after the loan is granted. This informational asymmetry creates a demand for the leader to hold a higher proportion of the loan as a function of the level of adverse selection and moral hazard problems. Conservatism increases the contracting value of accounting numbers because they provide timely information about the borrower's credit quality. Ball et al. (2008) find that the proportion of the loan retained by the leader declines as a function of the level of conservatism. This negative relation is stronger when the borrower does not have a credit rating and when the leader's reputation is low. If there is a pricing provision in the contract, the likelihood of this provision being an accounting ratio, rather than a credit rating, is increasing in conservatism.

Chen, Chen, Lobo, and Wang (2010) analyse the impact of state versus private ownership of borrowers and lenders on the association between conservatism and lending using a sample of Chinese firms. They find that lenders to state-owned firms demand less conservatism because the risk of default of state-owned firms is lower than that of privately-held firms. This evidence indirectly supports the role of conservatism on debt financing. They also find that borrowers report less conservatively as the fraction of total loans obtained from state-owned banks increases because these banks have lower demand for assurance of net assets to cover loan repayments than non-state-owned banks. Finally, Chen et al. (2010) document that borrowers supply more conservatism when they borrow from banks with foreign ownership, which provides direct support for the debt contracting explanation of accounting conservatism.

Erkens, Subramanyan, and Zhang (2014) provide indirect evidence of the debt-contracting value of conservatism through the analysis of borrowers' monitoring by lenders. The debt-contracting value hypothesis predicts that the information asymmetry between lenders and borrowers will cause the former to demand more conservative reporting. The information asymmetry can be reduced if the lender can monitor the borrower more closely. In this case, it is expected that the lender will demand less conservatism. Erkens et al. (2014) find that when a lender has representation on the board of directors of the borrower, firms report less conservatively. A close examination of the relation between covenant intensity and conservative accounting suggests that board representation decreases lenders' reliance on conservatism-facilitated control transfers. Finally, through an analysis that uses relationship lending as an alternative proxy of lender monitoring, they also find that what drives this result is not the presence of an affiliated banker on the board but heightened lender monitoring.

In relation to the association between accounting conservatism and debt maturity, Khurana and Wang (2015) explicitly examine the association between debt maturity structure and accounting conservatism in private debt contracts. Their analysis is based on the argument that short-term debt maturity may mitigate agency costs of debt stemming from information asymmetries and suboptimal investment inherently present in debt financing, so the demand for conservatism should be lower for shorter debt maturities in the debt contracting context. Their study directly focuses on conditional conservatism exhibited in the case of short-maturity debt contracts, and the findings indicate that short maturity in private debt contracts is negatively associated with accounting conservatism.

Donelson, Jennings, and McInnis (2017) survey commercial bank lenders to assess how they evaluate and react to variations in financial statements quality, including conservatism. The majority of respondents indicated both that they evaluate financial statements for conservatism and that they view conservatism favourably because conservative firms commit to not overstate assets, which makes covenants more binding. These responses fully support the claims in the literature on the importance of conservatism for debt contracting. The surveyed lenders also indicated that they evaluate conservatism by examining conservative accrual patterns (e.g. timely write-downs and adequate liability provisions). For a borrower with lower than average conservatism, more than two-thirds of respondents said that they would often or always require a loan guarantee or impose more restrictive covenants. Surprisingly, less than 17% of respondents mentioned that they increase interest rates for loans to firms with less conservative financial statements. The Donelson et al. (2017) study concentrates on lenders who make loans between $0.25 and $50 million, in contrast to archival studies that analyse very large loans to public firms or very small loans to private firms.

Sunder, Sunder, and Zhang (2018) analyse the impact of balance sheet conservatism (i.e. conservative valuation of assets as a result of all methods of conservatism, conditional and unconditional) on the design of debt contracts. They find that a higher level of balance sheet conservatism in the borrower's financial statements is associated with lower loan spreads, less reliance on covenants (especially balance sheet-based covenants), and looser covenant slack. Balance sheet conservatism reduces lenders' downside uncertainty about the liquidation value of assets and facilitates ex ante screening of borrowers. However, borrowers with high balance sheet conservatism are constrained in their ability to be conditionally conservative to signal negative economic news in the future, which adversely affects the lenders' ability to monitor. Consistent with this latter finding, Sunder et al. (2018) also document that conditional conservatism is associated with lower borrowing costs only when balance sheet conservatism is moderate. The also document that unconditional conservatism is not associated with lower cost of debt. Their overall conclusion is that unconditional conservatism reduces the debt contracting efficiency of conditional conservatism because it reduces its monitoring value for lenders.

In summary, the conclusions of this set of papers strongly suggest that there is a positive association between debt contracting and accounting conservatism. Being simple association studies, they are unable to clearly identify the causal effects of conservatism on the different economic outcomes of debt financing (i.e. better credit terms, fewer covenants, easier monitoring, etc.). Notice as well, that the research designs used in the above papers cannot assess the relative efficiency of conservatism for debt contracting because this requires an analysis of the costs and benefits of the suppliers of debt.

5.3. *Contracting benefits of conservatism*

A large number of papers examine economic benefits of conservative accounting to the contracting parties. A particularly important outcome is the cost of debt. If conservatism is beneficial, firms that report more conservatively should exhibit a lower cost of debt. Several pieces of evidence support this observation. Zhang (2008) finds that conservatism is associated with reduced interest rates for bank debt, after controlling for several earnings attributes such as quality, persistence, predictability, smoothness, timeliness, and relevance. Wittenberg-Moerman (2008) documents that timely recognition of losses in the earnings of borrowers is associated with lower bid-ask spreads in the secondary trading of syndicated loans. She also finds that timely gain recognition, which makes earnings more informative about the performance of borrowers, is not associated with reduced bid-ask spreads. Ahmed, Billings, and Morton (2002) find that conservatism is associated with better debt ratings. All this evidence does not necessarily contradict the findings of Donelson, Jennings, and McInnis (2017) about interest rates being the loan characteristic less likely to be affected ex post by reduced conservatism. When lenders make the loan granting decision, they assign borrowers with low conservatism to higher risk categories, which results in higher interest rates. In addition, the results of Donelson et al. (2017) apply to smaller loans and may not generalise to public debt markets, where interest rates are the key metric over which investors have control.

Another contracting benefit results from acceleration of the transfer of control rights. Zhang (2008) documents that conservatism makes it more likely that borrowers violate debt covenants after a negative price shock and facilitates timely signalling of default risk. Timely recognition of losses enhances the efficiency of debt contracting because it mitigates lenders' downside risk. Haw, Lee, and Lee (2014) study a sample of Korean private firms that issue public debt and find that they become more conditionally conservative after issuance, as opposed to public firms. The effect is stronger when information asymmetry and credit risk are high. This evidence is consistent with conservatism enhancing contract efficiency in settings with ex ante high agency costs. Along the same lines, Franke and Müller (2018) find that timely loss recognition significantly increases following the issuance of private debt. The effect is stronger for debt contracts with performance covenants and when the prospects of the firm are highly uncertain. Their evidence is consistent with conditional conservatism increasing debt contract efficiency because it accelerates the transfer of control rights to lenders.

Beatty and Liao (2011) show that conservatism helps banks to reduce pro-cyclical lending in recessionary periods. Using a sample of banks during the period after implementation of the 1988 Basel Risk Based Capital Regulation and the Federal Depository Insurance Corporation Improvement Act of 1991 (FDICIA), they find that banks that are more conditionally conservative and delay less the recognition of expected loan losses, experience lower reductions in lending during recessionary periods and are less affected by the capital crunch effect.

Conservatism can also serve as a governance tool that reduces the agency costs of firms. Ahmed and Duellman (2007) find that the percentage of inside directors is negatively related to conservatism, and the percentage of outside directors' shareholdings is positively related to conservatism. Beekes, Pope, and Young (2004) analyse a U.K. sample and reach similar conclusions. However, the endogenous nature of the choice of the level of governance and conservatism prevents them from showing causality. Garcia Lara, Garcia Osma, and Penalva (2009) show that firms with stronger governance, measured as low anti-takeover protection and low CEO involvement in board decisions, exhibit higher levels of conservatism. They also find that the increase in conservatism in strong-governance firms is driven by the discretionary component of reported accruals. This evidence is consistent with strong-governance firms using accruals to accelerate the recognition of bad news in earnings. Additionally, they document that the direction of causality flows from governance to conservatism, and not vice versa, indicating that governance and conservatism are not substitutes. Lim, Lee, Kausar, and Walker (2014) discover that banks that recognise losses timelier exhibit higher prudence in lending decisions, as evidenced by higher spreads charged, after controlling for a series of bank, borrower and deal characteristics, as well as corporate governance and bank return dispersion. Their results are consistent with the beneficial governance role of accounting conservatism.

Conservatism can affect investment efficiency because it facilitates access to debt financing. Garcia Lara, Garcia Osma, and Penalva (2016) argue that conservatism improves investment efficiency because it resolves debt-equity conflicts, facilitating a firm's access to debt financing and limiting underinvestment. This increases the financing of low-risk investments that otherwise might not be pursued. Their empirical results show that more conservative firms invest more and issue more debt in settings prone to underinvestment and that these effects are more pronounced in firms characterised by greater information asymmetry. They also find that conservatism is associated with reduced overinvestment, even for opaque investments such as research and development. Balakrishnan, Watts, and Zuo (2016) study the effect of accounting conservatism on firms' investment during the 2007–2008 global financial crisis. They find that less conservative firms experienced a steeper decline in investment activity following the onset of the crisis compared to more conservative firms. This relationship is stronger for firms with higher financial constraints, greater external financing needs and higher information asymmetry. More conservative firms experienced lower declines in both debt-raising activity and stock performance. The evidence in these two studies is consistent with conservatism alleviating underinvestment in the presence of information frictions because it facilitates access to debt financing.

Conservatism can improve creditors' recovery rate in case of borrowers' default. Donovan, Frankel, and Martin (2015) find that creditors of firms that are more conservative before default, have significantly higher recovery rates and that this positive relation is more pronounced for default firms that violated covenants before the default. They also find that conservative firms have shorter bankruptcy resolution and a much higher probability of reemerging from bankruptcy. Conservatism thus contributes to preserve firm value and to reduce the downside risk of lenders upon borrowers' default.

LaFond and Watts (2008) study the argument that the contracting value of accounting information depends on its verifiability. Hard-to-verify financial reports create information asymmetries between firm insiders and external contracting parties, which increases agency costs. They claim that 'the role of accounting is not to report equity values, but instead to provide verifiable information useful for assessing alternative information sources on equity values and mitigating agency cost' (LaFond and Watts, 2008, p. 476). They also document that conservatism plays a positive equity-contracting role. Using a proxy for information asymmetry between managers and outside equity investors, they find that firms in settings of higher information asymmetry are timelier in the recognition of losses and that conservatism increases following increases in information asymmetries. Given that the information asymmetry between managers and equity investors is likely to be higher than that between managers and debtholders, these results complement the beneficial debt-contracting role of conservatism.

Conservative firms tend to make less risky acquisitions. Kravet (2014) documents that firms with timelier loss recognition make less risky acquisitions and that this association is driven by firms with accounting-based debt covenants. Managers of conservative firms are more prudent in their investment decisions because potential large losses can trigger debt covenants. These results show that conservatism decreases the risk that managers transfer wealth from debtholders to equity holders and helps explain prior literature findings that more conservative firms obtain lower cost of debt. However, these results cannot answer the bigger question of whether this prudent investment policy is optimal or whether it is an undesirable outcome of conservative accounting, implying that there must be other benefits to conservatism in that case. Moreover, managers' prudence may be the cause of both more conservatism and less risky investments.

5.4. Causal evidence of role of conservatism on debt financing

The proxies for conservatism are inherently linked to the economic characteristics and performance of the firm. This is so because conservatism proxies are usually based on accounting numbers, and the objective of accounting systems is to measure economic performance. Separating conservatism from the underlying economics is a challenge (Leuz and Wysocki, 2016) and makes it hard to establish causality, that is, whether higher lenders' demand for conservatism 'causes' borrowers to supply more conservatism. Changes in the demand for conservatism are likely also due to changes in the economic conditions of the firm that, at the same time, also affect the measurement of conservatism.

There are several approaches to establish causality. A typical approach is to identify settings in which an exogenous shock causes changes in conservatism without affecting firms' underlying economics (Leuz and Wysocki, 2016). For example, one might exploit mandatory changes that affect conservatism but do not affect the economic characteristics of the firm. The majority of the studies discussed above are association studies that are unable to identify the causal effects of conservatism on the different economic outcomes. In what follows, we discuss several papers that try to address this problem by identifying exogenous shocks or other forms of identification. One of the first papers that explicitly test for causality is García Lara, Garcia Osma, and Penalva (2009) who show causality of corporate governance for conservatism using a lead-lag analysis and an external shock to governance.

Gormley, Kim, and Martin (2012) analyse the impact of the market entry of foreign banks in India during the 1990s on the reporting conservatism of local firms. The entry of foreign banks is an exogenous shock that likely changed the incentives of local firms to report more conservatively without affecting firm characteristics (therefore, not affecting the measures of conservatism) and other factors that may also affect reporting policies. This shock increases lenders' demand for conservatism, which drives borrowers' incentives to be more conservative. The entrant foreign banks have less access to soft information about local firms and have to rely more heavily on information contained in firms' financial statements, so they are likely to demand higher conservatism. Foreign banks tend to attract larger, more profitable local firms in developing countries. This lowers the average quality of the rest of borrowers seeking domestic loans, which raises the demand of local banks for conservative reporting. Local lenders also try to adopt better practices of foreign banks and increase their reliance on financial statements in the lending decision and likely demand more conservatism. Gormley et al. (2012) find that foreign bank entry is associated with more conservatism and this increase is positively related to firms' subsequent debt levels. The increase in conservatism is concentrated among firms that depend more on external financing: private firms, smaller firms, and nongroup firms. Their conclusion is that exogenous changes in the banking sector that increase the benefits of being more transparent to lenders cause local firms to report more conservatively.

Jayaraman and Shivakumar (2013) use a change of antitakeover laws in certain states as an exogenous shock to the agency costs of debt to study its effect on reporting conservatism. Prior research has documented that antitakeover laws entrench managers, and this increases lenders' agency costs of debt (Chava, Kumar, and Warga, 2010). They find that the passage of antitakeover laws results in lenders demanding higher conservatism and in borrowers supplying more conservatism, especially for firms with higher debt-based contracting pressures, that is, firms with increases in debt between the pre- and post-antitakeover periods. However, they find no increases in conservatism in firms without debt-contracting pressures or in firms that increase equity financing between the pre- and post-periods.

Tan (2013) analyses the impact of the transfer of control rights to lenders after a debt covenant violation on the reporting conservatism of borrowers. He uses a regression-discontinuity design in which the assignment variable is the continuous distribution of the values of the ratios used in debt covenants, such as the current ratio, and the treatment is the transfer of control rights after violation, which jumps discontinuously when a covenant is violated. Tan (2013) finds that firms' financial reporting becomes more conservative immediately after covenant violations and that this effect is economically strong and persists for at least eight quarters. He speculates that lenders exercise their information acquisition and control rights after a violation by demanding more reporting conservatism. The results support this specific channel through which lenders influence borrowers' financial reporting. Tan (2013) finds that the increase in conservatism is more pronounced when lenders possess greater bargaining power, when firms' operations are more volatile, and when lenders put chief restructuring officers in place.

Aier, Chen, and Pevzner (2014) show a strong causal link between lenders' demand for conservatism and borrowers supply of conservatism to meet lenders' demand. They use a natural experiment provided by a 1991 Delaware court ruling that expanded the scope of directors' fiduciary duties to include creditors when a Delaware incorporated firm is in the 'vicinity of insolvency.' This ruling had no effect on financial reporting per se or in firms' characteristics. They predict that firms subject to the ruling are likely to significantly increase their accounting conservatism. This exogenous variation in supply allows them to attribute any post-ruling change in conservatism by near insolvent Delaware companies to increased lenders' demand for conservatism. They find that, in the period following the court ruling in 1991, conservatism significantly increased for near insolvent Delaware firms. The results indicate that, in response to their increased fiduciary obligations to creditors, directors of firms subject to the court ruling influence managers to adopt more conservative financial reporting. This result is more pronounced for firms with stronger boards, showing that the board is the channel through which the response to the ruling occurs; that is, higher litigation pressure leads the board to require managers to report more conservatively.

Martin and Roychowdhury (2015) use lenders' initiation of credit default swaps (CDS) trading as an exogenous shock to borrowers' incentives to report conservatively. Engaging in CDS trading reduces lenders' incentives to continuously monitor borrowers and also their demand that borrowers report more conservatively. They find that lenders that insure their borrowers' default risk with CDS demand less conservatism and reduce monitoring because their payoffs are less risky and asymmetric. Consequently, borrowers whose loans are CDS-insured by their lenders report less conservatively. The results are more pronounced when lenders' reputation costs of reduced monitoring are lower, when loan contracts outstanding at the time of CDS trade initiation contain more covenants, and when lenders in the pre-CDS period monitored more regularly. However, lenders' reduced monitoring and borrowers' lower conservatism open the possibility for borrowers to transfer wealth from debtholders to equity holders, for example, via dividend overpayments. Martin and Roychowdhury (2015) rule out this possibility arguing that borrowers will not engage in such behaviours because they expect lenders to be more intransigent in renegotiations in case of default or covenant violations.

Kim (2018) studies the collapse of the junk bond market in the early 1990s as an exogenous shock to external capital for speculative-grade firms. The collapse of the junk bond market forced speculative-grade firms to switch to bank loans as a substitute for their publicly traded junk bonds. He shows that speculative-grade firms that recognise economic losses in a timely manner experience a smaller reduction in investment following the collapse. The effect is more pronounced for speculative-grade firms with a low level of asset liquidation value. Kim speculates that conservatism reduces financing frictions between speculative-grade firms and banks and, as a result, mitigates underinvestment that otherwise would arise following the collapse of the junk bond market. This identification strategy allows Kim (2018) to test for the effect of a variation in pre-collapse conservatism on post-collapse investment through the availability of debt financing. As he explains, the collapse of the junk bond market is not a shock to conservatism directly but to the availability of debt financing that connects conservatism to under-investment. If the pre-collapse level of conservatism explains an exogenous change in the availability of debt financing, which in turn explains underinvestment, it mitigates the concern that unobservable determinants of underinvestment correlated with the pre-collapse level of conservatism confound the identification of the effect of conservatism on underinvestment. Unfortunately, Kim only finds weak evidence of the effect of conservatism on the availability of debt financing, which is a caveat of his study. Nevertheless, Kim's (2018) research design is an attempt in a promising direction as he analyses the entire causal path (from conservatism to debt financing to investment) as recommended by Leuz and Wysocki (2016). Most studies cannot follow this approach and employ a reduced form in which they directly analyse the effect of conservatism on an outcome variable (investment, in this case).

Aghamolla and Li (2018) show that the use of conservative accounting in debt contracting depends on the enforceability of the contract. This effect is strongest for firms that increased their borrowings and for firms with high levels of tangible assets, consistent with a collateral-based explanation. Their evidence suggests that strong enforcement is necessary to generate lenders' demand for conservative accounting. Stronger enforcement allows lenders to effectively pursue covenant violations through the legal system, forcing borrowers to engage in renegotiation following violations. Similarly, strong enforcement makes collateral-based lending more appealing to lenders. These two channels lead to an increased emphasis on debt covenants and collateral in debt contracting, thus increasing lenders' demand for conservative reporting. To conduct their tests, Aghamolla and Li (2018) exploit a natural experiment based on the staggered introduction of debt recovery tribunals in India. The increase in enforcement is exogenous to firms' characteristics, accounting choices, and borrowing behaviour. This study provides strong causal evidence that firms adopt conservative accounting due to lenders' demand. Aghamolla and Li (2018) perform their analysis along the entire causal path, from increased enforcement to lenders' demand for conservatism to borrowers' supply of conservatism.

Deng, Li, Lobo, and Shao (2018) study whether loan sales in the secondary market affect borrowers' conservatism. They find that borrowing firms exhibit a significant decline in accounting conservatism after the initial loan sales. They also find that the decline in borrower conservatism is more pronounced for firms that borrow from lenders that have lower monitoring incentives and for firms that have lower incentives to supply conservatism. Their evidence corroborates the hypothesis that lead lenders have stronger monitoring incentives than secondary market participants to enforce accounting conservatism in the private debt market. Because the decision to sell a loan is endogenous and affected by firm, loan, and lender characteristics, Deng et al.'s (2018) identification strategy relies on a difference-in-differences design to control for the observable firm and loan characteristics that affect the probability of loan sales.

5.5. *Use of accounting-based covenants*

Several papers study conditional conservatism when accounting information is used in debt covenants, specifically the prompt exercise of control rights by lenders. The underlying reasoning is that conservatism facilitates the monitoring of debt contracts because it accelerates the triggering of debt covenants based on accounting numbers and the transfer of control rights to lenders (Ball and Shivakumar, 2005; Zhang, 2008; Nikolaev, 2010; Christensen and Nikolaev, 2012). Timely covenant violation thus can be an efficient mechanism for lenders to exercise their contractual rights and restrict decisions by loss-making managers that could further erode debt quality (Ball, Robin and Sadka, 2008). However, Leuz (2001) and Gigler, Kanodia, Sapra, and Venugopalan (2009) note that conservatism can push towards inefficient liquidation.

Dyreng, Vashishtha, and Weber (2017) address this tension. They analyse a small sample of firms that disclose the actual earnings definition used in performance debt covenants and find that the definitions are not conditionally conservative. The actual measures used are not based on net income but are similar to EBITDA. In addition, they document that the contractual adjustments made to earnings in debt covenants are economically large, income increasing, and change the information content of earnings. This is consistent with evidence in Li (2010, 2016) showing that net income is more likely to be defined different from GAAP when transitory earnings are less useful for debt contracting. Removing transitory earnings is one principal concern in the measurement of earnings but not in the measurement of net worth. Li (2016) finds that, in addition to conservative adjustments, definitions of performance covenants earnings also tend to include some non-conservative adjustments that allow for exclusion of noncash expenses but not noncash income. The results in Dyreng et al. (2017) contrast with earlier findings, but are consistent with the theoretical research in Gigler, Kanodia, Sapra, and Venugopalan (2009). There are three possible explanations for the differences to prior literature: (i) Dyreng et al.'s use of rolling-over (i.e. overlapping) quarterly earnings data as their measure of earnings in performance covenants causes observations for any firm to have an embedded MA(3) process, which renders the estimated standard errors inconsistent; (ii) their specific consideration of performance covenants but not that of other accounting-based covenants; and (iii) their small sample of firms that disclose realised (i.e. ex post) contractual earnings. In addition, as discussed earlier, modifications of assumptions used in Gigler et al. (2009) can lead to conservative accounting being preferable. So, the empirical research may pick up somewhat different economic settings.

Beatty, Cheng and Zach (2019) produce evidence consistent with the results of Dyreng et al. (2017). They analyse the determinants of excluding nonrecurring items from covenant calculations. They document that approximately 80% of debt contracts exclude certain nonrecurring items from covenant compliance calculations, which seems to indicate that nonrecurring items are not useful in the assessment of borrowers' future performance or creditworthiness. They find that nonrecurring items are more likely to be excluded from performance (i.e. income statement-based) covenants when the agency costs of debt are higher and more likely to be retained when they predict borrowers' performance. When they examine separately the exclusions of nonrecurring losses versus gains, and their interplay with setting the covenants' thresholds (slack), their results are consistent with the findings of Dyreng et al. (2017) that the earnings measures used in performance covenants are not conservative. Beatty et al. (2019) also show that firms with debt contracts that exclude nonrecurring items in covenant computations are less conservative and the loans are larger, with longer maturities, more likely to be secured and syndicated, and with higher spreads, compared to those that include nonrecurring items. Importantly, they provide initial evidence that lenders behave conservatively and treat nonrecurring losses and gains differentially not at the exclusion stage, but rather when determining the slack in covenants' thresholds: lenders may prefer to exclude these items and simultaneously increase covenants' tightness and loan spreads.

Callen, Chen, Dou, and Xin (2016) consider private debt financing and show that conservative accounting and performance covenants are complements in settings of high information asymmetry about the lender's proclivity to paying high dividends. The mechanisms reinforce themselves to allow good lenders to signal their type through the choice of the contract. Callen et al. (2016) also find that firms with high conservatism and tight performance covenants enjoy lower interest rate spreads.

5.6. *Fair value accounting and debt contracting*

Fair value accounting for balance sheet items without liquid markets leads to the recognition of unrealised gains in earnings that have a low verifiability. That is, fair value accounting is non-conservative, which can potentially reduce the debt contracting value of accounting reports that include more fair values (Christensen, Nikolaev, and Wittenberg-Moerman, 2016). Several studies provide evidence consistent with this assertion.

Demerjian (2011) documents a sharp decline in the use of balance sheet-based covenants in U.S. private debt contracts during the period 1996–2007, while the use of income statement-based covenants has remained stable. He attributes this result to the increased emphasis of the FASB on fair value, which has reduced the contracting usefulness of the balance sheet. Ball, Li, and Shivakumar (2015) find that the adoption of IFRS has led to a significant reduction in the use of accounting-based covenants in debt contracts. They conclude that the rise in the use of fair value brought about by IFRS, and the additional managerial discretion introduced, has reduced the contract value of accounting information.

Christensen and Nikolaev (2017) document a significant time-trend towards excluding GAAP changes from the determination of covenant compliance over the period 1994–2012. This trend is positively associated with proxies for the FASB's shift in focus towards relevance and international accounting harmonisation, which is consistent with the FASB de-emphasising the contractual role of accounting information in favour of a greater valuation role.

Other research reaches opposite conclusions. Demerjian, Donovan, and Larson (2016) investigate the impact of the adoption of SFAS 159 on debt contract design. Since 2007, SFAS 159 allows firms to record virtually all financial assets and liabilities at fair value. They find that the majority of debt contracts continue to include financial covenants affected by the standard without modification, suggesting that in many cases fair value is useful for contracting. In the few cases in which fair value can be detrimental, lenders modify the contracts to exclude it. Demerjian et al. (2016) conclude that the evidence of limited modification of financial covenants – but no change in the use of financial covenants – shows that contracting parties responded to SFAS 159 differently than to the changes examined in prior studies (Demerjian, 2011; Ball, Li, and Shivakumar, 2015). They speculate that the shift toward a balance sheet approach was perhaps too far reaching to be addressed via modifications in covenant definitions and it was less costly to reduce to usage of balance sheet-based covenants.

Badia, Duro, Penalva, and Ryan (2017) provide evidence that firms holding larger proportions of financial instruments measured at fair value based on Level 2 and 3 inputs report more conditionally conservative earnings. Fair values based on Level 2 and Level 3 inputs are far less reliable than those measured using Level 1 inputs. This introduces uncertainty in the reported fair values and investors price protect by discounting the stock price. The evidence in Badia et al. (2017) suggests that firms attempt to mitigate investors' discounting of the measurements by using inputs that produce more conservative earnings and fair values. This is an important result because it shows that conservatism and fair value are not opposites and that fair value does not destroy the contracting value of conservatism. In addition, this evidence indicates that the demand for conservative financial reporting can also originate in the equity market.

6.   Conclusions

We survey theoretical and empirical research on the costs and benefits of conservative accounting for debt financing and in debt covenants. The theory literature has come up with different conceptualisations of conservatism and the use of accounting information in specific debt contract settings. While many studies establish net benefits of conservative accounting, others find the contrary that conservative accounting is undesirable. That depends on different uses of accounting information in debt financing, on the set of available information, the possibility of renegotiation, and other conditions. The benefit of this literature is that it helps to understand the economic effects that arise with a variation of the degree of conservatism in a particular setting. Some results seem counter-intuitive to many, such as the result in Gigler, Kanodia, Sapra, and Venugopalan (2009) who show that liberal (non-conservative) accounting is desirable in earnings-based debt covenants that allocate control. Yet the underlying economics are quite persuasive and robust. Follow-up theoretical literature added other features, such as renegotiation or additional agency problems and show that conservative accounting can be optimal. But there is a lack of models that, for example, include more detailed financing contracts, study multi-period settings and overlapping projects or include the decision whether to use debt or equity financing in the first place. Overall, the main takeaway from the theoretical literature is that it is not the case that conservative (or liberal) accounting is always best in a debt contracting setting, but that depends on the specific conditions. In this sense, it would not be surprising to find mixed results. These insights open avenues for more differentiated and sophisticated hypotheses and empirical tests.

The empirical literature takes a more holistic approach and constructs proxies that relate to the basic effects of conservatism, which are the early recognition of bad news and the understatement of net assets. Most of the empirical work finds overwhelming support for the beneficial debt-contracting role of conservatism. Given the mixed predictions from theoretical work, this is a surprising and distinct insight. Conservatism appears to be driven primarily by debt markets and less so by equity markets, the latter particularly in the case of fair value measurement of financial assets. Conservatism reduces the cost of debt, enhances the efficiency of debt contracts by accelerating the transfer of control rights to lenders, reduces pro-cyclical lending in recessionary times, serves as a useful governance mechanism, improves investment efficiency and reduces the risk in acquisitions, reduces information asymmetries among contracting parties, and increases the lenders' recovery rate in case of borrowers' default. Over time, empirical work has refined the identification strategies in an attempt to show the causal impact of conservatism. However, there are still unresolved questions and controversial results that need to be further investigated.

Over the years, analytical research has identified many settings in which conservatism is beneficial, and empirical research has provided evidence from many different settings that conservatism is associated with, or even caused, by lenders' demand. Empirical designs have evolved to provide better and more rigorous tests that aid in understanding the paths through which conservative accounting acts to improve the efficiency of debt financing. Yet it is a challenge for future empirical research to test the richer and more specific predictions resulting from the theoretical literature.

Many intriguing research questions still wait to be addressed in future research. For example, what are the causes of mixed empirical findings – is it different theories or empirical designs? Can we find conditions under which conservatism is beneficial for some firms and not for others and what are key features of these firms? What is the primary economic friction that debt covenants address and can researchers identify firms/situations where such frictions exist? What are the reasons debt covenants are combined in specific ways? Why debt covenants compliance calculations tend to exclude nonrecurring items that can act as trip wires for debtholders? Can unconditional conservatism enhance the efficiency of debt contracting and, if so, how? In this regard, empirical work has failed to find supporting evidence, but we do not yet know whether the reason is the conceptual inadequacy of this form of conservatism or the lack of good proxies to measure unconditional conservatism. We know that the demand for timely recognition of bad news comes from debtholders, but there is also certain demand from equityholders and even from regulators. Current evidence is still scarce, and this is an area worth exploring. The effects of the adoption of fair value on the contracting usefulness of conservatism has not yet been extensively examined. Fair value seems to influence the design of debt contracts but the findings are inconclusive. In this review, we have focused on the debt contracting value of conservatism but other contracting settings can be studied in more depth: compensation contracts, supplier contracts, government contracts, etc. Good theories and empirical identification are challenges and creative research designs to establish the causal effect of conservatism on the outcomes of interest are always welcome. Finally, from a larger perspective, investment, financing and governance choices are endogenous, but we usually consider only few elements of the broader decision problem.

Acknowledgements

We thank the organiser, Edward Lee, the sponsor of the Symposium, *Accounting and Business Research*, and two anonymous reviewers for helpful comments.

Funding

Fernando Penalva acknowledges financial assistance from research project ECO2016-77579-C3-1-P funded by the Ministry of Economy Industry and Competitiveness.

Disclosure statement

No potential conflict of interest was reported by the authors.

Notes

1. Dickhaut, Basu, McCabe, and Waymire (2010) even suggest 'that the ultimate explanation for the *Conservatism* principle may derive from how gains and losses are differentially processed by neurons within the human brain' (p. 244).
2. Further examples are discussed in Barker and McGeachin (2013) and Wagenhofer (2014).
3. This is a limitation not imposed by conditional conservatism but by current accounting standards, which prevent the use of fair value for most assets with the exception of financial assets. But even in the case of financial assets, Badia, Duro, Penalva and Ryan (2017) show that firms are conditionally conservative in the measurement of the fair value of Level 2 and Level 3 financial assets, where there is more uncertainty.
4. It is worth noting that the use of accelerated depreciation among U.S. firms has experienced a sharp, monotonic decline over the last decades (Jackson, Liu, and Cecchini, 2009). This trend persists until 2018.
5. DeFond et al. (2016) use the proxies of unconditional conservatism developed by Penman and Zhang (2002), which are based on capitalised and amortised research and development and advertising expenditures.
6. For a more detailed survey see Ewert and Wagenhofer (2011).
7. Gigler, Kanodia, Sapra, and Venugopalan (2009) provide a definition for continuous signals in the same spirit. Gao (2013) suggests a more elaborate procedure with two steps: step 1, in which transactions are recorded and differentially verified, and step 2, in which management biases the report by earnings management.
8. Such disclosure models have become known as Bayesian persuasion games. See Kamenica and Gentzkow (2011).
9. Jiang and Yang (2016) show a similar result.
10. Francis and Martin (2010) argue that conservatism induces managers to abandon poorly performing projects earlier. If a manager does not benefit from continuing the project ($B = 0$) then it is not clear why biasing information for managerial decision making should be beneficial.
11. The reverse result holds as well: If the net present value were negative, then a conservative accounting system would be optimal. But in this case the firm would not invest in the first place.
12. Beyer (2012) considers aggregation of signals and finds that conservatism is beneficial when the amount of debt financing is high because it improves efficient liquidation.
13. In another asset substitution model, Burkhardt and Strausz (2009) find that less information, e.g., pure historical-cost based accounting, is preferable to more information, e.g., lower-of-cost-or market accounting.
14. Neither Gao and Liang (2018) nor Laux (2017) explicitly consider accounting biases.
15. See also Guay and Verrecchia (2006).

ORCID

FERNANDO PENALVA ⓘ http://orcid.org/0000-0002-5206-3754
ALFRED WAGENHOFER ⓘ http://orcid.org/0000-0001-5919-942X

References

Aghamolla, C., and Li, N., 2018. Debt contract enforcement and conservatism: evidence from a natural experiment. *Journal of Accounting Research*, 56 (5), 1383–1416.

Aghion, P., and Bolton, P., 1992. An incomplete contracts approach to financial contracting. *The Review of Economic Studies*, 59 (3), 473–494.

Ahmed, A. S., Billings, B. K., Morton, R. M., and Stanford-Harris, M., 2002. The role of accounting conservatism in mitigating Bondholder-Shareholder conflicts over dividend policy and in reducing debt costs. *The Accounting Review*, 77 (4), 867–890.

Ahmed, A. S., and Duellman, S., 2007. Accounting conservatism and board of director characteristics: an empirical analysis. *Journal of Accounting and Economics*, 43 (2–3), 411–437.

Aier, J. K., Chen, L., and Pevzner, M., 2014. Debtholders' demand for conservatism: evidence from changes in directors' fiduciary duties. *Journal of Accounting Research*, 52 (5), 993–1027.

Amir, E., Guan, Y., and Livne, G., 2010. Auditor independence and the cost of capital before and after Sarbanes-Oxley: the case of newly issued public debt. *European Accounting Review*, 19 (4), 633–664.

Amir, E., Guan, Y., and Livne, G., 2018. Abnormal fees and timely loss recognition – a long-term perspective. *Auditing: A Journal of Practice & Theory*. Available from: https://doi.org/10.2308/ajpt-52348

Antle, R., and Nalebuff, B., 1991. Conservatism and auditor-client negotiations. *Journal of Accounting Research*, 29 (Suppl.), 31–54.

Armstrong, C. S., Guay, W. R., and Weber, J. P., 2010. The role of information and financial reporting in corporate governance and debt contracting. *Journal of Accounting and Economics*, 50 (2–3), 179–234.

Badia, M., Duro, M., Penalva, F., and Ryan, S., 2017. Conditionally conservative fair value measurements. *Journal of Accounting and Economics*, 63 (1), 75–98.

Balakrishnan, K., Watts, R., and Zuo, L., 2016. The effect of accounting conservatism on corporate investment during the global financial crisis. *Journal of Business Finance and Accounting*, 43 (5–6), 513–542.

Ball, R., 2001. Infrastructure requirements for an economically efficient system of public financial reporting and disclosure. *Brookings-Wharton Papers on Financial Services*, 127–169.

Ball, R., Bushman, R. M., and Vasvari, F. P., 2008. The debt-contracting value of accounting information and loan syndicate structure. *Journal of Accounting Research*, 46 (2), 247–287.

Ball, R., Li, X., and Shivakumar, L., 2015. Contractibility and transparency of financial statement information Prepared under IFRS: evidence from debt contracts Around IFRS adoption. *Journal of Accounting Research*, 53 (5), 915–963.

Ball, R., Kothari, S. P., and Nikolaev, V. A., 2013a. On estimating conditional conservatism. *The Accounting Review*, 88 (3), 755–787.

Ball, R., Kothari, S. P., and Nikolaev, V. A., 2013b. Econometrics of the Basu asymmetric timeliness coefficient and accounting conservatism. *Journal of Accounting Research*, 51 (5), 1071–1097.

Ball, R., Robin, A., and Sadka, G., 2008. Is financial reporting shaped by equity markets or by debt markets? An international study of timeliness and conservatism. *Review of Accounting Studies*, 13 (2–3), 168–205.

Ball, R., and Shivakumar, L., 2005. Earnings quality in UK private firms: comparative loss recognition timeliness. *Journal of Accounting and Economics*, 39 (1), 83–128.

Barker, R., 2015. Conservatism, prudence and the IASB's conceptual framework. *Accounting and Business Research*, 45 (4), 514–538.

Barker, R., and McGeachin, A., 2013. Why is there inconsistency in accounting for liabilities in IFRS? An analysis of recognition, measurement, estimation and conservatism. *Accounting and Business Research*, 43 (6), 579–604.

Basu, S., 1997. The conservatism principle and the asymmetric timeliness of earnings. *Journal of Accounting and Economics*, 24, 3–37.

Baylis, R. M., Burnap, P., Clatworthy, M. A., Gad, M. A., and Pong, C. K., 2017. Private lenders' demand for audit. *Journal of Accounting and Economics*, 64 (1), 78–97.

Beatty, A., Cheng, L., and Zach, T., 2019. Nonrecurring items in debt contracts. *Contemporary Accounting Research*, 36 (1), 139–167.

Beatty, A., and Liao, S., 2011. Do delays in expected loss recognition affect banks' willingness to lend? *Journal of Accounting and Economics*, 52 (1), 1–20.

Beatty, A., Weber, J., and Yu, J. J., 2008. Conservatism and debt. *Journal of Accounting and Economics*, 45 (2–3), 154–174.

Beaver, W., and Ryan, S., 2005. Conditional and unconditional conservatism: concepts and modeling. *Review of Accounting Studies*, 10 (2–3), 269–309.

Beekes, W., Pope, P. F., and Young, S., 2004. The link between earnings timeliness, earnings conservatism and board composition: evidence from the UK. *Corporate Governance*, 12 (1), 47–59.

Beyer, A., 2012. Conservatism and aggregation: the effect on cost of equity capital and the efficiency of debt contracts. Working paper, Stanford University.

Bliss, J. H., 1924. *Management Through Accounts*. New York: The Ronald Press Co.

Burkhardt, K., and Strausz, R., 2009. Accounting transparency and the asset substitution problem. *The Accounting Review*, 84 (3), 689–712.

Callen, J. L., Chen, F., Dou, Y., and Xin, B., 2016. Accounting conservatism and performance covenants: a signaling approach. *Contemporary Accounting Research*, 33 (3), 961–988.

Callen, J.L., Segal, D., and Hope, O.-K., 2010. The pricing of conservative accounting and the measurement of conservatism at the firm-year level. *Review of Accounting Studies*, 15 (1), 145–178.

Caskey, J., and Hughes, J. S., 2012. Assessing the impact of alternative fair value measures on the efficiency of project selection and continuation. *The Accounting Review*, 87 (2), 483–512.

Chava, S., Kumar, P., and Warga, A., 2010. Managerial agency and bond covenants. *Review of Financial Studies*, 23 (3), 1120–1148.

Chen, H., Chen, J. Z., Lobo, G. L., and Wang, Y., 2010. Association between borrower and lender state ownership and accounting conservatism. *Journal of Accounting Research*, 48 (5), 973–1014.

Chen, Q., Hemmer, T., and Zhang, Y., 2007. On the relation between conservatism in accounting standards and incentives for earnings management. *Journal of Accounting Research*, 45 (3), 541–565.

Christensen, H. B., and Nikolaev, V., 2012. Capital versus performance covenants in debt contracts. *Journal of Accounting Research*, 50 (1), 75–116.

Christensen, H. B., and Nikolaev, V., 2017. Contracting on GAAP changes: large sample evidence. *Journal of Accounting Research*, 55 (5), 1021–1050.

Christensen, H. B., Nikolaev, V., and Wittenberg-Moerman, R., 2016. Accounting information in financial contracting: the incomplete contract theory perspective. *Journal of Accounting Research*, 54 (2), 397–435.

DeFond, M.L., Lim, C.Y., and Zang, Y., 2016. Client conservatism and auditor-client contracting. *The Accounting Review*, 91 (1), 69–98.

Demerjian, P. R., 2011. Accounting standards and debt covenants: Has the "balance sheet approach" led to a decline in the use of balance sheet covenants? *Journal of Accounting and Economics*, 52 (2), 178–202.

Demerjian, P. R., 2017. Uncertainty and debt covenants. *Review of Accounting Studies*, 22 (3), 1156–1197.

Demerjian, P., Donovan, J., and Larson, C. R., 2016. Fair value accounting and debt contracting: evidence from adoption of SFAS 159. *Journal of Accounting Research*, 54 (4), 1041–1076.

Deng, S., Li, Y., Lobo, G. J., and Shao, P., 2018. Loan sales and borrowers' accounting conservatism. *Contemporary Accounting Research*, 35 (2), 1166–1194.

Diamond, D., 1991. Monitoring and reputation: the choice between bank loans and directly placed debt. *Journal of Political Economy*, 99 (4), 689–721.

Dickhaut, J., Basu, S., McCabe, K. A., and Waymire, W. B., 2010. Neuroaccounting: consilience between the biologically evolved brain and culturally evolved accounting principles. *Accounting Horizons*, 24 (2), 221–255.

Dietrich, J. R., Muller, K. A., and Riedl, E. J., 2007. Asymmetric timeliness tests of accounting conservatism. *Review of Accounting Studies*, 12 (1), 95–124.

Donelson, D. C., Jennings, R., and McInnis, J., 2017. Financial statement quality and debt contracting: evidence from a survey of commercial lenders. *Contemporary Accounting Research*, 34 (4), 2051–2093.

Donovan, J., Frankel, R. M., and Martin, X., 2015. Accounting conservatism and creditor recovery rate. *The Accounting Review*, 90 (6), 2267–2303.

Dutta, S., and Patatoukas, P., 2017. Identifying conditional conservatism in financial accounting data: theory and evidence. *The Accounting Review*, 92 (4), 191–216.

Dyreng, S. D., Vashishtha, R., and Weber, J., 2017. Direct evidence on the informational properties of earnings in loan contracts. *Journal of Accounting Research*, 55 (2), 371–406.

Erkens, D. H., Subramanyam, K. R., and Zhang, J., 2014. Affiliated banker on board and conservative accounting. *The Accounting Review*, 89 (5), 1703–1728.

Ettredge, M., Huang, Y., and Zhang, W., 2012. Earnings restatements and differential timeliness of accounting conservatism. *Journal of Accounting and Economics*, 53 (3), 489–503.

Ewert, R., and Wagenhofer, A., 2011. Earnings management, conservatism, and earnings quality. *Foundations and Trends® in Accounting*, 6 (2), 65–186.

Financial Accounting Standards Board (FASB), 2010. Conceptual framework for financial reporting. Statement of Financial Accounting Concepts No. 8. Norwalk, CT.

Francis, J., and Martin, X., 2010. Acquisition profitability and timely loss recognition. *Journal of Accounting and Economics*, 49 (1–2), 161–178.

Franke, B., and Müller, S., 2018. Private debt and timely loss recognition. *European Accounting Review*, doi:10.1080/09638180.2018.1476168.

Gao, P., 2013. A measurement approach to conservatism and earnings management. *Journal of Accounting and Economics*, 55 (2–3), 251–268.

Gao, P., and Liang, P. J., 2018. Accounting information, renegotiation, and debt contracts. Working paper, University of Chicago.

García Lara, J., García Osma, B., and and Penalva, F., 2009. Accounting conservatism and corporate governance. *Review of Accounting Studies*, 14 (1), 161–201.

Garcia Lara, J., Garcia Osma, B., and and Penalva, F., 2016. Accounting conservatism and firm investment efficiency. *Journal of Accounting and Economics*, 61 (1), 221–238.

Gigler, F., Kanodia, K., Sapra, H., and Venugopalan, R., 2009. Accounting conservatism and the efficiency of debt contracts. *Journal of Accounting Research*, 47 (3), 767–797.

Givoly, D., and Hayn, C., 2000. The changing time-series properties of earnings, cash flows and accruals: Has financial reporting become more conservative? *Journal of Accounting and Economics*, 29 (3), 287–320.

Givoly, D., Hayn, C. K., and Natarajan, A., 2007. Measuring reporting conservatism. *The Accounting Review*, 82 (1), 65–106.

Glover, J. C., and Lin, H. H., 2018. Accounting conservatism and incentives: intertemporal considerations. *The Accounting Review*, 93 (6), 181–201.

Gormley, T.A., Kim, B.H., and Martin, X., 2012. Do firms adjust their timely loss recognition in response to changes in the banking industry? *Journal of Accounting Research*, 50 (1), 159–196.

Göx, R., and Wagenhofer, A., 2009. Optimal impairment rules. *Journal of Accounting and Economics*, 48 (1), 2–16.

Göx, R., and Wagenhofer, A., 2010. Optimal precision of accounting information in debt financing. *European Accounting Review*, 19 (3), 579–602.

Guay, W., and Verrecchia, R. E., 2006. Discussion of an economic framework for conservative accounting and Bushman and Piotroski. *Journal of Accounting and Economics*, 42 (1–2), 149–165.

Guay, W. R., and Verrecchia, R. E., 2018. Conservative disclosure. *Journal of Financial Reporting*, 3 (1), 73–92.

Haw, I.-M., Lee, J. J., and Lee, W.-J., 2014. Debt financing and accounting conservatism in private firms. *Contemporary Accounting Research*, 31 (4), 1220–1259.

International Accounting Standards Board (IASB), 2010. *The Conceptual Framework for Financial Reporting 2010*. London: IFRS Foundation.

International Accounting Standards Board (IASB), 2018. *Conceptual Framework for Financial Reporting*. London: IFRS Foundation.

International Accounting Standards Committee (IASC), 1989. *Framework for the Preparation and Presentation of Financial Statements*. London: International Accounting Standards Committee.

Jackson, S. B., Liu, K., and Cecchini, M., 2009. Economic consequences of firms' depreciation method choice: evidence from capital investments. *Journal of Accounting and Economics*, 48 (1), 54–68.

Jayaraman, S., and Shivakumar, L., 2013. Agency-based demand for conservatism: evidence from state adoption of antitakeover laws. *Review of Accounting Studies*, 18 (1), 95–134.

Jenkins, D. S., and Velury, U., 2008. Does auditor tenure influence the reporting of conservative earnings? *Journal of Accounting and Public Policy*, 27 (2), 115–132.

Jiang, X., and Yang, M., 2016. Optimal disclosure rule and efficient liquidation. Working paper, Duke University.

Kamenica, E., and Gentzkow, M., 2011. Bayesian persuasion. *American Economic Review*, 101 (6), 2590–2615.

Khan, M., and Watts, R., 2009. Estimation and empirical properties of a firm-year measure of accounting conservatism. *Journal of Accounting and Economics*, 48 (2–3), 132–150.

Khurana, K.I., and Wang, C., 2015. Debt maturity structure and accounting conservatism. *Journal of Business, Finance and Accounting*, 42 (1–2), 167–203.

Kim, J., 2018. Asymmetric timely loss recognition, adverse shocks to external capital, and underinvestment: evidence from the collapse of the junk bond market. *Journal of Accounting and Economics*, 65 (1), 148–168.

Kothari, S. P., Ramanna, K., and Skinner, D., 2010. Implications for GAAP from an analysis of positive research in accounting. *Journal of Accounting and Economics*, 50 (2–3), 246–286.

Kothari, S., Shu, S., and Wysocki, P., 2009. Do managers withhold bad news? *Journal of Accounting Research*, 47 (1), 241–276.

Kravet, T. D., 2014. Accounting conservatism and managerial risk-taking: corporate acquisitions. *Journal of Accounting and Economics*, 57 (2–3), 218–240.

Krishnan, G.V., 2007. Did earnings conservatism increase for former Andersen clients? *Journal of Accounting, Auditing & Finance*, 22 (2), 141–163.

LaFond, R., and Watts, R. L., 2008. The information role of conservatism. *The Accounting Review*, 83 (2), 447–478.

Laux, V., 2017. Debt covenants, renegotiation, and accounting manipulation. Working paper, University of Texas at Austin.

Leuz, C., 2001. *Comment on Infrastructure Requirements for an Economically Efficient System of Public Financial Reporting and Disclosure*. Brookings-Wharton Papers on Financial Services, edited by R. Litan and R. Herring, Washington, DC: Brookings Institution Press, 170–177.

Leuz, C., and Wysocki, P. D., 2016. The economics of disclosure and financial reporting regulation: evidence and suggestions for future research. *Journal of Accounting Research*, 54 (2), 525–622.

Lev, B., and Sougiannis, T., 1996. The capitalization, amortization, and value-relevance of R&D. *Journal of Accounting and Economics*, 21, 107–138.

Li, J., 2013. Accounting conservatism and debt contracts: efficient liquidation and covenant renegotiation. *Contemporary Accounting Research*, 30 (3), 1082–1098.

Li, N., 2010. Negotiated measurement rules in debt contracts. *Journal of Accounting Research*, 48 (5), 1103–1144.

Li, N., 2016. Performance measures in earnings-based financial covenants in debt contracts. *Journal of Accounting Research*, 54 (4), 1149–1186.

Lim, C. Y., Lee, E., Kausar, A., and Walker, M., 2014. Bank accounting conservatism and bank loan pricing. *Journal of Accounting and Public Policy*, 33 (3), 260–278.

Maltby, J., 2000. The origins of prudence in accounting. *Critical Perspectives on Accounting*, 11 (1), 51–70.

Mansi, S. A., Maxwell, W. F., and Miller, D. P., 2004. Does auditor quality and tenure matter to investors? Evidence from the bond market. *Journal of Accounting Research*, 42, 755–793.

Martin, X., and Roychowdhury, S., 2015. Do financial market developments influence accounting practices? Credit default swaps and borrowers' reporting conservatism. *Journal of Accounting and Economics*, 59 (1), 80–104.

Milgrom, P. R., 1981. Good news and bad news: representation theorems and applications. *The Bell Journal of Economics*, 12 (2), 380–391.

Milgrom, P., and Roberts, J., 1992. *Economics, Organization & Management*. Englewood Cliffs, NJ: Prentice Hall.

Mora, A., and Walker, M., 2015. The implications of research on accounting conservatism for accounting standard setting. *Accounting and Business Research*, 45 (5), 620–650.

Nan, L., and Wen, X., 2014. Financing and investment efficiency, information quality, and accounting biases. *Management Science*, 60 (9), 2308–2323.

Nikolaev, V., 2010. Debt covenants and accounting conservatism. *Journal of Accounting Research*, 48 (1), 137–176.

Patatoukas, P. N., and Thomas, J. K., 2011. More evidence of bias in the differential timeliness measure of conditional conservatism. *The Accounting Review*, 86 (5), 1765–1793.

Patatoukas, P. N., and Thomas, J. K., 2016. Placebo tests of conditional conservatism. *The Accounting Review*, 91 (2), 625–648.

Penman, S., and Zhang, X., 2002. Accounting conservatism, the quality of earnings, and stock returns. *The Accounting Review*, 77, 237–264.

Ryan, S. G., 2006. Identifying conditional conservatism. *European Accounting Review*, 15 (4), 511–525.

Ruch, G. W., and Taylor, G., 2015. Accounting conservatism: a review of the literature. *Journal of Accounting Literature*, 34 (C), 17–38.

Shivakumar, L., 2013. The role of financial reporting in debt contracting and in stewardship. *Accounting and Business Research*, 43 (4), 362–383.

Smith, C. W. and Warner, J. B., 1979. On financial contracting: An analysis of bond covenants. *Journal of Financial Economics*, 7 (2), 117–161.

Sterling, R., 1967. Conservatism: the fundamental principle of valuation in traditional accounting. *Abacus*, 3 (2), 109–132.

Sunder, J., Sunder, S. V., and Zhang, J., 2018. Balance sheet conservatism and debt contracting. *Contemporary Accounting Research*, 35 (1), 494–524.

Tan, L., 2013. Creditor control rights, state of nature verification, and financial reporting conservatism. *Journal of Accounting and Economics*, 55 (1), 1–22.

Thoman, L., 1996. Legal damages and auditor efforts. *Contemporary Accounting Research*, 13 (1), 275–306.

Tirole, J., 2006. *The Theory of Corporate Finance*. Princeton, NJ: Princeton University Press.

Verrecchia, R., 1983. Discretionary disclosure. *Journal of Accounting and Economics*, 5 (1), 179–194.

Verrecchia, R., 1990. Information quality and discretionary disclosure. *Journal of Accounting and Economics*, 12 (4), 365–380.

Vuolteenaho, T., 2002. What drives firm-level stock returns? *The Journal of Finance*, 57, 233–264.

Wagenhofer, A., 2014. The role of revenue recognition in performance reporting. *Accounting and Business Research*, 44 (4), 349–379.

Watts, R., 2003a. Conservatism in accounting Part I: explanations and implications. *Accounting Horizons*, 17 (3), 207–221.

Watts, R., 2003b. Conservatism in accounting Part II: evidence and research opportunities. *Accounting Horizons*, 17 (4), 287–301.

Watts, R., and Zimmerman, J., 1986. *Positive Accounting Theory*. Englewood Cliffs, NJ: Prentice-Hall.

Wittenberg-Moerman, R., 2008. The role of information asymmetry and financial reporting quality in debt trading: evidence from the secondary loan market. *Journal of Accounting and Economics*, 46 (2–3), 240–260.

Zhang, J., 2008. The contracting benefits of accounting conservatism to lenders and borrowers. *Journal of Accounting and Economics*, 45 (1), 27–54.

Zhong, Y., and Li, W., 2017. Accounting conservatism: a literature review. *Australian Accounting Review*, 27 (2), 195–213.

The impact of filing micro-entity accounts and the disclosure of reporting accountants on credit scores: an exploratory study

MICHAEL J. PEEL

There is a dearth of evidence regarding the potential costs incurred by small private companies that opt to publish only an unaudited abbreviated balance sheet. This paper provides new evidence regarding whether UK companies that publish reduced balance sheet information in micro-entity annual accounts are allocated lower credit scores by a credit rating agency. Recently, for the smallest companies, a new exemption category for 'micro-entities' was introduced. Qualifying companies may elect to file even less unaudited balance sheet information than their small company counterparts. Consistent with the conjecture that publishing micro accounts conveys a negative signal to the credit scorer, there is systematic evidence that micro-entities are assigned worse credit scores. This result is robust to the employment of statistical methods that account for observed and unobserved bias. Based on both assurance and signalling tenets, the second novel conjecture examined in this study is that companies which disclose their annual accounts are prepared by an accountancy firm (reporting accountant) will attract higher credit scores. Contrary to extant research which reports that companies that opt for voluntary audits receive higher credit scores, there is no evidence that the credit scorer rewards companies whose accounts bear the imprimatur of a reporting accountant.

1. Introduction

This empirical paper presents new evidence on whether UK private companies which publish reduced balance sheet information in micro-entity annual accounts are allocated lower credit scores by a credit rating agency (hereafter referred to as the credit scorer). The paper also provides novel evidence on whether companies whose annual statutory accounts disclose they are prepared by an accountancy firm (hereafter referred to as a reporting accountant) obtain higher credit scores. As demonstrated in the next section, UK small companies rely heavily on debt financing, so credit ratings are important in terms of their potential influence on the availability and cost of debt. The study is exploratory in that, to the author's knowledge, extant archival studies do not investigate the relationship between corporate outcomes and reduced financial disclosure under the small/micro-company reporting regimes – nor the disclosure that companies have a reporting accountant. Hence, as well as being of academic interest, it is hoped that the results of this study will prove informative for policy-makers/regulators and small company accountants.

Despite its economic importance, and the perennial intervention of policy-makers, the small company sector has received relatively little (but growing) attention from accounting researchers (see Kitching et al. 2011, Collis 2012, Kitching et al. 2015). A recent ICAEW report (Singleton-Green 2015), which contains a review of extant SME survey and archival accounting research, stresses (p. 9) that 'Valuable though this research is, it tells us remarkably little about the effects of regulating or deregulating SME financial reporting'. Though providing important evidence and insights, prior archival accounting research concentrates on the minority of small companies which voluntarily publish full accounts and then examines the association between voluntarily audits and various corporate outcomes, including the cost of debt and credit scores (Singleton-Green 2015). In contrast, and given the diminishing proportion of companies opting for voluntary audits, this study focuses on the vast majority of small UK companies which publish unaudited accounts, containing only an abbreviated balance sheet.

All UK companies must file annual accounts at Companies House (CH, the UK repository for company filings) where they are then available for public inspection. However, in the UK (and the EU) small private companies are exempt from the requirements to publish full audited annual accounts (as their larger counterparts must do) on the grounds of lifting the administrative burden on the small company sector. The company size criteria for claiming these exemptions have been relaxed through time (Collis 2012). Clatworthy and Peel (2013) report that a minority (17.9%) of small UK companies with year ends in 2009/2010 voluntarily filed full or audited accounts, with the typical small company opting to file only an unaudited abbreviated balance sheet (hereafter referred to as small company accounts). Following an EU directive aimed at reducing the administrative burden still further for the smallest companies (see DBIS 2013, Kitching et al. 2015), a new exempt category, 'micro-entities', was recently introduced. Small UK private companies which meet specific (smaller) size criteria need only file an unaudited abbreviated balance sheet (hereafter referred to as micro-company accounts), which contains even less financial information than small company accounts.

Intuitively, and as explicitly stated (DBIS 2013, p. 5), the motivation underpinning these exemptions is that, given the lack of divorce between ownership and control, audits/full accounts are of less import, since most small companies do not suffer substantive agency problems. However, as discussed below, in such a reporting environment, increased voluntary accounting disclosures may act as a signal (see eg Toms 2002, Watson et al. 2002) to outsiders (including credit rating agencies) that the company is of higher quality (lower risk). In line with this, the first conjecture examined in the current study is that, relative to small companies publishing abbreviated accounts, those which opt to file micro-company accounts, which divulge even less information, will be assigned worse credit scores. In this context, and with reference to the new micro-entities' exemption, Collis (2012, p. 442) comments that 'there is a paucity of up-to-date research on the benefits that might be lost', and that 'A further limitation is that previous impact assessment studies on raising the thresholds in the UK have necessarily focused on predicted behaviour rather than the actual choices made' (p. 443). The current study provides new archival evidence regarding the filing choice exercised.

Extant archival research finds that voluntary audits are associated with higher credit scores (Dedman and Kausar 2012, Lennox and Pittman 2011). This is consistent with the credit scorer viewing audited accounts as being of higher quality (the company being of lower risk) in accord with assurance/signalling principles.

Similarly, small and micro companies in the current study may voluntarily appoint an accountancy firm to compile their annual accounts. On the same tenets (assurance/signalling) obtaining to voluntary audits, the second conjecture examined in this paper is that companies whose annual accounts contain the imprimatur of an accountancy firm (reporting accountant) will be rewarded with higher credit scores.

The remainder of this paper is organised as follows: Section 2 presents background information and provides motivation for the conjectures examined in the empirical study. Section 3 describes the research design and data, as well as reporting descriptive statistics. Section 4 presents the results of the empirical study, before the paper concludes in Section 5.

2. Background and study conjectures

Based on survey evidence from 4500 SME businesses (employees $\leq$249), BDRC provides detailed information on financing in the UK SME sector. For 2016, it reports (BDRC 2017, p.11 and p. 58) that only 63% of SMEs used any form of external finance (including debt finance, trade credit and 'injections of personal funds'), with 38% receiving 'core' external debt finance (bank overdrafts, loans/commercial mortgages and credit cards) and with 15% of SMEs relying solely on trade credit (p. 82). Risk ratings show (p. 24) that, as with the current study, larger businesses are associated with better risk ratings. In addition, SMEs with superior risk ratings were more likely to receive trade credit (p. 74). However, the information provided by BDRC does not differentiate companies from other forms of business ownership. At the start of 2016, official government estimates indicate that there were about 5.5 million UK businesses, of which around 60% were sole proprietorships, 8% were ordinary partnerships and 32% were actively trading companies (DBEI 2016a).

The use of debt finance by small UK companies appears to be much higher than that reported for all businesses in the BDRC surveys. In particular, Clatworthy and Peel (2013, p.11) express 'surprise' that the median gearing ratio (as defined in this study) of all small UK independent private companies (n = 1,067,577) with year ends falling in 2009/2010 amounted to 0.78, with 41.4% (21.8%) of small companies exhibiting negative working capital (negative equity). Contemporary evidence is consistent with these findings. Table 1 reports gearing statistics for a sample of 100,000 UK companies randomly selected from all (n = 1,101,600) UK private independent (not held as a subsidiary) live companies (not failed/dormant) available on the FAME database (see below). Data was collected in September 2017 and relates to companies with year ends in the corporate fiscal year to March 2017. Statistics are reported for size categories based on total assets (TA), including those corresponding to the TA limits of £316k (£3.26 m) which, as discussed below, are applicable to the micro (small) company reporting regimes. As shown in the table, because mean gearing levels (GEAR) – defined as the ratio of total liabilities to TA – are skewed heavily upwards for smaller companies, as well as median GEAR values, mean winsorised gearing ratios (WINGEAR) are presented where GEAR values $\geq$3 are winsorised at a value of 3.

In general, and consistent with the findings of Clatworthy and Peel (2013), Table 1 reveals that small private companies exhibit high gearing levels. Compared to the largest private companies (TA>£3.26 m), with median (mean WINGEAR) gearing values of 0.562 (0.550), those for the smallest ones (TA $\leq$ £100,000) are substantially higher at 0.852 (0.942), respectively. Because the median is not influenced by outliers, it is informative that, for all UK private companies, the median gearing ratio of 0.768 emphasises the important role of debt financing in this market. As reported in Table 1, 2.2% of all companies have no debt financing (GEAR = 0),

Table 1. Summary gearing statistics for UK private independent companies for the corporate fiscal year to March 2017.

Total assets (TA)	GEAR[a] Mean	WINGEAR[a,b] Mean	GEAR[a] Median	GEAR = 0[c] Mean	Negative equity[d] Mean
All companies ($n = 100,000$)	1.384	0.839	0.768	0.022	0.185
TA≤ £3.26 m ($n = 98,331$)	1.399	0.844	0.772	0.023	0.187
TA ≤ £316,000 ($n = 84,882$)	1.527	0.885	0.808	0.025	0.203
TA > £3.26 m ($n = 1669$)	0.551	0.550	0.562	0.007	0.063
TA > £316,000 & ≤ £3.26 m ($n = 13,449$)	0.586	0.581	0.571	0.004	0.089
TA > £100,000 & ≤ £316,000 ($n = 15,209$)	0.642	0.627	0.590	0.006	0.117
TA ≤ £100,000 ($n = 69,673$)	1.721	0.942	0.852	0.030	0.222

Notes: Data was downloaded in September 2017 from the FAME database. The sample of 100,000 companies was randomly selected from all ($n = 1,101,600$) UK private independent (not held as a subsidiary) live companies (not failed/dormant) available on FAME.
[a]GEAR is defined as the ratio of total liabilities to total assets.
[b]WINGEAR denotes that GEAR values ≥3 are winsorised at a value of 3.
[c]The mean represents the proportion of companies that have zero values for total liabilities (GEAR = 0).
[d]The mean represents the proportion of companies that have negative equity (total liabilities > total assets).

with 18.5% exhibiting negative equity. The proportions of companies with zero gearing (negative equity) are inversely related to company size (TA), with values of 0.7% (6.3%) for the largest companies, rising to 3.0% (22.2%) for the smallest ones. In summary, the high use of debt finance by small private independent companies suggests that credit scores may be important, to the extent that they influence the cost and availability of external finance, including trade credit and potential equity investors.

CH classifies (as does the FAME database used in this study) companies filing micro accounts as 'micro-entity accounts' and small companies filing only an unaudited abbreviated balance sheet as 'total exemption small'. Micro companies may voluntarily file an abbreviated profit and loss account and/or may voluntarily appoint an auditor. As explained below, such companies are excluded from the analysis, so that only micro companies filing an unaudited abbreviated balance sheet remain.

At the time of this study,[1] private independent companies were classified as small, and could elect to file only an unaudited abbreviated balance sheet, if they met at least two of the following criteria: sales ≤£6.5 m, TA ≤£3.26 m and number of employees ≤50. Recently, a new UK statutory filing category aimed at the smallest (micro) companies was introduced for account year ends falling after 30 September 2013. Companies are classified as micro-entities if they meet at least two of the following criteria: sales ≤£632,000, TA ≤£316,000 and number of employees ≤10. Micro companies need only file an abbreviated balance sheet which contains less financial information than those companies classified as small. Hence micro companies can choose to opt out of the small company reporting regime and file annual accounts which contain less balance sheet information.[2] As mentioned above, the (then) government's rationale for the new micro reporting category is that it 'eases burdens on the very smallest of companies' (DBIS 2013, p. 5).

However, based on survey evidence, it did acknowledge (DBIS 2013, p.11) that 'clearly, the owners and directors of micro-entities will need to assess the possible effect of reduced disclosures on their company and decide which form of financial statement … best meets their company's needs'. Note that, other than with regard to increased privacy (less information available to competitors), it is not obvious how the costs (financial or otherwise) are reduced when companies are permitted to file abbreviated accounts. In fact, given full accounts must be prepared to derive abbreviated ones, and that (in the UK) information from full accounts is required for tax purposes, the cost of filing abridged ones is marginally higher (see Dedman and Lennox 2009, p. 211, Collis 2012, p. 446).

Table 2 shows the difference in disclosure requirements for small and micro companies filing abbreviated annual accounts, together with the legislation governing the disclosures. It shows that, whereas small companies are required to show the elements of current and fixed assets, micro ones need only reveal the totals. The other difference is with regard to shareholders' funds. Unlike micro companies, small ones must report its constituents. As shown, both micro and small companies are not required to disclose the components of current and long-term liabilities in the balance sheet or in notes to the balance sheet; nor are they required to disclose the number of their employees. In this context, although Dedman and Kausar (2012) employ (as does the current study) a variable denoting a company has negative equity (shareholders' funds), neither Lennox and Pittman (2011) nor Dedman and Kausar (2012) incorporate variables based on the individual elements of current assets or shareholders' funds when examining the relationship between voluntary audits and credit scores on the FAME database. In any event, endogeneity concerns are addressed using appropriate econometric techniques in the empirical analysis below.

Regarding the preceding discussion, signalling theory (eg Spence 1973, Toms 2002) suggests that companies may make voluntary disclosures to signal to outsiders that they are of higher quality (lower risk). The credibility of this signal may be enhanced if the company incurs disclosure costs (Melumad and Thoman 1990). Such corporate costs include the loss of confidentiality (from competitors) associated with fuller disclosure. Given this, the first conjecture of this study is that, relative to small companies filing abbreviated accounts, those which exercise their option to file micro ones will be penalised by the credit scorer. This is hypothesised to occur because the credit scorer is aware that the typical small company files abbreviated accounts under the small company regime. By opting out of this regime, and divulging even less balance sheet information,

Table 2.   Micro and small company abbreviated balance sheets.

Small company balance sheet[a]	Micro-company balance sheet[b] (NR = not required)
Fixed assets	**Fixed assets**
Intangible assets	NR
Tangible assets	NR
Investments	NR
Current assets	**Current assets**
Stocks	NR
Debtors	NR
Investments	NR
Cash at bank and in hand	NR
Current liabilities (due within one year)	**Current liabilities** (due within one year)
Net current assets (liabilities)	Net current assets (liabilities)
Total assets less current liabilities	Total assets less current liabilities
Long-term liabilities (due after more than one year)	**Long-term liabilities** (due after more than one year)
Capital and reserves (Shareholders funds)	**Capital and reserves (Shareholders funds)**
Called up share capital	NR
Share premium account	NR
Revaluation reserve	NR
Other reserves	NR
Profit and loss account	NR

[a]Disclosure under The Small Companies and Groups (Accounts and Directors' Report) Regulations 2008.
[b]Disclosure under The Small Companies (Micro-Entities' Accounts) Regulations 2013.

the filing of micro accounts is postulated to convey a negative signal to the credit scorer that companies who do so are of lower quality (higher risk). In addition, by electing to be known publicly as a micro-entity may per se be viewed negatively by the credit scorer with reference to corporate strategic orientation/ambition/growth prospects. This leads to the first hypothesis[3]:

H1: Companies filing micro-entity annual accounts will receive lower credit scores.

Despite the benefits which have been found to accrue to small companies which voluntarily appoint auditors (Singleton-Green 2015), the proportion doing so has shrunk through time (Collis 2012, Clatworthy and Peel 2013). As Dedman and Kausar (2012, p. 146) stress, 'by allowing progressive size-based audit exemptions for private firms, the UK has been steadily moving towards a largely audit-exempt private sector'. This emphasises the increasing import of the market for reporting accountants in the small company sector (FRC 2006). Clatworthy and Peel (2013) show that the UK small company reporting environment was dominated by companies restricting their accounts to include only an unaudited abbreviated balance sheet. Of all small UK independent private companies with year ends in 2009/2010 ($n = 1,067,577$), they report (p. 11) that 84.7% filed small company unaudited abbreviated accounts. Only 3.2% of small companies had appointed an auditor. Also, although (generally) there is no divorce between ownership and control in private companies, the Financial Reporting Council (FRC 2006, p. 37) reported that at least 67% of SME companies check potential customer credit worthiness before issuing credit; and 'accountants told us that their clients may use a credit rating agency for this purpose'.

As commented by Singleton-Green (2015, p. 26), 'Audits should lead to higher financial reporting quality, which should ultimately lead to other benefits, in particular for SMEs a lower cost of borrowing.' In reviewing the literature, Singleton-Green (2015) documents that voluntary audits are associated with a lower cost, and the increased availability, of debt finance. Importantly, in examining UK small companies on the FAME database which voluntarily filed full accounts, studies by Dedman and Kausar (2012) and Lennox and Pittman (2011) report that, consistent with the value of audit assurance (credibility of financial reporting), voluntary audits are associated with higher credit scores. Lennox and Pittman (2011) also find that companies which were subject to mandatory audits, but which retained their auditors following a relaxation in mandatory auditee size requirements, were rewarded with credit score upgrades. They postulate this occurs 'because their decision to remain audited conveys an incrementally positive signal about their credit risk' (p. 1657). Note that signalling is credible in that it is costly (audit fees); so that 'the decision to bear the cost of an audit enables the low-risk types to better differentiate themselves from the high-risk types' (Lennox and Pittman 2011, p. 1660).

The directors of small or micro audit-exempt companies are not required to use an accountant to prepare statutory annual accounts (or for any other purpose). Under the company acts, it is the directors who are responsible for keeping adequate accounting records, for producing and filing statutory accounts in the appropriate regulatory format and for signing (approving) the accounts to the effect that they provide a true and fair view.[4] However, companies may voluntarily appoint an accountancy firm (reporting accountant) to prepare their statutory annual accounts and to state (publish) the accountancy firm's details therein. Where this is the case, UK professional accounting bodies recommend that the annual accounts should include an accountant's report (see FRC 2006, ICAEW 2017, ACCA 2017). For instance, the Association of Chartered Certified Accountants (ACCA 2017, p. 1) 'recommends that the ACCA accounts preparation report should be given where the practitioner's or firm's name is associated in any way with the financial statements which have been prepared by them'. As explained further below, for general interest, and to inform potential future research, Table 3 contains a reproduction of a typical accountant's

Table 3. Reproduction of accountant's report.

Note that the text in bold is as per the original report.

Chartered Certified Accountant's Report to the Directors on Unaudited Financial Statements of XX Limited

The following reproduces the text of the report prepared for the directors in respect of the company's annual unaudited financial statements, from which the unaudited abbreviated accounts have been prepared.

In order to assist you to fulfil your duties under the Companies Act 2006, we have prepared for your approval the financial statements of XX Limited for the year ended 31st October 2014 which comprise the Profit and Loss Account, the Balance Sheet, and the related notes from the company's accounting records and from information and explanations you have given us.

As a practising member firm of the Association of Chartered Certified Accountants, we are subject to its ethical and other professional requirements which are detailed at http://rulebook.accaglobal.com.

This report is made solely to the directors of XX Limited in accordance with our terms of engagement. Our work has been undertaken solely to prepare for your approval the financial statements of XX Limited and state those matters that we have agreed to state to the directors of XX Limited in this report in accordance with the requirements of the Association of Chartered Certified Accountants as detailed at http://www. accaglobal.com/factsheet163. To the fullest extent permitted by law, we do not accept or assume responsibility to anyone other than the company and its directors for our work or for this report.

It is your duty to ensure that XX Limited has kept adequate records and to prepare statutory financial statements that give a true and fair view of the assets, liabilities, financial position and profit of XX Limited. You consider that XX Limited is exempt from the statutory audit requirement for the year.

We have not been instructed to carry out an audit or a review of financial statements of XX Limited. For this reason, we have not verified the accuracy or completeness of the accounting records or information and explanations you have given to us and we do not, therefore, express any opinion on the statutory financial statements.

Accountancy firm name

Address

Date

---

report[5] included in the annual accounts of a company sampled for the current study. As shown, the report sets out the directors' duties, the basis on which the accounts are prepared and the exclusion of liability beyond the company and its directors.

With regard to private companies, Clatworthy and Peel (2013, p. 3) state that outsiders rely on the information in annual accounts for debt contracting and supplying trade credit[6]; and that 'the accuracy of the information filed by private companies is potentially important to these users and to credit rating agencies that are a primary source of information to lenders'. On the same tenets (assurance/signalling) obtaining to voluntary audits discussed previously, the second conjecture of this study is that companies whose financial statements disclose they have voluntary appointed a reporting accountant will receive higher credit scores.

As discussed above, it is expected that the credit scorer will reward companies based on the assurance tenet (an accountant endorsing the integrity of a company's annual accounts) and/or based on the positive signal[7] (as per Lennox and Pittman 2011) conveyed to the credit scorer when the annual accounts bear the imprimatur of an accountancy firm. Though the signalling/assurance value associated with a reporting accounting is expected to be less than that of a voluntary audit[8] (see Table 3), it is predicted that companies with a reporting accountant will be associated with higher credit scores; given that in the absence of a reporting accountant, the credit scorer is unaware who prepared the annual accounts.

H2: Companies whose annual accounts disclose they have appointed a reporting accountant will receive higher credit scores.

The focus of this study in terms of research design/empirical analysis is companies in their start-up phase. The influential study of Berger and Udell (1998) emphasises that small start-up firms are the most informationally opaque, in that they lack a track record and so 'may have difficulty building reputations to signal high quality … to overcome informational opacity' (p. 16). When investigating the financing of Belgian manufacturing corporate start-ups, Huyghebaert and Van de Gucht (2007) stress that 'At the start-up stage, outside financiers have no historical data about the firm, which leads to a higher asymmetry in information compared to established firms' (p. 102); and find that 'entrepreneurs who provide a credible quality signal … have a larger fraction of bank debt' (p. 129). Similar points obtain in the literature relating to initial public offerings (IPOs), when information asymmetries are pronounced (eg Holland and Horton 1993, Firth and Liau-Tan 1998). In examining UK IPOs in the (then) Unlisted Securities Market, Holland and Horton (1993, p. 19) state that in 'the context of information asymmetry … the status of the professional advisers employed by the company is used as a signal of the quality of the IPO.' They find evidence in support of this conjecture, in that the appointment of 'higher quality' (larger) auditors is associated with smaller initial share price discounts. In accord with this literature, any signalling/assurance value associated with filing choice (*H1*) and reporting accountants (*H2*) is likely to be especially valuable to the credit scorer (and hence empirically detectable) when assigning credit scores to young, informationally opaque small companies.

3.   Research design, data and descriptive statistics

3.1   *Data and sample design*

All data for this study were downloaded from the FAME internet database, which contains information for all UK companies, in January 2016. The database is prepared for Bureau Van Dijk by Jordans Limited (see below). Companies were initially selected if they were 'live' (not failed/dormant[9]), private, independent (not held as a subsidiary) and had account year ends falling in the corporate fiscal year to March 2015 (the latest available on FAME). A total of 35,983 private independent companies meeting these requirements had filed micro-entity accounts,[10] with 822,087 having filed small abbreviated unaudited ones, of which 712,631 (86.7%) had TA ≤£316,000. As described below, to ensure broad initial size homogeneity, only micro/small companies with TA ≤£316,000 (the upper qualifying TA limit for a micro-entity) are included in the estimation sample.

The original research objective of this study was to examine only company start-ups which had filed their first set of accounts, since (as discussed above) start-ups are the most informationally opaque companies, information asymmetries are especially marked – and hence their initial credit scores, and the signalling/assurance value associated with filing micro accounts and the disclosure of reporting accountants, may be of particular import (Berger and Udell 1998). However, on downloading some initial data, it became clear that no credit scores were allocated to start-ups whose accounts disclosed negative equity[11] (TA < total liabilities). In consequence, this data was abandoned since empirical models and inferences would be restricted (atypical). Rather, data was collected for micro and small companies which had filed their second and fifth set of accounts. These companies are in the early stage of their life cycle, and as mentioned previously, their allocated credit scores may be especially important with regard to raising finance.

In addition, as argued above, evidence in support of *H1* or *H2* is more likely to be detected when information asymmetries (for young companies) are pervasive; and hence when the value (to the credit scorer) of signalling/assurance is especially pronounced. Companies that had filed their fifth set of accounts were selected with a view to examining whether more established companies (though still in their start-up phase) are rewarded with higher credit scores

(Dedman and Kausar 2012). Furthermore, restricting the sample to companies filing their second/fifth set of accounts ensures a reasonable degree of uniformity when estimating regression/matching models,[12] whilst facilitating an examination (below) of the robustness of the empirical findings when models are estimated separately for companies which had filed their second/fifth set of accounts. Specifically, companies which had filed their second or fifth set of accounts are still in their start-up phase, but the latter are more mature (having filed an additional three sets of accounts), providing a reasonable basis to examine whether the findings relating to the experimental variables persist across the two subsamples.

Data for all micro companies on FAME ($n = 6996$) who had filed either their second ($n = 4965$) or their fifth set of accounts ($n = 2031$) was downloaded. Using FAME random sampling software, data was also collected for a random sample of 8000 small companies with TA $\leq£316,000$. These comprise a random of 4000 small companies who had filed their second set of accounts, together with a random sample of 4000 companies which had submitted their fifth set of accounts (see Section 4.5 for a discussion of the limitations of this study). However, as discussed below, in addition to the primary samples, basic information (variables) for all 35,983 micro companies, together with that for a random sample of 40,000 small companies drawn from the available 822,087 mentioned above, was also downloaded from FAME. As reported in Table 6, statistics indicate that credit scores differences between micro and small companies are persistent across these extended samples.

Table 4 shows how the final estimation sample is constructed. To ensure broad size homogeneity, micro companies with TA $>£316,000$ are excluded ($n = 135$). Note that, as described above, the initial sample of small companies was restricted to those with TA $\leq£316,000$ with this in mind. In addition, the application of this size filter ensures that most (if not all) of the sampled small companies could have opted to file micro accounts. This is because even if some have sales above the micro regulatory limit (£632,000), they are highly likely to have 10 or fewer employees. Specifically, official data estimates (DBEI 2016b) reveal that 87.9% of all UK companies had nine or fewer employees (the definition of a micro-company used in UK official statistics) at the start of 2016. As the table reveals, a further 3(4) micro (small) companies which had auditors (a negative gearing ratio) are also excluded[13]; and 59(76) had not been allocated credit scores.[14]

A total of 228 micro companies are omitted because they voluntarily filed a profit and loss statement, with a further 8 small companies excluded because they disclosed profit and loss data – and had therefore been incorrectly classified by CH as 'total exemption small' (see above). Hence, all small and micro companies in the final sample had filed only an unaudited abbreviated balance sheet at CH. Lastly, a relatively large number of micro (1069) and small (312) companies are excluded because they have no (zero) current liabilities; and hence the

Table 4. Sample construction.

	Micro sample		Small sample		All companies	
	Lost	Remaining	Lost	Remaining	Lost	Remaining
Initial samples		6996		8000		14,996
Total assets >£316,000	(135)	6861		8000	(135)	14,861
Missing credit score	(59)	6802	(76)	7924	(135)	14,726
Has audited accounts	(3)	6799		7924	(3)	14,723
Disclosed profit and/or sales	(228)	6571	(8)	7916	(236)	14,487
Has negative gearing ratio	(4)	6567		7916	(4)	14,483
Current liabilities = zero	(1069)	5498	(312)	7604	(1381)	13,102

current ratio (below) could not be computed. However, as a robustness test, results are reported where these companies are included in the estimation sample via a dummy (binary) variable approach.

3.2 Model specification and variables

Variable labels and definitions are reported in Table 5. The full model specification is:

$$\begin{aligned}
\text{Credit score (CREDSCR)} = {} & a_0 + b_1\text{MICRO} + b_2\text{REPACC} + b_3\text{SIZE} + b_4\text{GEAR} \\
& + b_5\text{CACL} + b_6\text{NEGEQ} + b_7\text{NEGWC} + b_8\text{FATA} + b_9\text{COURT} \\
& + b_{10}\text{DEFLT} + b_{11}\text{CHARGE} + b_{12}\text{DIVERS} + b_{13}\text{DUM5} \\
& + b_{14}\text{LNSHR} + b_{15}\text{LNDIR} + b_{16}\text{SHRDIR} + b_{17}\text{IND} + e
\end{aligned}$$

where IND represents a vector of industry dummy variables.

FAME credit scores are developed and maintained by CRIF Decision Solutions Limited in conjunction with Jordans Limited, who also prepare FAME data. As well as the credit scores being available to subscribers to FAME (such as banks), they are also included in credit reports which can be purchased (eg by creditors or potential creditors) from Jordans Limited, a

Table 5.   Variable labels, definitions and means.

Label	Definition	Mean ($n = 13{,}102$)
CREDSCR	Credit score	33.535
MICRO	1 = Filed micro abbreviated accounts, 0 = filed small abbreviated accounts	0.420
REPACC[a]	1 = Accounts disclose accountant's name (reporting accountant)	0.284
TA	Total assets (£)	42,877
SIZE	Natural log of TA	9.838
GEAR	Total liabilities to total assets	0.966
CACL	Current assets to current liabilities	1.374
NEGEQ[a]	1 = Negative equity (total liabilities > total assets)	0.245
NEGWC[a]	1 = Negative working capital (currents assets < current liabilities)	0.394
FATA	Fixed assets to total assets	0.199
COURT[a]	1 = Court judgment for debt against company in past year	0.014
DEFLT[a]	1 = Defaulted on filing annual accounts and/or annual returns on time	0.011
CHARGE[a]	1 = Creditor has a registered charge against company assets	0.036
DIVERS[a]	1 = Has additional standard industrial classification code	0.077
DUM5	1 = Fifth set of accounts, 0 = second set of accounts	0.419
LNSHR	Natural log of number of shareholders	0.149
LNDIR	Natural log of number of directors	0.246
SHRDIR	Number of shareholders to number of directors	0.984
AGRI[a]	1 = Agricultural and fisheries industrial sector	0.004
MINING[a]	1 = Mining industrial sector	0.002
MAN[a]	1 = Manufacturing industrial sector	0.042
UTILI[a]	1 = Utilities industrial sector	0.005
CONS[a]	1 = Construction industrial sector	0.103
RET[a]	1 = Retail/wholesale industrial sector	0.107
OTHSER[a]	1 = Service industrial sector, other than financial services	0.712
FINSER[a]	1 = Financial service industrial sector (base case)	0.020
NOIND[a]	1 = If no standard industry code disclosed	0.007

[a]Indicates a binary variable where a company without the characteristic is coded as zero.

major UK business information provider. The credit scores range from 0 to 100 and are a measure of the likelihood that a company will become bankrupt in the next 12 months – with lower scores indicating higher failure risk. For company year ends commencing on or after 1 April 2014 (as per the company year ends in the current study), credit scores are allocated on the basis of a new[15] scoring model. The FAME online literature states that as well as financial data being used to determine credit scores, other factors taken into account include industry SIC data, director and shareholder information, county court judgements and the timeliness with which a company files its accounts. *Inter alia*, the explanatory variables in the current study endeavour to capture all of these factors.

The experimental binary variables employed in the study are MICRO and REPACC, with the former coded 1 for micro companies filing abbreviated accounts and 0 for small companies filing abbreviated accounts. REPACC is coded as 1 if a company's annual accounts disclose they are prepared by an accountancy firm (as provided as a variable on FAME) and 0 otherwise. To check the accuracy of the FAME scanning process for this variable, and to ascertain the frequency with which an accountant's report is included in the annual accounts, the accounts filed at CH for random samples of 20 micro and 20 small companies (drawn from those reported in Table 6) where FAME indicated they had an accountant[16] were examined. In all cases, the name of the accountancy firm had been correctly scanned. The accounts of 11 companies (27.5%) contained an accountant's report, 6 of which were micro companies, with the remaining 5 being small ones. Typically, the accountant's name and address is included in the company information page under the heading 'Accountants', with the contents page indicating that the accounts contained an 'Accountant's Report'.

Following Dedman and Kausar (2012), the model includes control variables reflecting corporate size (which is expected to be positively associated with CREDSCR), gearing, liquidity, solvency and asset tangibility. More specifically, SIZE is the natural log of TA, GEAR is the ratio of total liabilities to TA, CACL is the ratio of current assets to current liabilities,[17] NEGEQ (NEGWC) indicates that a company has negative equity (negative working capital) and FATA is the ratio of fixed to TA. Theodossiou (1993) reports that the latter is negatively associated with corporate failure. As commented by Bessler et al. (2011, p. 24), 'a high ratio of fixed to TA provides debtors with a high level of security since they can liquidate assets in case of bankruptcy'. For these reasons, FATA is expected to be positively related to CREDSCR. Additional variables include whether a county court order for non-payment of debt has been issued against a company in the preceding 12 months (COURT); and whether FAME indicates that a company has defaulted (DEFLT) on its obligation to file its annual accounts/returns within prescribed time limits, thus incurring penalties (see eg Clatworthy and Peel 2016). In this context, Experian (2013) warns that late filing may lead to inferior credit ratings. Hence, both variables are predicted to be negatively related to CREDSCR, with COURT expected (intuitively) to have a particularly strong association.

A further variable (CHARGE) denotes whether a creditor has registered a charge against a company's assets. The presence of a registered charge has been found to be positively related to corporate failure (Wilson and Wright 2013). This may arise in cases of debt default, where secured creditors are more likely to instigate insolvency proceedings to recover the value of their collateralised loans. In this context, Wilson and Wright (2013, p. 956) note that a charge may be registered against high-risk companies in order to mitigate default risk. In consequence, CHARGE and CREDSCR are expected to be negatively related. DIVERS is a binary variable denoting whether or not a company has more than one standard industrial classification (SIC) code (ie operates in more than one industrial sector). Other things equal (and in line with portfolio theory), companies with diversified operations (revenue streams) may be perceived by the credit

Table 6. Statistics for all micro companies and a random sample of 40,000 small companies.

| Years of accounts (YR) | MICRO: means unbracketed, with number of companies bracketed | | | SMALL: means unbracketed, with number of companies bracketed | | | CREDSCR difference |
| | Total assets (TA) ≤£316,000 | | | Total assets (TA) ≤£316,000 | | | |
	CREDSCR	TA £000	REPACC	CREDSCR	TA £000	REPACC	
Panel A: Summary statistics							
YR1	22.15 (6585)	20.34 (8128)	0.070 (8128)	31.38 (4512)	32.11 (5766)	0.358 (5766)	−9.23
YR2	28.26 (4846)	29.38 (4895)	0.118 (4895)	36.25 (4766)	38.61 (4804)	0.368 (4804)	−7.99
YR3	27.90 (3547)	35.44 (3581)	0.134 (3581)	36.76 (3866)	44.62 (3897)	0.389 (3897)	−8.86
YR4	28.36 (2588)	40.69 (2618)	0.158 (2618)	36.27 (3023)	51.58 (3049)	0.403 (3049)	−7.91
YR5	28.12 (1953)	42.74 (1963)	0.144 (1963)	36.31 (2419)	52.25 (2439)	0.382 (2439)	−8.19
YR6	31.35 (1663)	41.59 (1685)	0.124 (1685)	39.98 (1843)	53.07 (1864)	0.386 (1864)	−8.63
YR7	34.91 (1702)	45.52 (1718)	0.137 (1718)	44.69 (1764)	57.29 (1785)	0.406 (1785)	−9.78
YR8	39.23 (1929)	50.02 (1946)	0.114 (1946)	47.70 (1819)	57.97 (1831)	0.410 (1831)	−8.47
YR9	39.97 (1562)	52.02 (1576)	0.108 (1576)	47.61 (1290)	64.32 (1298)	0.423 (1298)	−7.64
YR ≥ 10	38.26 (6575)	58.76 (6654)	0.153 (6654)	51.48 (7848)	75.03 (7907)	0.445 (7907)	−13.22
All years	30.69 (32,950)	38.69 (34,764)	0.120 (34,764)	40.99 (33,150)	52.35 (34,640)	0.398 (34,640)	−10.30
Panel B: TA > £316,000							
All years	40.63 (1169)	775.39 (1207)	0.253 (1207)	56.90 (5246)	1251.55 (5360)	0.471 (5360)	−16.27
Panel C: Regression model (TA ≤£316,000)							

(Continued)

Table 6. Continued.

Years of accounts (YR)	MICRO: means unbracketed, with number of companies bracketed Total assets (TA) ≤ £316,000			SMALL: means unbracketed, with number of companies bracketed Total assets (TA) ≤ £316,000			CREDSCR difference
	CREDSCR	TA £000	REPACC	CREDSCR	TA £000	REPACC	

OLS ($n = 66,100$): CREDSCR $= 5.922$(Constant) $+ 2.715$SIZE $- 0.018$REPACC $- 8.469$MICRO $+ 4.631$YR2 $+ 4.228$YR3 $+ 3.740$YR4 $+ 3.549$YR5 $+ 6.969$YR6 $+ 10.891$YR7 $+ 14.295$YR8 $+ 14.531$YR9 $+ 15.383$YR10 Model $R^2 = 0.404$

MICRO ($n = 4177$)   SMALL ($n = 13,770$)

Panel D: Top 5 reporting accountants' market shares (TA ≤ £316,000)
Carnegie Knox: 4.93%   SJD Accountancy: 1.89%
Grant Harrod: 3.85%   Churchill Knight: 0.73%
Burrows Scarborough Silk: 3.14%   Paystream Accounting Services: 0.61%
Pipeline Accountants: 2.39%   Danbro Accounting: 0.54%
Limelight Accountancy: 2.38%   JSA Services: 0.47%

Notes: Variable definitions: SIZE = natural log of total assets (TA) and YR = number of annual accounts filed since incorporation. Panels A and B: mean values of CREDSCR, TA and REPACC differ significantly at $p < 0.001$ between the micro and small company samples on the basis of t-tests for CREDSCR and TA and χ^2 tests for REPACC (two-tailed tests) for individual years (YR) and for all years. Panel C: YR2 to YR10 are binary variables where unity corresponds to the number of annual accounts filed, with YR1 being the base case. On the basis of robust standard errors, all regression model coefficients are statistically significant at $p \leq 0.001$, other than that for REPACC which is statistically insignificant ($p = 0.873$).

scorer to have a lower failure likelihood. If this is the case, a positive association between DIVERS and CREDSCR is anticipated.

As mentioned above, DUM5 represents a binary variable, where one (zero) denotes a company which had filed its fifth (second) set of annual accounts. If more mature companies are perceived to be associated with lower risk, then DUM5 and CREDSCR are expected to be positively related. As shown in Table 5, three variables focus on directors and shareholders.[18] Other things equal, companies with larger boards (LNDIR) have more human capital/resources to devote to managing their enterprises and in inconsequence may be less failure prone, thereby attracting higher credit scores. Similarly, *ceteris paribus*, companies with a larger number of shareholders (LNSHR) have a larger potential pool of equity finance to draw on and may thereby be less likely to fail. However, it is also possible that the credit scorer penalises companies with a higher ratio of shareholders to directors (SHRDIR). This variable is a proxy for agency problems associated with the divorce between ownership and control and may therefore be positively associated with corporate failure – and hence negatively related to CREDSCR. Finally, as revealed in Table 5, with reference to their SIC codes, nine industry dummy variables were computed.

As with the studies of Lennox and Pittman (2011) and Dedman and Kausar (2012), the hypotheses of this paper are evaluated with reference to empirical models estimated with FAME credit scores as the dependent variable. Note, however, that banks may utilise their own internal SME credit scoring systems (Resti 2016), though this does not preclude them from also referencing external credit scores such as those provided by FAME. Furthermore, a potential limitation of this study is that other UK company credit rating agencies (CreditSafe, Dun & Bradstreet, Equifax, Experian and Graydon UK) may formulate credit scores employing different criteria from FAME ones.

3.3 *Descriptive statistics*

Prior to focusing on the primary estimation samples, Table 6 presents descriptive statistics for the sample of all micro companies[19] ($n = 35,971$) and the random sample of 40,000 small companies described previously. These descriptive statistics aim to provide a backdrop to the current study (as well as for potential future research) by reporting the stylised facts for the micro and small company sectors. For companies with TA ≤£316k, Panel A shows the mean values of CREDSCR, TA and REPACC for the micro and small subsamples, according to the number of annual accounts (YR) they had filed at CH since incorporation (ranging from 1 to ≥10). As reported, for all values of YR, the differences between the subsample means of the three variables are highly significant in all cases ($p ≤ 0.001$), with micro companies being smaller, substantially less likely to have a reporting accountant and attracting lower credit scores than their small company counterparts. In general, the three variables increase with YR, though for both subsamples, this occurs only from Y6 for CREDSCR. More specifically, for micro (small) companies, mean values for CREDSCR, TA and REPACC rise from 22.15 (31.38), £20.34k (£32.11k) and 0.070 (0.358) for YR1 to 38.26 (51.48), £58.76k (£75.03k) and 0.153 (0.455) for YR10. As shown in the last column of Table 6, noteworthy is the lower credit scores systematically assigned to micro companies relative to small ones, with the difference in credit scores varying between −7.64 and −13.22.

Panel B reports statistics for all companies with TA >£316k. Unsurprisingly, for both subsamples, it shows that the mean values of CREDSCR, TA and REPACC are substantially higher than those for companies with TA ≤£316k. For the latter, Panel C presents results for a simple ordinary least squares (OLS) regression model where CREDSCR is regressed on SIZE, REPACC, MICRO and nine binary YR variables (YR2 to YR10), with YR1 being the base (omitted) case.[20] As shown, the explanatory power of the model is reasonably high ($R^2 = 0.404$). Other than for REPACC, which exhibits a statistically insignificant ($p = 0.873$) small negative coefficient which is close to zero (and thus not supporting H2), the variable coefficients are highly significant ($p \leq 0.001$). After controlling for SIZE and YR, the coefficient for MICRO implies that, on average, the credit scores of micro companies are some 8.5 points lower than those of small companies. Hence, the OLS results in Table 6 are supportive of H1. For both sub-samples, noteworthy is the pattern of the coefficients for the YR dummies, which suggest that credit scores increase from YR6 onwards.[21] Finally, Panel D shows that the market shares of the top five reporting accountants are relatively small. However, there is evidence of a higher degree of specialisation in the micro market, with the leading accountancy firms in the micro (small) company sectors being Carnegie Knox (SJD Accountancy) having market shares of 4.9% (1.9%).

Turning to the primary estimation samples, Tables 5 and 7 provide summary statistics for the combined sample and the subsamples of micro and small companies, respectively. As Table 5 shows, the mean TA value (£42,877) of the sampled companies is comparatively small, as is the mean credit score (33.54), which varies from a minimum of 16 to a maximum of 69, with the median being 32. Consistent with the evidence presented in Table 1, the gearing (GEAR)

Table 7. Subsample variable means.

	MICRO (n = 5498)	SMALL (n = 7604)
CREDSCR	29.038**	36.786**
REPACC	0.138**	0.390**
TA	36,702**	47,343**
SIZE	9.658**	9.969**
GEAR	0.976	0.958
CACL	1.405**	1.351**
NEGEQ	0.262**	0.233**
NEGWC	0.379**	0.405**
FATA	0.205**	0.195**
COURT	0.016*	0.012*
DEFLT	0.010	0.011
CHARGE	0.025**	0.043**
DIVERS	0.090**	0.070**
DUM5	0.305**	0.502**
LNSHR	0.132**	0.161**
LNDIR	0.243	0.248
SHRDIR	0.969**	0.995**
AGRI	0.004	0.003
MINING	0.001	0.002
MAN	0.045	0.040
UTILI	0.005	0.005
CONS	0.099	0.106
RET	0.103	0.109
OTHSER	0.722*	0.704*
FINSER	0.015**	0.023**
NOIND	0.007	0.007

Notes: All variables are defined in Table 5.
**,*Indicate means differ significantly between the MICRO and SMALL subsamples at $p \leq 0.01$ and $p \leq 0.05$ on the basis of χ^2 tests for binary variables and t-tests for non-binary variables (two-tailed tests). No variables differed significantly at the 0.10 statistical level.

sample mean of 0.966 is very high, though the median value is somewhat lower (0.858). In addition, a high proportion of companies exhibit negative equity (NEGEQ) and negative working capital (NEGWC), at 0.245 and 0.394, respectively.

As Table 5 reveals, 28.4% of companies disclosed that they had a reporting accountant, 1.4% had received a court order for non-payment of debt, 1.1% had defaulted with regard to filing their annual accounts or returns on time and 3.6% had a charge registered against their assets. Of note is the large proportion of companies operating in the service sector (73.2%), with only 4.2% classified as being in the manufacturing sector. As anticipated, the mean ratio (0.984) of the number of directors to shareholders is approaching unity.

Using t-tests (chi-squared tests) for difference between variable means (proportions), Table 7 reveals that the small and micro subsamples differ significantly in a number of dimensions. Small companies are larger, are less likely to exhibit negative equity or to have received a court order for non-payment of debt. Micro companies exhibit higher liquidity (CACL), have higher asset tangibility (FATA) and are more likely to operate in more than one industrial sector (DIVERS). In addition, small companies have more shareholders and a higher ratio of shareholders to directors than micro ones. As also shown in Table 7, noteworthy is that the proportion of small companies with reporting accountants (0.390) is substantially higher than that for micro ones[22] (0.138). Given that micro companies opted to disclose less balance sheet information than their small company counterparts, this may result from them being less aware of (or less concerned with) the potential benefits[23] in terms of assurance/signalling. Furthermore, a significantly higher proportion of small companies (0.043) than micro ones (0.025) had a creditor's registered charge against their assets. It is likely that these charges contain restrictive covenants, one of which may be that a reporting accountant must be appointed. This would then contribute to the finding that small companies are more likely to have appointed a reporting accountant. Finally, the table reveals that the mean credit score of small companies (36.79) is 7.75 points higher (in percentage terms, 26.7% higher) than that of their micro counterparts (29.04).

Table 8 reports a Pearson's correlation matrix for the explanatory variables, together with CREDSCR. Most of the explanatory variables are significantly correlated with the latter and display their expected signs. On a univariate basis, MICRO and REPACC are negatively ($r = -0.340$) and positively ($r = 0.104$) associated with CREDSCR. GEAR and NEGEQ exhibit the highest degree of correlation with CREDSCR, with coefficients of -0.460 and -0.412, respectively. As expected, the strongest correlations are between GEAR and NEGEQ ($r = 0.774$) and CACL and NEGWC ($r = -0.732$). However, as discussed below, there is no evidence that multicollinearity poses a problem in the regression models.

4. Empirical study

4.1 *Multivariate regression results*

Table 9 presents standard OLS regression results with CREDSCR as the dependent variable. Model 1 reports the estimated parameters for the full model specification, with Models 2 and 3 showing the stability of the parameters when insignificant variables are omitted. The reported variance inflation factors (VIFs) are a measure of the degree of correlation (collinearity) between each variable and the remaining variables. As shown, the VIFs are relatively low, with the highest being for GEAR (CACL) at 3.70 (3.03). In terms of collinearity, the statistical literature suggests VIFs exceeding 10 are unacceptable (Chatterjee and Price, 1991). Worthy of note is that Model 1 appears well determined, with an R^2 of 0.395, which is higher than the adjusted R^2 (0.286) reported by Dedman and Kausar (2012) for their cross-sectional credit score model.

Consistent with *H1* and the univariate findings, the coefficient of MICRO is negative (−7.516) and highly significant ($t = 47.64, p < 0.001$). This implies that if micro companies had filed abbreviated accounts under the small company regime, on average, they would have benefitted from a 7.52 points rise (a 25.9% increase) in their credit scores.

However, unlike for audited accounts (Dedman and Kausar 2012), there is no evidence that the credit scorer rewards companies whose accounts bear the imprimatur of a reporting accountant. The coefficient of REPACC is negative[24] (−0.024) and indistinguishable from zero ($t = 0.13$, $p = 0.898$). Hence, *H2* is rejected. As described above, note that the simple regression model estimated in the extended samples (Panel C, Table 6) also supports this finding.

Model 1 shows that the shareholder/director variables and DIVERS are statistically insignificant, with DUM5 exhibiting a relatively small negative coefficient (−0.310), which is significant at the 10% level. The latter indicates that older companies that filed their fifth set of accounts have marginally lower credit scores than their younger counterparts who filed their second set of accounts.[25] LNSHR, LNDIR and SHRDIR are also statistically insignificant[26] when entered singularly or in pairs in Model 1. It is possible, however, that the credit scorer employs variables reflecting shareholder/director characteristics for larger (eg listed) companies where substantive agency/governance issues arise in consequence of the divorce between ownership and control (see Ashbaugh-Skaife et al. 2006).

The remaining control variables exhibit their expected signs and are statistically significant at the 1% level, other than for CHARGE which attains significance at the 5% level. In addition, on the basis of an *F*-test, the industry dummies are jointly significant ($p < 0.001$). As the table reveals, smaller companies with higher gearing, lower asset tangibility, lower liquidity, negative equity or negative working capital attract significantly lower credit scores. As anticipated, the coefficients of DEFLT, CHARGE and COURT are negative. Unsurprisingly, COURT has the largest association, with its coefficient implying that companies issued with a court order for non-payment of debt have a mean credit score some 11.74 points lower than those who had not received such a an order.[27] Models 2 and 3 show that the inferences for Model 1 are highly robust to the omission of the insignificant variables. Model 2 reveals that when LNSHR, LNDIR and SHRDIR are excluded, the remaining variable coefficients are similar in size and significance to their counterparts in Model 1. Similar findings obtain for Model 3, where all statistically insignificant variables are excluded. The latter parsimonious specification is therefore employed in the analysis reported in the following sections.

As mentioned previously, a number of companies which had not incurred current liabilities were excluded from the sample. As a robustness test, and following Black and Smith (2006), a dummy variable (NOCL) – coded 1 if a company has zero current liabilities (0, otherwise) – is included in the regression model. In addition, CACL is coded as zero for these missing observations. In the regression model, NOCL captures the mean difference in credit scores for companies not incurring current liabilities relative to those that did, whilst facilitating the inclusion of all explanatory variables (including CACL) for the expanded sample. Appendix 1 to this paper reports regression results for the full specification. Though the coefficient for MICRO declines marginally to −7.30, Appendix 1 shows that the mean credit score of companies without current liabilities (NOCL) is 1.79 points lower; and that the remaining variables exhibit similar signs and significance levels as their counterparts in Model 1. The OLS regression results are therefore robust to this specification change.[28]

Finally, as discussed above, to examine the robustness of the regression results, Appendix 2 reports OLS models estimated separately for companies which had filed their second (Year 2) and fifth (Year 5) set of accounts. For both models, it shows that the control variables exhibit their expected signs and are statistically significant, other than for DEFLT and CHARGE which lose statistical significance in the Year 2 model. However, both are significant at the 10% level

($p = 0.08$ and $p = 0.07$, respectively) on the basis of a one-sided directional test. Importantly, the inferences for the experimental variables are stable across the Year 2 and 5 models, with the coefficients for MICRO being -7.18 and -8.09, respectively; and with both being highly significant ($p < 0.001$). In contrast, the coefficients for REPACC are close to zero and statistically insignificant for both the Year 2 ($t = 0.15$, $p = 0.883$) and Year 5 ($t = 0.01$, $p = 0.997$) specifications. Hence, these results strongly support those reported in Table 9. *Inter alia*, Section 4.5 discusses potential reasons for the statistical insignificance of REPACC; and hence the lack of empirical support for *H2*.

4.2. *Heckman selection models*

The Heckman treatment (endogenous selection) two-step model aims to control/test for unobserved selection bias (see eg Leuz and Verrecchia 2000, Tucker 2010, Bayar and Chemmanur 2012). In the current study, this would arise if an unobserved (hidden) variable is jointly and significantly correlated with CREDSCR and MICRO leading to biased estimates for MICRO. The rationale of the Heckman approach is that the errors (residuals) from a first-step probit selection model can be employed as a surrogate for potential hidden (omitted) variables. In the current study, a first-step probit selection model with MICRO as the dependent variable is used to compute generalised model residuals (Gourieroux et al. 1987), which are known as inverse Mills ratios (IMRs). The IMR for each company is then included in the second-step CREDSCR regression specification (Model 3, Table 9) as a proxy for hidden variables. For credible implementation, an instrumental variable is required. Such a variable is a significant determinant of MICRO, but is not significantly correlated with CREDSCR, other than via its association with MICRO. In the current study, REPACC meets these empirical requirements. Table 10 reports Heckman two-step estimates employing the Stata *treatreg* command.

In consequence of the (unintended) sample distribution of DUM5 for small companies,[29] three models are presented. As shown in Table 7, because the same number of small companies was randomly selected which had filed their second and fifth set of annual accounts, the proportion (0.5) filing their fifth set is overstated. Table 6 reveals that the actual proportion is around 0.34 (2419/7185). Table 10 therefore presents models including/excluding DUM5. In all cases, the IMR coefficients are statistically insignificant, suggesting that the standard regression results reported in Table 9 are preferred. For all probit models, the coefficients of REPACC are negative, stable and highly significant, with the reported Wald tests also confirming that REPACC is an effective instrumental variable.[30]

As discussed above, the higher likelihood of small companies appointing a reporting accountant may result from these companies (or their accountants) being more aware of the associated potential benefits[31] (eg in providing a degree of assurance to banks and trade creditors). Importantly, the coefficient of the IMR (-0.299) in Model 1 is statistically insignificant ($p = 0.428$), with the remaining variables exhibiting stable coefficients and significance levels when compared to the standard regression estimates in Table 9. Model 2 reports parameters where DUM5 is omitted from both the probit and OLS regression specifications. It shows that the estimated parameters[32] are similar to those in Model 1, with the coefficient of the IMR being identical to three decimal places – and exhibiting a similar level of insignificance ($p = 0.429$). Finally, for completeness, Model 3 includes DUM5 in both the probit and OLS specifications. Its parameters are consistent with those reported for Models 2 and 3. In summary, based on the Heckman estimates, there is no evidence of hidden selection (endogeneity) bias.

Table 8. Correlation matrix.

	CREDSCR	MICRO	REPACC	SIZE	GEAR	CACL	NEGEQ	NEGWC	FATA	COURT	DEFLT	CHARGE	DIVERS	DUM5	LNSHR	LNDIR	SHRDIR
CREDSCR	1																
MICRO	−0.340*	1															
REPACC	0.104*	−0.276*	1														
SIZE	0.344*	−0.109*	0.111*	1													
GEAR	−0.460*	0.012*	−0.019*	−0.378*	1												
CACL	0.367*	0.028*	−0.024*	0.272*	−0.650*	1											
NEGEQ	−0.412*	0.034*	−0.036*	−0.272*	0.774*	−0.472*	1										
NEGWC	−0.344*	−0.026*	0.008	−0.203*	0.576*	−0.732*	0.591*	1									
FATA	−0.057*	0.018*	−0.026*	−0.006	0.203*	−0.458*	0.208*	0.494*	1								
COURT	−0.149*	0.017*	−0.022*	−0.005	0.057*	−0.051*	0.055*	0.050*	0.062*	1							
DEFLT	−0.046*	−0.005	−0.005	−0.048*	0.042*	−0.040*	0.030*	0.015	0.016	0.025*	1						
CHARGE	0.016	−0.047*	0.037*	0.212*	0.028*	−0.062*	0.033*	0.057*	0.091*	0.033*	−0.012	1					
DIVERS	−0.015	0.045*	−0.039*	−0.047*	0.023*	0.009	0.031*	0.003	0.010	0.019*	−0.003	0.003	1				
DUM5	0.071*	−0.197*	0.063*	0.135*	0.016	0.011	0.008	0.017*	0.003	−0.019*	−0.011	0.077*	0.018*	1			
LNSHR	0.054*	−0.043*	0.056*	0.172*	−0.017*	0.024*	−0.017	−0.015	0.018*	−0.029*	−0.021*	0.073*	0.013	0.062*	1		
LNDIR	0.026*	−0.006	0.003	0.106*	−0.001	0.012	0.002	−0.001	0.032*	−0.019*	−0.024*	0.069*	0.022*	0.133*	0.380*	1	
SHRDIR	0.018*	−0.025*	0.035*	0.066*	−0.001	0.003	−0.001	−0.003	−0.001	−0.005	−0.001	0.016	−0.010	−0.037*	0.588*	−0.369*	1

Notes: All variables are defined in Table 5 ($n = 13,102$).
*Indicates correlation coefficient is significant at $p \leq 0.05$ (two-tailed tests).

Table 9. Credit score regression models.

	VIF	Model 1	Model 2	Model 3
MICRO	1.137	−7.516	−7.514	−7.499
		(47.64)**	(47.59)**	(49.27)**
REPACC	1.102	−0.024	−0.025	
		(0.13)	(0.13)	
SIZE	1.366	1.170	1.170	1.164
		(18.23)**	(18.43)**	(18.43)**
GEAR	3.698	−2.766	−2.766	−2.766
		(17.95)**	(17.97)**	(17.97)**
CACL	3.028	1.724	1.724	1.731
		(11.64)**	(11.65)**	(11.71)**
NEGEQ	2.979	−2.967	−2.967	−2.959
		(11.93)**	(11.94)**	(11.92)**
NEGWC	2.869	−2.584	−2.583	−2.586
		(10.25)**	(10.25)**	(10.26)**
FATA	1.454	5.480	5.482	5.494
		(18.68)**	(18.69)**	(18.75)**
COURT	1.013	−11.740	−11.744	−11.727
		(21.07)**	(21.11)**	(21.11)**
DEFLT	1.006	−2.247	−2.250	−2.255
		(3.55)**	(3.56)**	(3.57)**
CHARGE	1.077	−0.995	−0.993	−0.985
		(2.48)*	(2.48)*	(2.46)*
DIVERS	1.015	0.426	0.427	
		(1.44)	(1.44)	
DUM5	1.081	−0.310	−0.304	−0.297
		(1.89)†	(1.87)†	(1.83)†
LNSHR	1.294	0.034		
		(0.64)		
LNDIR	1.613	0.091		
		(0.49)		
SHRDIR	1.378	−0.059		
		(0.48)		
Constant		25.611	25.555	25.617
		(26.33)**	(27.48)**	(27.57)**
Industry dummies		✓	✓	✓
R^2		0.395	0.395	0.395
N=		13,102	13,102	13,102

Notes: VIF = Variance inflation factor. All variables are defined in Table 5. Coefficients are unbracketed, with t-values (based on robust standard errors) shown in parentheses.
**,*Indicate coefficients are statistically significant at $p \leq 0.01$ and $p \leq 0.05$ (two-tailed tests).
†Indicate coefficients are statistically significant at $p \leq 0.10$ (two-tailed tests).

4.3. Matching and regression adjustment

Matching is an intuitive method which controls for potential observed bias associated with regression model estimates. More specifically, it does not rely on model functional form, nor does it require the linearity assumption, since estimates are confined to the common support; that is, where treated (in this study micro companies) and control subjects have similar character-istics.[33] Because it is usually impossible to match closely on more than one continuous variable (known as the curse of dimensionality), the method of propensity score matching (PSM) is widely employed in accounting studies (Tucker 2010). Rosenbaum and Rubin's (1983) seminal research demonstrates that matching on propensity scores (selection model probabilities) is equivalent to

Table 10. Heckman credit score selection models.

	Model 1		Model 2		Model 3	
	OLS	Probit	OLS	Probit	OLS	Probit
SIZE	1.184 (17.59)***	-0.085 (9.29)***	1.170 (17.49)***	-0.085 (9.29)***	1.186 (18.10)***	-0.063 (6.72)***
GEAR	-2.755 (13.67)***	-0.059 (1.97)**	-2.777 (13.80)***	-0.059 (1.97)**	-2.759 (13.71)***	-0.020 (0.67)
CACL	1.718 (12.15)***	0.045 (2.18)**	1.706 (12.08)***	0.045 (2.18)**	1.708 (12.03)***	0.064 (3.02)***
NEGEQ	-3.002 (9.65)***	0.215 (4.71)***	-2.992 (9.62)***	0.215 (4.71)***	-3.015 (9.71)***	0.195 (4.22)***
NEGWC	-2.552 (9.52)***	-0.183 (4.60)***	-2.565 (9.57)***	-0.183 (4.60)***	-2.544 (9.51)***	-0.160 (3.99)***
FATA	5.439 (16.41)***	0.234 (4.87)***	5.439 (16.41)***	0.234 (4.87)***	5.418 (16.35)***	0.230 (4.72)***
COURT	-11.760 (17.93)***	0.132 (1.35)	-11.735 (17.90)***	0.132 (1.35)	-11.763 (17.95)***	0.090 (0.91)
DEFLT	-2.233 (3.04)***	-0.141 (1.28)	-2.224 (3.02)***	-0.141 (1.28)	-2.220 (3.02)***	-0.154 (1.38)
CHARGE	-0.958 (2.23)**	-0.164 (2.47)**	-0.991 (2.31)**	-0.164 (2.47)**	-0.961 (2.24)**	-0.106 (1.58)
DUM5	-0.297 (1.86)*				-0.177 (0.92)	-0.481 (20.23)***
MICRO	-7.044 (11.83)***		-6.991 (11.76)***		-6.845 (11.25)***	
Constant	25.292 (25.49)***	0.519 (3.86)***	25.334 (25.53)***	0.519 (3.86)***	25.182 (25.57)***	0.409 (3.01)***
REPACC		-0.804 (29.78)***		-0.804 (29.78)***		-0.800 (29.30)***
IMR	-0.299 (0.79)		-0.299 (0.79)		-0.427 (1.11)	
Industry dummies	✓	✓	✓	✓	✓	✓
R^2 or χ^2	0.395	1,252.03***	0.395	1,252.03***	0.395	1,666.13***
N=	13,102	13,102	13,102	13,102	13,102	13,102

Models 1 and 2: Wald test REPACC=0; χ^2 = 887.01 ($p < 0.001$)
Model 3: Wald test REPACC=0; χ^2 = 858.73 ($p < 0.001$)

Notes: All variables are defined in Table 5. IMR = the inverse Mills ratio. The dependent variables are CREDSCR and MICRO for the OLS and probit specifications, respectively. Coefficients are unbracketed, with t-values (OLS) and z-values (probit) shown in parentheses. All models are estimated with the Stata treatreg command. ***, **, *Indicate coefficients are statistically significant at $p \leq 0.01$, $p \leq 0.05$ and $p \leq 0.10$ (two-tailed tests).

matching on the individual variables included in the selection model. Hence, PSM circumvents the curse of dimensionality. After PSM, the 'treatment effect' (in this study, MICRO) is estimated as a simple difference in the means of the outcome of interest in the matched samples (see eg Bayar and Chemmanur 2012).

As reported in Appendix 1, PSM is implemented with a probit selection model (with MICRO as the dependent variable), which contains the explanatory variables specified in Table 11. Using the Stata *psmatch* module, nearest neighbour (NN) matching without replacement is employed, where the predicted probability for each micro-company is matched to the closest value of that predicted for a small company. To ensure close NN matching, a fine calliper of 0.01 is applied. This specifies the maximum difference in selection probabilities for micro and small companies which can be matched. As a robustness test, results are also reported where an even finer calliper (0.005) is applied.

Table 11 reports covariate balance statistics for the NN matched micro and small companies for PSM with a 0.01 calliper (n= 8710) and for the finer calliper of 0.005 (n = 8164). For both cases, it reveals that the variable means are similar for the micro and small subsamples, with none of the differences approaching statistical significance at conventional levels. After matching, for the 0.01 (0.005) calliper samples, the mean credit scores for micro companies are 29.038 (29.067), compared to 37.015 (37.192) for small ones, with the mean differences of −7.977 (−8.125) being highly significant[34] (both at $p<0.001$); and hence supporting *H1*.

As a robustness test, a typical approach in accounting research is to estimate regression models in the NN matched samples (eg Ittonen et al. 2015). Regression adjustment is applied for two reasons. Firstly, to account for any covariate imbalance after matching; and secondly, because estimates are doubly robust 'in the sense that if either the matching or the parametric

Table 11.   Covariate balance (means).

	Matched propensity scores: calliper = 0.01			Matched propensity scores: calliper = 0.005		
	MICRO (n = 4355)	SMALL (n = 4355)	Mean difference (p-value)[a]	MICRO (n = 4082)	SMALL (n = 4082)	Mean difference (p-value)[a]
SIZE	9.972	9.959	0.624	10.033	10.031	0.945
GEAR	0.955	0.934	0.161	0.951	0.931	0.192
CACL	1.344	1.357	0.517	1.340	1.350	0.586
NEGEQ	0.230	0.217	0.150	0.223	0.212	0.227
NEGWC	0.389	0.386	0.708	0.391	0.389	0.838
FATA	0.182	0.186	0.531	0.182	0.186	0.505
COURT	0.009	0.011	0.332	0.009	0.011	0.577
DEFLT	0.012	0.011	0.762	0.012	0.011	0.610
CHARGE	0.031	0.030	0.950	0.032	0.032	0.900
DUM5	0.385	0.385	0.982	0.410	0.410	1.000
AGRI	0.002	0.002	0.818	0.002	0.002	0.808
MINING	0.002	0.002	1.000	0.002	0.002	1.000
MAN	0.037	0.035	0.688	0.035	0.034	0.716
UTILI	0.005	0.006	0.554	0.005	0.006	0.545
CONS	0.104	0.103	0.916	0.104	0.104	0.942
RET	0.104	0.109	0.445	0.104	0.111	0.317
OTHSER	0.721	0.717	0.721	0.721	0.715	0.572
FINSER	0.019	0.018	0.937	0.020	0.019	0.936
NOIND	0.007	0.007	0.899	0.008	0.007	0.898

Notes: All variables are defined in Table 5.
[a]Difference between means probabilities (p-values) are based on χ^2 tests for binary variables and t-tests for non-binary variables (two-tailed tests). No means differ significantly at $p \leq 0.10$.

model is correct, but not necessarily both, causal estimates will still be consistent' (Ho et al. 2007, p. 215). Using the same specification as Model 3 in Table 9 for the full sample, Models 1 and 3 in Table 12 report standard regression results estimated in the NN matched samples. Both models exhibit the same patterns of coefficient signs and significance levels as their counterparts estimated in the full (unmatched) sample. In particular, the coefficients of MICRO are −7.868 (−7.999) for Models 1 (3), thus supporting *H1*.

Finally, the IMR for each matched company (estimated from Model 1 in Table 10 using the full sample[35]) is included as an additional variable in the NN matched regression specification. As with the full sample Heckman selection estimates, Models 2 and 4 in Table 12 show that the IMR regression coefficients are statistically insignificant in the matched samples. In summary, results for the PSM and the adjusted regression models (with/without IMRs) support the full sample standard/Heckman regression findings. Furthermore, the estimates of the relationship between MICRO and CREDSCR reported in this section are similar to those of their full sample counterparts. In summary, there is no evidence of observed or unobserved bias.

Table 12. Credit score regression models for propensity score matched samples.

	Matched calliper = 0.01		Matched calliper = 0.005	
	Model 1	Model 2	Model 3	Model 4
MICRO	−7.868	−7.233	−7.999	−7.465
	(43.33)***	(10.66)***	(42.73)***	(10.75)***
SIZE	1.053	1.082	1.018	1.042
	(12.44)***	(12.06)***	(11.44)***	(11.11)***
GEAR	−2.582	−2.566	−2.554	−2.541
	(12.68)***	(12.56)***	(11.78)***	(11.68)***
CACL	1.931	1.915	2.050	2.036
	(10.25)***	(10.11)***	(10.40)***	(10.29)***
NEGEQ	−2.408	−2.468	−2.327	−2.378
	(7.86)***	(7.86)***	(7.24)***	(7.22)***
NEGWC	−2.977	−2.926	−3.071	−3.028
	(9.98)***	(9.68)***	(10.09)***	(9.83)***
FATA	6.285	6.206	6.651	6.586
	(15.85)***	(15.34)***	(15.92)***	(15.47)***
COURT	−13.453	−13.500	−13.506	−13.545
	(20.47)***	(20.52)***	(19.68)***	(19.72)***
DEFLT	−1.301	−1.272	−1.348	−1.324
	(1.79)*	(1.75)*	(1.84)*	(1.81)*
CHARGE	−1.067	−1.033	−1.049	−1.021
	(2.17)**	(2.09)**	(2.13)**	(2.06)**
DUM5	−0.641	−0.641	−0.774	−0.774
	(3.32)***	(3.32)***	(3.90)***	(3.90)***
IMR		−0.417		−0.351
		(0.98)		(0.80)
Constant	26.498	26.047	26.776	26.395
	(22.64)***	(20.72)***	(21.96)***	(20.25)***
Industry dummies	✓	✓	✓	✓
R^2	0.400	0.400	0.403	0.403
N=	8710	8710	8164	8164

Notes: All variables are defined in Table 5. IMR = inverse Mills ratio. Coefficients are unbracketed, with *t*-values (based on robust standard errors) shown in parentheses.
***,**,*Indicate coefficients are statistically significant at $p \leq 0.01$, $p \leq 0.05$ and $p \leq 0.10$ (two-tailed tests).

4.4.   *Further analysis: credit ratings*

As a further robustness test, this section extends the analysis to estimate models where the dependent variable is specified as companies' credit ratings. Based on credit scores, FAME assigns credit ratings on a five-point ordered scale. Specifically, the ratings are defined in the FAME online literature as follows (with credit scores in parentheses): *Secure* (81–100): 'Companies in this sector tend to be large and successful public companies. Failure is very unusual and normally occurs only as a result of exceptional changes within the company or its market'; *Stable* (61–80): 'Here again, company failure is a rare occurrence and will only come about if there are major company or marketplace changes'; *Normal* (41–60): 'This sector contains many companies that do not fail, but some that do'; *Cautious* (21–40): 'Here, as the name suggests, there is a significant risk of company failure'; and *High Risk* (0–20): 'Companies in the high risk sector may have difficulties in continuing trading unless significant remedial action is undertaken, there is support from a parent company, or special circumstances apply'.

Using credit scores, companies were assigned into these categories on an ordered scale ranging from 1 = high risk to 4 = stable. Panel A in Table 13 shows the distribution of the credit rating for the full sample as well as for the micro and small subsamples. Unsurprisingly, no companies have scores in the secure rating category and only 17 are classified as being

Table 13.   Credit ratings and ordered logit models.

	1: (High risk)	2: (Cautious)	3: (Normal)	4: (Stable)
Panel A: Distribution of credit ratings[a]				
MICRO	$n = 240$ (4.37%)	$n = 4968$ (90.36%)	$n = 289$ (5.26%)	$n = 1$ (0.02%)
SMALL	$n = 192$ (2.52%)	$n = 4587$ (60.23%)	$n = 2809$ (36.94%)	$n = 16$ (0.21%)
All	$n = 432$ (3.30%)	$n = 9555$ (72.93%)	$n = 3098$ (23.65%)	$n = 17$ (0.13%)
Panel B: Ordered logit models (credit ratings 1 to 3)				
	Model 1	Model 2	Model 3[b] PSM calliper = 0.01	Model 4[b] PSM calliper = 0.005
MICRO	−2.321***	−2.332***	−2.434***	−2.441***
REPACC	0.055			
SIZE	0.250***	0.249***	0.210***	0.209***
GEAR	−0.911***	−0.913***	−0.922***	−0.910***
CACL	0.172***	0.170***	0.158***	0.185***
NEGEQ	−0.550***	−0.550***	−0.543***	−0.514***
NEGWC	−0.887***	−0.886***	−0.932***	−0.926***
FATA	1.463***	1.457***	1.454***	1.492***
COURT	−8.311***	−8.306***	−9.037***	−8.936***
DEFLT	−0.714***	−0.712***	−0.393	−0.453
CHARGE	−0.214*	−0.214*	−0.302*	−0.311*
DIVERS	0.050			
DUM5	−0.027	−0.027	−0.076	−0.096
LNSHR	−0.035			
LNDIR	−0.002			
SHRDIR	−0.011			
Industry dummies	✓	✓	✓	✓
Model χ^2	5,557.66***	5,555.76***	3,483.99***	3,267.11***
N=	13,085	13,085	8705	8159

Notes: All variables are defined in Table 5. Coefficients are reported. Cut-off points (constants) are omitted.
[a]Distributions for MICRO and SMALL samples differ significantly: χ^2 =1,791.37 ($p < 0.001$).
[b]PSM = the propensity score matched samples employing callipers of 0.01 and 0.005 as reported in Table 12.
***,*Indicate coefficients are statistically significant at $p \leq 0.01$ and $p \leq 0.10$ levels, respectively, on the basis of z-values (two-tailed tests).

stable, 16 of which are small companies. As reported, the distributions of micro and small company credit ratings differ significantly, with a substantially larger proportion of small companies being in the lower risk categories.

Due to the difficulty in interpreting the effects of ordered probit model coefficients (Greene and Hensher 2009, p. 113), ordered logit models are often employed in accounting studies (eg Ashbaugh-Skaife et al. 2006, Altin et al. 2016). In particular, as shown below, the log odds coefficients of the ordinal logit model can be readily interpreted in terms of odds ratios (eg Yin and Zhang 2014). Panel B in Table 13 presents ordered logit models with identical (full and parsimonious) specifications to those which were used in the OLS credit score models reported in Table 9. Because of the small number of companies (and only one micro-company) in the stable category, they are excluded from the analysis, so that the ordered dependent variable contains three rating categories.[36] As shown in Table 13, other than for DUM5 which is statistically insignificant, the full (Model 1) and parsimonious (Model 2) specifications exhibit the same coefficient signs and similar significance levels as their OLS counterparts; with the coefficient of REPACC in Model 1 again being close to zero (0.055) and statistically insignificant ($z = 1.09$, $p = 0.277$). As Models 3 and 4 reveal, similar findings obtain when the estimates are confined to the two matched samples described above. Importantly, the coefficients of MICRO are stable and highly significant across all reported models.

Taking the exponential of a logit coefficient gives its odds ratio. For the coefficient (-2.321) of MICRO in Model 1, the associated odds ratio is calculated as: exponential (-2.321) = 0.099:1. More specifically, after controlling for other factors, small companies are 10.1 times (1/0.099) more likely to be assigned a higher credit rating than their micro counterparts. This clearly demonstrates the negative influence of filing micro accounts on credit ratings, with the relationship being more pronounced than for the credit score models.

Controlling for potential unobserved selection bias with ordered outcome models is more complex than the Heckman approach. As explained by Miranda and Rabe-Hesketh (2006), though based on the same principles as the Heckman model (above), due to distributional assumptions, for consistent estimated parameters, it requires maximum likelihood simultaneous estimation of a probit selection model (Model 1, Table 10) and an ordered probit outcome model. In doing so, as with the Heckman approach, it accounts for correlated errors between the models. Using the Stata *ssm* command (Miranda and Rabe-Hesketh 2006), Table 14 presents endogenous ordered probit selection models, together with standard ordered probit model estimates for comparison. Model 1 shows that the standard ordered probit estimates are the same in terms of coefficient signs and statistical significance as the corresponding ordered logit ones. As explained by Greene and Hensher (2009, p. 114), in comparing the coefficients of ordered probit and ordered logit models, the relationship between the two is $\beta_{\text{logit}} \approx 1.81\beta_{\text{probit}}$. For the coefficient of MICRO in Model 1, the associated logit coefficient is $-1.196 \times 1.81 = -2.165$. This compares to the actual logit coefficient of -2.332 for the same specification (Model 2 in Table 13). Hence, there is a good degree of congruence between the models.

Model 2 reports the results for the endogenous ordered probit specification.[37] It shows that the degree of correlation (rho) between the probit and ordered probit model errors (0.085) is statistically insignificant ($p = 0.668$). This result suggests that the standard ordered probit estimates for MICRO in Model 1 are apposite. For completeness, since DUM5 is statistically insignificant in all specifications, Model 3 omits this variable. As shown, the estimates are similar to their Model 2 counterparts. Consistent with the Heckman model findings, the results presented in Table 14 indicate an absence of hidden selection bias. Finally, as per the OLS credit score models, Appendix 2 reports separate ordered logit specifications for companies which had filed their second (Year 2) and fifth (Year 5) set of accounts. The results are highly congruent with those reported above, with the coefficients of MICRO being highly significant and negative in both specifications – and

Table 14.   Ordered probit and ordered probit endogenous selection models.

	Credit ratings 1 to 3		
	1. Probit	2. Endogenous probit	3. Endogenous probit
MICRO	−1.196***	−1.323***	−1.321***
SIZE	0.134***	0.129***	0.128***
GEAR	−0.434***	−0.436***	−0.436***
CACL	0.132***	0.135***	0.135***
NEGEQ	−0.228***	−0.216***	−0.216***
NEGWC	−0.437***	−0.446***	−0.446***
FATA	0.755***	0.769***	0.769***
COURT	−4.100***	−4.083***	−4.083***
DEFLT	−0.403***	−0.408***	−0.408***
CHARGE	−0.122*	−0.130*	−0.131*
DUM5	−0.010	−0.009	
Industry dummies	✓	✓	✓
Model χ^2	5,280.77***		
$N=$	13,085	13,085	13,085
Rho[a]		0.085	0.085
Rho significance[b]		$p=0.668$	$p=0.664$

Notes: All variables are defined in Table 5. Coefficients are reported. Cut-off points (constants) are omitted. Using the Stata *ssm* module (Miranda and Rabe-Hesketh 2006), parameters for Models 2 and 3 are obtained by jointly estimating, via maximum likelihood, the ordered probit models with a probit selection model (Model 1, Table 10).
[a]Rho is the estimated degree of correlation between the errors of the ordered probit model and the probit selection model.
[b]Significance is with reference to a likelihood ratio test (Miranda and Rabe-Hesketh 2006).
***,*Indicate coefficients are statistically significant at $p \le 0.01$ and $p \le 0.10$ levels, respectively, based on z-values (two-tailed tests).

being of a similar magnitude to those reported in Table 13 – and hence providing further empirical support for *H1*. Consistent with prior results relating to *H2*, the coefficients of REPACC are close to zero and statistically insignificant in the Year 2 ($z=0.91$, $p=0.361$) and Year 5 ($z=0.68$, $p=0.496$) models.

4.5.   *Summary of results and study limitations*

In support of *H1*, this study finds systematic empirical evidence that companies filing micro accounts are associated with lower credit scores. In contrast, there is no empirical support for *H2*, in that REPACC is statistically insignificant in all the reported regression models, including the simple regression specification estimated in extended samples (Table 6). It is not unusual for archival accounting studies to report that empirical evidence does not support hypotheses/ expected relationships (eg Liberty and Zimmerman 1986, DeFond et al. 2002, Armstrong et al. 2010, Lawrence et al. 2011, Minutti-Meza 2013). For instance, the influential study of Bowen et al. (1987) reports that, unlike for cash flows, there was no evidence to support the hypothesis that accruals have 'incremental information content relative to that contained in earnings' (p. 723). More recently, Vergauwe and Gaeremynck (forthcoming) find that some conjectures relating to fair value disclosures and information asymmetry are not supported empirically. As with the aforementioned research, it is important that the veracity of empirical findings of the current research are examined across different samples[38]/jurisdictions and employing alternative methodologies (such as survey, interview and case study approaches). This is especially pertinent with regard to the current exploratory study, where (to the author's knowledge) the hypotheses have not been investigated in prior research.

One potential explanation for the absence of empirical support for *H2* is that the credit scorer has not considered whether REPACC should influence credit scores. However, though this is a possible explanation (that the credit scorer has simply overlooked this variable), it is, perhaps, an unlikely one – given REPACC (whether a company has a reporting accountant) is readily available to the credit scorer as a variable on the FAME database. The fact that prior research (above) indicates that the FAME credit scorer gives cognisance to voluntary audits also makes this rationale less likely. A more plausible explanation is that the credit scorer has considered REPACC, but does not believe that the imprimatur of a reporting accountant carries sufficient weight (in terms of signalling/assurance) to warrant an upgrade in credit scores. This may occur if the credit scorer presumes that the statutory accounts of companies without reporting accountants have been prepared (at least largely) by accountants; and hence that the signalling/assurance value associated with REPACC is inconsequential. Specifically, in this case, though not knowing who prepared the accounts, it is conjectured that the credit scorer assumes that all (or for the most part) statutory annual accounts are prepared by accountants.[39] Note, however, that REPACC may provide some assurance for trade creditors, banks, tax authorities and other credit rating agencies.

Related to the above, in terms of sample design, this study focuses on young companies where information asymmetries are pervasive. In consequence (and as previously argued), any signalling/assurance value associated with the experimental variables is likely to be at its highest for companies in their start-up phase – and in consequence, empirically detectable. Despite this, it follows that a potential limitation of this study is that the empirical findings may not generalise to all small/micro companies. As already mentioned, further research is warranted to establish the validity of the empirical findings of this study; and especially with regard to reporting accountants. However, *a priori*, it seems unlikely that the credit scorer would fail to upgrade credit scores for companies with a reporting accountant in their start-up phase, when information asymmetries are at their most palpable, but (*ceteris paribus*) reward more mature companies with a reporting accountant when such asymmetries are less pronounced.

A more general limitation of this study relates to causation. As with all studies which employ archival data, empirical inferences may not equate with causation. Strictly speaking, observational (non-experimental) studies cannot prove/establish causation, even when appropriate methods/models are used. Rather, the archival data used in the current study can be employed to establish whether hypotheses are supported in terms of the statistical association between variables.

5.   Conclusion

Given it economic significance, the small business sector is one that continually exercises policymakers and attracts perennial government and statutory intervention. This is primarily aimed at encouraging entrepreneurship, new business formation and promoting and enhancing small firm growth. In the UK (and the EU), it also extends to 'lifting the burden' (costs) from small private companies of the requirements to file full annual accounts and to appoint an auditor. As described above, there is little evidence-based policy regarding the deregulation of financial reporting requirements for small private companies (Singleton-Green, 2015). Though important, prior archival evidence concentrates on the influence of voluntary audits on credit scores and the cost and availability debt finance. In contrast, and given the dwindling market for voluntary corporate audits, this paper focuses on the vast majority of small UK companies which publish unaudited accounts, containing only an abbreviated balance sheet.

Consistent with signalling theory, this study finds that, relative to small companies filing abbreviated accounts, there is systematic evidence that the credit scorer penalises companies which file micro-entity abbreviated accounts. This is consistent with the conjecture that the filing of micro accounts conveys a negative signal to the credit scorer that micro companies are of lower quality (higher risk). This finding is robust to statistical methods that accounts for both observed and unobserved (endogeneity) bias. Based on assurance and signalling tenets, the second conjecture examined in this paper is that companies which disclose their annual accounts are prepared by reporting accountant are expected to attract higher credit scores. However, contrary to extant research which reports that companies which opt for voluntary audits receive superior credit scores, there is no evidence that the credit scorer rewards companies whose accounts bear the imprimatur of a reporting accountant with better credit scores.

It is hoped the results of this exploratory study will stimulate further research in a wider context and across other jurisdictions. In particular, more qualitative and quantitative research is required into the motivation of small companies to file micro accounts and to appoint reporting accountants. In addition, research is required into whether small/micro companies which voluntarily publish fuller information in their annual accounts (including those that adopt higher financial reporting standards than those in FRS105 or Section 1A of FRS 102) benefit in terms of credit scores, debt finance and trade credit. In a similar vein, further archival and survey research is warranted into the potential benefits which may accrue to companies with reporting accountants. For instance, extant research reports that voluntary audits are associated with less costly debt finance (Kim et al. 2011), higher measures of financial reporting quality (Dedman and Kausar 2012) and fewer errors in statutory annual accounts (Clatworthy and Peel 2013). Such studies could be extended to examine whether these beneficial outcomes extend (though to an expected lower degree than obtaining to voluntary audits) to companies with a reporting accountant.

Notes

1. For accounting periods on or after 01/01/2016, the size limits for small company filing exemptions for sales (total assets) were increased to £10.2 million (£5.1 million). In addition, for accounting periods on or after 01/01/2016, small (but not micro) companies are subject to a new reporting regime. As described by Price Bailey (PB 2017), though the regulations are more complex, small companies need only file an abridged balance sheet, the contents of which are similar to those obtaining to abbreviated accounts (as studied in this paper) under the former small company reporting regime.

2. Certain financial service companies – such as those providing insurance, banking or investment services – are not permitted to file micro or small company abbreviated accounts and are therefore naturally excluded from the current study.

3. Although not affecting the current study, for accounting periods beginning on or after 01/01/2016, new UK financial reporting standards (FRS) were introduced. Companies filing abbreviated accounts under the micro regime must adopt FRS 105; whereas those filing accounts under the small company regime must apply Section 1A of FRS 102, which is of a higher standard (see FRC 2015a, p. 12, FRC 2015b, p. 4). Small companies (including those which qualify as micro-entities) may choose to voluntarily file full accounts which are subject to higher reporting standards. In terms of potential future research, the higher standard (quality) of reporting under Section 1A of FRS 102, as compared with that of FRS 105, would strengthen $H1$, in that the credit scorer may upgrade credit scores to reflect superior reporting standards.

4. However, CH does advise small/micro companies that 'you may wish to consult a professional accountant before you prepare accounts' (CH 2015, p. 20).

5. The FAME database used in this study only includes a variable containing the accountants name and not whether the accounts include an accountant's report. It is therefore highly unlikely that the FAME credit scorer uses the latter in determining scores (see also footnote 24).

6. In this context, Kitching et al. (2011, p. 28) state that around '935,000 abbreviated accounts are downloaded annually' from CH by users. Survey research of UK SMEs (Collis 2008, p. 35) reports that directors considered the main users of their annual accounts were suppliers and other trade creditors (64%), credit rating agencies (62%), competitors (57%) and bank and other lenders (46%).

7. Though this study cannot disentangle assurance and signalling influences, as do Lennox and Pittman (2011) for voluntary audits, both are postulated to be positively associated with credit scores. Note also

with regard to costly signalling (Dharan 1992, Lennox and Pittman 2011), that the cost of hiring an auditor is higher than that for a reporting accountant.

8. Employing a cross-sectional regression model (as in the current study), Dedman and Kausar (2012) report that voluntary audits are associated with an 11.9 increase in FAME credit scores. Hence, the predicted increase in credit scores associated with the disclosure of a reporting accountant would be expected to be less than this.

9. Unsurprisingly, credit scores are not allocated to companies which fail.

10. Note that, although the number filing micro accounts is comparatively small, it had increased substantially to 81,917 when the FAME database was examined a year later (with the same sampling criteria, but for micro companies with year ends falling in the fiscal year to March 2016). This may indicate an increasing awareness amongst directors of the relatively new micro-entity filing option.

11. This strongly suggests that negative equity may be an important variable in the credit scoring model (below). Note also that on checking data on FAME one year later (fiscal year to March 2016), start-up companies with negative equity were still not being awarded credit scores. Hence, exclusion of the latter by the credit scorer is a permanent feature.

12. A further reason is that FAME data discs are no longer available. The discs facilitated the downloading of unlimited data. However, based on the number of companies/variables, the FAME internet database imposed a limit on the number of companies/variables that could be downloaded; requiring several file downloads. Hence, focusing on all micro companies which had filed their second or fifth set of accounts, together with 8000 small companies which had similarly filed their second or fifth set of accounts, appeared to be a reasonable research approach.

13. FAME has a variable indicating whether a company has an audit. This variable was also checked with regard to small companies to ascertain if any had incorrectly filed unaudited small abbreviated accounts. None had done so.

14. There was no obvious reason for this. It is possible that some of these companies had failed, but that this had not been recorded when the data was downloaded. It is also possible that the credit scorer had not yet allocated new credit scores.

15. In the past, the database contained historical credit scores for prior accounting years. These have now been deleted from the FAME database. Similarly, for the new scoring model, historical credit scores are not available on the FAME database.

16. The accounts of random samples of 12 micro and 12 small companies where no accounting firm name had been recorded on FAME were also checked. In all cases, no accountant's name appeared in the accounts.

17. To mitigate the influence of outliers, values of GEAR and CACL are winsorised at a value of 3. Note that ratio values for FATA lie naturally in the range of zero to one.

18. It is accepted that these are experimental variables and that ownership/governance variables may be more apposite for larger public/quoted companies with numerous/diverse shareholders (see e.g. Ashbaugh-Skaife et al. 2006).

19. From the original sample of 35,983, 12 micro companies are omitted because they had voluntarily appointed auditors.

20. Note that given credit scores are not assigned to newly incorporated companies with negative equity, other things equal, YR1 mean credit scores would be expected to be even lower if the credit scorer had allocated credit scores to them.

21. This would imply that the credit scorer penalises companies in the early part (to YR5) of their life cycle, when failure risk may be higher.

22. The difference in proportions can be converted into an odds ratio by estimating the following simple logit model: MICRO = 0.022(Constant) − 1.384(REPACC). The odds ratio associated with REPACC is calculated as the exponential of the coefficient (−1.384) giving odds of 0.251:1.This implies that small companies are 3.99 times more likely (1/0.251) than micro ones to disclose they have a reporting accountant. This result holds after controlling for company size, as the following logit estimates reveal: MICRO =1.221(Constant) − 0.123(SIZE) − 1.349(REPACC). All model coefficients are significant at $p < 0.001$.

23. Of course, more generally, as with voluntary audits, companies may choose not to hire a reporting accountant if the estimated cost is higher than the perceived benefits.

24. Though not investigated in the current study, it is highly unlikely that the credit scorer only awards a higher credit score to companies whose accounts contain an accountant's report. If this was the case, REPACC would still be expected to attract a positive coefficient.

25. This result is consistent with the simple regression model reported in Table 6, which shows that credit scores increase monotonically with the filing of the sixth set of accounts onwards. This suggests a non-linear relationship between age and credit scores and therefore the DUM5 result is not necessarily inconsistent with the finding of Dedman and Kausar (2012) that company age is positively associated with credit scores.

26. Similar results obtain when the number of directors and shareholders are employed in place of their logged values.

27. Note that the association between MICRO and CREDSCR is not insubstantial, the size of its coefficient amounting to 0.64 (7.52/11.74) of that for COURT.

28. Similar results were found when this procedure was repeated for Models 2 and 3 in Table 9, with the coefficients of MICRO being −7.298 and −7.292, respectively (both significant at $p < 0.001$).

29. Note this issue only affects the probit model and not the other regression models.

30. Consistent with the univariate results, the other statistically significant probit model coefficients suggest that small companies are larger, are more highly geared, are less likely to exhibit negative working capital and are more likely to have a charge against their assets. Micro companies are associated with higher liquidity, higher asset tangibility and have a higher likelihood of displaying negative equity.

31. The fact that micro companies chose not to file small company accounts may also indicate that they are less concerned about the potential benefits of having reporting accountant or of disclosing that fact. As highlighted in the Conclusion, further research is warranted into why companies appoint a reporting accountant.

32. For direct comparison with the OLS results for Model 2, Model 3 in Table 9 was re-estimated with DUM5 omitted. The results are quantitatively similar to those for Model 3, with the coefficient for MICRO being −7.445 ($p < 0.001$).

33. Regression results may be biased if the linearity assumption does not hold outside the common support and/or if the model functional form is incorrect.

34. The associated t-values are 36.54 (36.11).

35. The Stata *treatreg* command enables IMRs to be saved as an additional variable in the dataset.

36. Note, however, that similar results to those reported obtain when the models are estimated in the full sample (ordered ratings 1–4). For instance, for Models 1(2), the coefficients of MICRO are −2.318 (−2.329), and are both highly significant at $p < 0.001$.

37. For brevity, the probit selection parameters are omitted. They are similar to those reported for Model 1 in Table 10.

38. Using FAME credit scores, an example of this is the study of Dedman and Kausar (2012) which confirms the findings of Lennox and Pittman (2011) that voluntary audits are associated with superior credit scores. In addition, the method of meta-analysis is employed to evaluate empirical evidence from multiple studies with regard to outcomes/hypotheses (see Hay et al. 2006, for an accounting research example).

39. Though not supported by the empirical results of this study, a counter argument is that if a credit scorer supposes that company accountants will only allow their name to appear on statutory annual accounts if they have prepared them, and/or consider they are accurate, then credit scores may be uplifted in line with the signalling/assurance tenets associated with REPACC.

Acknowledgements

I am grateful to two anonymous reviewers for their detailed comments and suggestions. I am also grateful to Edward Lee, the Editor, for helpful guidance. However, any errors are solely those of the author.

Disclosure statement

No potential conflict of interest was reported by the author.

References

ACCA, 2017. Audit Exempt Companies: ACCA Accounts Preparation Report. London: Association of Chartered Certified Accountants. Available from: www.accaglobal.com/content/dam/ACCA_Global/Technical/fact/technical-factsheet-163.pdf [Accessed 4 June 2017].

Altin, M., Kizildag, M. and Ozdemir, O., 2016. Corporate governance, ownership structure, and credit ratings of hospitality firms. *Journal of Hospitality Financial Management*, 24 (1), 5–19.

Armstrong, C., Jagolinzer, A., and Larcker, D., 2010. Chief executive officer equity incentives and accounting irregularities. *Journal of Accounting Research*, 48 (2), 225–271.

Ashbaugh-Skaife, H., Collins, D., and LaFond, R., 2006. The effects of corporate governance on firms' credit ratings. *Journal of Accounting and Economics*, 42 (2), 203–243.

Bayar, O. and Chemmanur, T., 2012. What drives the valuation premium in IPOs versus acquisitions? An empirical analysis. *Journal of Corporate Finance*, 18 (3), 451–475.

BDRC, 2017. *SME Finance Monitor2016*. London: BDRC Continental. Available from: http://bdrc-continental. com/BDRCContinental_SME_Finance_Monitor_Q4_2016_Final.pdf [Accessed 3 September 2017].

Berger, A. and Udell, G., 1998. The economics of small business finance: the roles of private equity and debt markets in the financial growth cycle. *Journal of Banking and Finance*, 22 (6), 613–73.

Bessler, W., Drobetz, W., and Kazemieh, R., 2011. Factors affecting capital structure decisions. In: H. Baker and G. Martin, eds. *Capital Structure and Corporate Financing Decisions: Valuation, Strategy and Risk Analysis for Creating Long-Term Shareholder Value*. Hoboken: John Wiley & Sons, 17–39.

Black, D. and Smith, J., 2006. Estimating the returns to college quality with multiple proxies for quality. *Journal of Labor Economics*. 24 (3), 701–728.

Bowen, R., Burgstahler, D., and Daley L., 1987. The incremental information content of accrual versus cash flows. *Accounting Review* 62 (4), 723–747.

CH, 2015. *Life of a Company: Part 1 Annual Requirements*. Cardiff: Companies House. Available from: www.gwaccounting.co.uk/uploads/1/1/2/7/11279084/gp2_life_of_a_company_part_1_v4_5.pdf [Accessed 17 January 2016].

Chatterjee, S. and Price, B., 1991. *Regression Analysis by Example*. New York: John Wiley & Sons.

Clatworthy, M. and Peel, M., 2013. The impact of voluntary audit and governance characteristics on accounting errors in private companies. *Journal of Accounting and Public Policy*. 32 (3), 1–25.

Clatworthy, M. and Peel, M., 2016. The timeliness of UK private company financial reporting: regulatory and economic influences. *British Accounting Review*, 48 (3), 297–315.

Collis, J., 2008. *Directors' Views on Accounting and Auditing Requirements for SMEs*. London: Department for Business Enterprise & Regulatory Reform. Available from: http://webarchive.nationalarchives.gov. uk/20090609004520/http://www.berr.gov.uk/whatwedo/businesslaw/corp-gov-research/current-research-proj/page18121.html [Accessed 17 September 2017].

Collis, J., 2012. Determinants of voluntary audit and voluntary full accounts in micro and non-micro small companies in the UK. *Accounting and Business Research*. 42 (4), 441–468.

DBEI, 2016a. *Business Population Estimates for the UK 2016*. London: Department for Business, Energy & Industrial Strategy. Available from: https://www.gov.uk/government/statistics/business-population-estimates-2016 [Accessed 28 September 2017].

DBEI, 2016b. *Detailed Data Tables: BPE 2016*. London: Department for Business, Energy & Industrial Strategy. Available from: https://www.gov.uk/government/statistics/business-population-estimates-2016 [Accessed 28 September 2017].

DBIS, 2013. *Simpler Financial Reporting for Micro-Entities: the UK's Proposal to Implement the Micros Directive*. London: Department for Business, Innovation and Skills. Available from: www.gov.uk/government/consultations/simpler-financial-reporting-for-micro-entities-the-uks-proposal-to-implement-the-micros-directive [Accessed 31 May 2017].

Dedman, E. and Kausar, A., 2012. The impact of voluntary audit on credit ratings: evidence from UK private firms. *Accounting and Business Research*, 42 (4), 397–418.

Dedman, E. and Lennox, C., 2009. Perceived competition, profitability and the withholding of information about sales and the cost of sales. *Journal of Accounting and Economics*, 48 (2), 210–230.

DeFond, M., Raghunandan, K., and Subramanyam, K., 2002. Do non-audit service fees impair auditor independence? Evidence from going concern auditor opinions. *Journal of Accounting Research* 40 (4), 1247–1274.

Dharan, B., 1992. Auditing as a signal in small business lending. *Journal of Small Business Finance*, 2 (1), 1–11.

Experian, 2013. Seven Steps to a Heavenly Commercial Credit Score. Available from: http://www.experian. co.uk/blogs/latest-thinking/7-steps-to-a-heavenly-commercial-credit-score/ [Accessed 20 May 2017].

Firth, M. and Liau-Tan, C., 1998. Auditor quality, signaling, and the valuation of initial public offerings. *Journal of Business Finance and Accounting*, 25 (1&2), 145–166.

FRC, 2006. *Review of how Accountants Support the Needs of Small and Medium-Sized Companies and Their Stakeholders*. London: Financial Reporting Council. Available from: www.frc.org.uk/Our-Work/Publications/POB/Review-of-How-Accountants-Support-the-needs-of-(1).pdf [Accessed 30 May 2017].

FRC, 2015a. *FRS 102: The Financial Reporting Standard Applicable in the UK and Republic of Ireland*. London: Financial Reporting Council. Available from: www.frc.org.uk/getattachment/e1d6b167-6cdb-4550-bde3-f94484226fbd/FRS-102-WEB-Ready-2015.pdf [Accessed 3 September 2017].

FRC, 2015b. *FRS 105: The Financial Reporting Standard Applicable to the Micro-Entities Regime in the UK and Republic of Ireland*. London: Financial Reporting Council. Available from: www.frc.org.uk/getattachment/fb775a35-08b0-41ad-b164-ff0414a61e33/FRS-105-WEB-READY-2015.pdf [Accessed 5 September 2017].

Greene, W. and Hensher, D., 2009. *Modelling Ordered Choices*. New York: Stern School of Business. http://pages.stern.nyu.edu/~wgreene/DiscreteChoice/Readings/OrderedChoiceSurvey.pdf [Accessed 22 April 2017].

Gourieroux, C., Monfort, A., Renault, E., and Trognon, A., 1987. Generalised residuals. *Journal of Econometrics*, 34 (1), 5–32.

Hay, D., Knechel, W., and Wong, N., 2006. Audit fees: a meta-analysis of the effect of supply and demand attributes. *Contemporary Accounting Research*, 23 (1), 141–91.

Ho, D., Kosuke, I., King, G., and Stuart, E., 2007. Matching as nonparametric preprocessing for improving parametric causal inference. *Political Analysis*, 15 (3), 199–236.

Holland, K. and Horton, J., 1993. Initial public offerings on the unlisted securities market: the impact of professional advisers. *Accounting and Business Research*, 24 (93), 19–34.

Huyghebaert, N. and Van de Gucht, L., 2007. The determinants of financial structure: new insights from business start-ups. *European Financial Management*, 13 (1), 101–133.

ICAEW, 2017. *Compilation Guidance Updated*. London: Institute of Chartered Accountants in England and Wales. Available from: www.icaew.com/en/technical/audit-and-assurance/working-in-the-regulated-area-of-audit/compilation-guidance-updated [Accessed 4 June 2017].

Ittonen, K., Johnstone, K., and Myllymäki, E., 2015. Audit partner public-client specialisation and client abnormal accruals. *European Accounting Review*, 24 (3), 607–633.

Kim, J., Simunic, D., Stein, M., and Yi, C., 2011. Voluntary audits and the cost of debt capital for privately held firms: Korean evidence. *Contemporary Accounting Research*, 28 (2), 585–615.

Kitching, J., Kašperová, E., Blackburn, R. and Collis, J., 2011. *Small Company Abbreviated Accounts: a Regulatory Burden or a Vital Disclosure?* Edinburgh: Institute of Chartered Accountants of Scotland. Available from: www.icas.com/__data/assets/pdf_file/0017/10583/9-Small-Company-Abbreviated-Accounts-A-Regulatory-Burden-Or-A-VitalDisclosure-ICAS.pdf [Accessed 5 June 2017].

Kitching, J., Kašperová, E., and Collis, J., 2015. The contradictory consequences of regulation: the influence of filing abbreviated accounts on UK small company performance. *International Small Business Journal*, 33 (7), 671–688.

Lawrence, A., Minutti-Meza, M., and Zhang, P., 2011. Can big 4 versus non-big 4 differences in audit quality proxies be attributed to client characteristics? *Accounting Review*, 86 (1), 259–286.

Lennox, C. and Pittman, J., 2011. Voluntary audits versus mandatory audits. *Accounting Review*, 86 (5), 1655–1678.

Leuz, C. and Verrecchia, R., 2000. The economic consequences of increased disclosure. *Journal of Accounting Research*, 38 (supplement), 91–124.

Liberty, S. and Zimmerman, J., 1986. Labor union contract negotiations and accounting choices. *Accounting Review*, 61 (4), 692–712.

Melumad, N. and Thoman L., 1990. On auditors and the courts in an adverse selection setting. *Journal of Accounting Research*, 28 (1), 77–120.

Minutti-Meza, M., 2013. Does auditor industry specialization improve audit quality? *Journal of Accounting Research*, 51 (4), 779–817.

Miranda, A. and Rabe-Hesketh, S., 2006. Maximum likelihood estimation of endogenous switching and sample selection models for binary, count, and ordinal variables. *Stata Journal*, 6 (3), 285–308.

PB, 2017. Moving on from Abbreviated Accounts to Abridged and Filleted Accounts. Available from: www.pricebailey.co.uk/blog/abbreviated-abridged-filleted-accounts/ [Accessed 19 March 2018].

Resti, A., 2016. *Banks' Internal Rating Models: Time for a Change?* Brussels: European Parliament. www.europarl.europa.eu/RegData/etudes/IDAN/2016/587366/IPOL_IDA(2016)587366_EN.pdf [Accessed 4 September 2017].

Rosenbaum, P. and Rubin, D., 1983. The central role of the propensity score in observational studies for causal effects. *Biometrika*, 70 (1), 51–55.

Spence, M., 1973. Job market signaling. *Quarterly Journal of Economics*, 87(8), 355–374.

Singleton-Green, B., 2015. *SME Accounting Requirements: Basing Policy on Evidence*. London: Institute of Chartered Accountants in England and Wales. Available from: http://www.icaew.com/en/archive/technical/financial-reporting/information-for-better-markets/sme-accounting-requirements-basing-policy-on-evidence [Accessed 28 May 2017].

Theodossiou, P., 1993. Predicting shifts in the mean of a multivariate time series process: an application in predicting business failures. *Journal of the American Statistical Association*, 88 (422), 441–449.

Toms, J., 2002. Firm resources, quality signals and the determinants of corporate environmental reputation: some UK evidence. *British Accounting Review*, 34 (3), 257–282.

Tucker, J., 2010. Selection bias and econometric remedies in accounting and finance research. *Journal of Accounting Literature*, 29, 31–57.

Vergauwe, S. and Gaeremynck, A., Forthcoming. Do measurement-related fair value disclosures affect information asymmetry? *Accounting and Business Research*. Available from: https://doi.org/10.1080/00014788.2018.1434608 [Accessed 6 March 2018].

Watson, A., Shrives, P., and Marston, C., 2002. Voluntary disclosure of accounting ratios in the UK. *British Accounting Review*, 34 (4), 289–313.

Wilson, N. and Wright, M., 2013. Private equity, buy-outs and insolvency risk. *Journal of Business Finance and Accounting*, 40 (8), 949–990.

Yin, H. and Zhang, H., 2014. Tournaments of financial analysts. *Review of Accounting Studies*, 19 (2), 573–605.

Appendix 1: OLS and probit regression models.

	OLS model	Probit model
MICRO	−7.299***	
REPACC	0.009	
SIZE	1.183***	−0.092***
GEAR	−1.968***	−0.025
CACL	1.980***	0.094***
NEGEQ	−3.179***	0.227***
NEGWC	−2.623***	−0.174***
FATA	4.923***	0.309***
COURT	−10.895***	0.141
DEFLT	−1.975***	−0.144
CHARGE	−1.012***	−0.113*
DIVERS	0.374	
DUM5	−0.287*	−0.486***
LNSHR	0.110	
LNDIR	−0.027	
SHRDIR	−0.105	
NOCL	−1.789***	
Constant	24.534***	0.434***
Industry dummies	✓	✓
R^2 or χ^2	0.411	758.34***
$N=$	14,483	13,102

Notes: Variables are defined in Table 5 in the paper. NOCL is a binary variable coded 1 if a company has zero current liabilities, 0 otherwise. As referred to in this paper, the dependent variable in the OLS model is CREDSCR and the model includes NOCL as an additional explanatory variable. As also referred to in the paper, the dependent variable for the probit model is MICRO. It is used to estimate the propensity scores (probabilities) for the matching analysis.
***,*Indicates coefficients are statistically significant at $p \leq 0.01$ and $p \leq 0.10$ (two-tailed tests).

Appendix 2: Regression models for companies filing their second and fifth set of accounts

	OLS credit score models[a]		Ordered logit credit rating models[a,b]	
	Year 2	Year 5	Year 2	Year 5
MICRO	−7.175**	−8.094**	−2.371**	−2.257**
REPACC	−0.036	0.001	0.064	0.049
SIZE	1.070**	1.322**	0.226**	0.275**
GEAR	−3.153**	−2.303**	−0.938**	−0.827**
CACL	1.916**	1.455**	0.204**	0.159**
NEGEQ	−3.099**	−2.692**	−0.715**	−0.411**
NEGWC	−2.051**	−3.359**	−0.794**	−0.990**
FATA	5.192**	5.945**	1.490**	1.472**
COURT	−10.665**	−13.682**	−9.264**	−7.332**
DEFLT	−1.204	−4.055**	−0.314	−1.451**
CHARGE	−0.935	−1.111*	−0.419*	−0.134
Constant	26.201 **	24.258**		
Industry dummies	✓	✓	✓	✓
R^2 or χ^2	0.402	0.385	3,222.43**	2,271.12**
$N =$	7,607	5,495	7,607	5,478

Notes: All variables are defined in Table 5.
[a]Year 2 (Year 5) denote companies which had filed their second (fifth) set of accounts respectively.
[b]Credit ratings are 1–3 as per Table 13. Cut-off points (constants) are omitted.
**,*Indicate coefficients are statistically significant at $p \leq 0.01$ and $p \leq 0.05$ levels, respectively, based on z-values for ordered logit models and t-values (robust standard errors) for OLS models (two-tailed tests).

Reflections on the development of the FASB's and IASB's expected-loss methods of accounting for credit losses[†]

NOOR HASHIM, WEIJIA LI AND JOHN O'HANLON

After the financial and banking crisis of the late 2000s, the FASB and the IASB aimed to develop methods of accounting for credit losses that would give more timely recognition of those losses. The IASB (in 2009) and the FASB (in 2010) each initially issued its own exposure draft proposing separate approaches to achieving this. They then attempted to agree a converged expected-loss-based method for accounting for credit losses, but failed to achieve convergence. They then each issued an accounting standard that included its own expected-loss method, with effective dates of 2018 for the IASB and 2020/21 for the FASB. This paper provides an overview of the development of proposals and standards in relation to accounting for credit losses issued by the standard setters from 2009 to 2016. It then offers reflections on difficulties that the standard setters faced in this area and on problems that might arise after the new standards become effective. It raises the question of whether a route based on 'expected loss', which in relation to credit losses is a concept that originally became prominent for the purpose of setting banks' capital requirements, was helpful to the process of improving the accounting for credit losses.

1. Introduction

The financial and banking crisis of the late 2000s prompted the Financial Accounting Standards Board (FASB) and the International Accounting Standards Board (IASB) to emphasise jointly

[†]This paper is based on a presentation at an *Accounting and Business Research* symposium on The Role of Accounting Information in Debt Markets at the European Accounting Association Congress, Valencia (May 2017). The paper is informed by work carried out within a project for which some results are reported in an ICAEW research briefing (O'Hanlon et al. 2018). The authors gratefully acknowledge the financial support of the ICAEW's Charitable Trusts for that project. This paper has benefited from the comments of Kees Camfferman on a preliminary version and from the detailed comments and suggestions of an anonymous reviewer.

'the importance of working cooperatively and in an internationally coordinated manner to consider accounting issues emerging from the crisis' and to say that 'the FASB and the IASB recognize that the urgency of the credit crisis requires unprecedented action'.[1] An issue that attracted particular attention was a perceived lack of timeliness in the then-current methods of accounting for credit losses, which is a highly material item for banks.[2] The FASB and the IASB moved quickly to address this issue. In light of elements of the history of accounting for credit losses and relevant prior literature, we reflect on the process that standard setters went through in the aftermath of the crisis in order to achieve more timely accounting recognition of credit losses. Within this, we consider the difficulties that the standard setters faced, including in relation to their failure to achieve a converged common solution on accounting for credit losses.

At the time of the financial and banking crisis, both U.S. GAAP and IFRS required that credit losses should be accounted for using incurred-loss (hereinafter, IL) methods: credit losses should only be recognised where there was evidence based on past events that a loss had been incurred. The IL methods in place at that time were more heavily weighted towards limiting earnings management and the associated overstatement of loss allowances than towards permitting the exercise of discretion that might facilitate timely recognition of credit losses and ensure loss-allowance adequacy. At the time of the crisis, concern that the restrictive IL methods had contributed to delay in recognition of credit losses prior to the crisis prompted calls for more forward-looking methods that would result in the more timely recognition of losses, including from a prudential-regulatory perspective from the Financial Stability Board's report to G20 leaders (Financial Stability Board 2009) and the Basel Committee on Banking Supervision (hereinafter, BCBS) (BCBS 2009). Consistent with advice from these sources and from the Financial Crisis Advisory Group (2009), the FASB and the IASB each pursued the development of more forward-looking methods of accounting for credit losses, including methods described as expected-loss (hereinafter, EL) methods. With regard to accounting for credit losses, the crisis appears to have prompted a shift in relative emphasis away from limiting earnings management and the associated overstatement of loss allowances and towards permitting the exercise of discretion that might facilitate timely recognition of credit losses and help to ensure that loss allowances are adequate.

The standard setters' process of developing methods that would lead to the more timely recognition of credit losses included the initial issue of separate IASB and FASB exposure drafts (IASB 2009, FASB 2010a), the issue of a joint supplementary document and follow-up proposals aimed at achieving a converged common solution (FASB/IASB 2011a,b), and the eventual failure of the attempt to achieve convergence. The standard setters then issued separate final exposure drafts (FASB 2012, IASB 2013a) and separate accounting standards (IASB 2014a, FASB 2016) with an effective date of 2018 for the IASB and 2020 or 2021 for the FASB.

Within their development of more timely methods of accounting for credit losses, the standard setters aimed to address the issue of the breadth of the information set that could be used to support the recognition of credit-loss impairment. They also aimed to address the perhaps less obvious issue that, when loans are made, the lender expects to suffer some as-yet-unidentified credit losses that are compensated within the interest revenue that is typically accrued in full from year 1 onwards. Under the IL regimes in place, recognition of the associated initially-expected losses was delayed until loss events occurred, which typically resulted in some of the credit-premium-inclusive interest revenue being recognised in advance of the associated losses. In their initial exposure drafts (IASB 2009, FASB 2010a), the two standard setters each proposed a credit-loss-accounting method that would allow expected losses to be recognised in advance of the occurrence of the type of loss events required by pre-existing IL methods. The methods proposed in those two exposure drafts were based on different objectives. The FASB's objective was to ensure that loss allowances at each reporting date were sufficient to cover all estimated credit losses for the remaining life of in-scope financial assets. This led to a proposed method involving the establishment of loss allowances at the first reporting date after origination or purchase, sometimes referred to as 'day 1', which would immediately reflect initial expectations of all future credit losses expected to occur over the full contractual life of assets. The IASB's objective was to reflect initially-expected credit losses within the calculation of the effective interest rate on financial assets. This led to a proposed method that explicitly linked initially-expected credit losses with the pricing of financial assets at origination, and would result in the recognition of initially-expected losses being spread over the life of assets. Like the FASB's proposed method, this method would require credit losses to be recognised in advance of the type of loss events required under pre-existing IL methods. However, it was less conservative than the FASB's proposed method in that recognition of initially-expected losses would be spread over the life of assets rather than occurring immediately at day 1. The initial IASB method was widely regarded as conceptually strong in the sense that it reflected the economic substance of the relationship between the contractual interest rate and initially-expected losses.[3] However, it was also widely regarded as posing a significant implementation challenge.

Subsequent joint deliberations by the FASB and the IASB based on FASB/IASB (2011a,b) were aimed at achieving a compromise converged solution that would partially address the objectives of each standard setter. Within these joint deliberations, the FASB and the IASB achieved straightforward and converged agreement that the information set that could be used to support credit-loss impairment would henceforth be broadened to include reasonable and supportable forecasts. This should address to a significant degree the concerns raised in the aftermath of the financial and banking crisis about delay in the accounting recognition of information about credit losses. However, the standard setters encountered a serious problem in their attempts to reach a converged solution for the treatment of initially-expected losses, and this contributed significantly to their inability to achieve a converged overall solution with respect to accounting for credit losses. The joint deliberations eliminated from consideration methods that explicitly spread the recognition of initially-expected losses across time. They produced a proposal that financial assets should be categorised with regard to whether or not their credit quality had significantly deteriorated since initial recognition: at each reporting date, allowances would recognise lifetime expected losses for assets that had significantly deteriorated since initial recognition ('bad book'); at each reporting date, including day 1, they would recognise 12-month expected losses for assets that had not significantly deteriorated since initial recognition ('good book'). The IASB accepted this proposal, seeing the 12-month allowance for good-book assets as a means of achieving in a practicable way an approximation to the recognition of initially-expected losses over time, which was a central feature of IASB (2009). However, after extensive involvement in the deliberations, the FASB indicated that it could not accept this proposal and that it could only accept full recognition at each reporting date, including at day 1, of all expected losses over the full contractual life of assets. The IASB's preferred approach was seen by the FASB as insufficiently conservative; the FASB's preferred approach was seen by the IASB as excessively conservative. There is evidence that the FASB's more conservative preference was due in part to pre-existing practice that reflected prudential-regulatory-related influence. After their failure to agree on this issue, the two standard setters proceeded to develop standards containing separate EL methods based on their respective preferences (IASB 2014a, FASB 2016). The process of developing the FASB and IASB standards on credit-loss impairment has been controversial both because of the failure to achieve a converged common solution and because of some of the proposals themselves. Both standard setters' requirements for the immediate establishment of loss allowances at day 1, 12-month expected losses in the case of the IASB and full-contractual-life losses in the case of the FASB, attracted significant criticism on conceptual grounds.

In this paper, we describe the events outlined above in the context of the history of accounting for credit losses and relevant prior literature and drawing on our confidential conversations with senior observers of the process. We then highlight two issues that may give rise to problems when the new credit-loss-impairment standards are implemented: the FASB's requirement for lifetime loss allowances and the day-1 loss requirements of both standard setters. We then consider whether, in light of issues arising during the development of the new EL credit-loss-impairment methods, improved methods of accounting for credit losses might have been more straightforwardly achieved through an alternative route to the type of EL route that was followed. In particular, we raise the question of whether, after the elimination from consideration of spreading-based EL approaches that did not involve day-1 losses, satisfactory more-forward-looking methods of accounting for credit losses that did not involve day-1 losses and that might have presented a lower barrier to FASB/IASB convergence might have been developed by following a less radical broader-information-set-based modified-IL-type route rather than by continuing to follow an EL route.

The paper is structured as follows. Section 2 provides background on the IL method of accounting for credit losses under U.S. GAAP and IFRS, provides background on bank regulation relating to credit losses and provides an outline of elements of prior academic literature that are relevant to the matters addressed in this paper. Section 3 outlines the development since 2009 by the FASB and the IASB of more timely methods of accounting for credit-loss impairment, including with reference to important elements of feedback on the standard setters' various proposal documents. Section 4 discusses issues that have arisen during the standard setters' development of their EL methods of accounting for credit losses that may present problems when the standards become effective. Section 5 considers whether a route based on EL was helpful to the process of improving the accounting for credit losses. Section 6 concludes.

2.   Background and literature review

This section provides a summary of background and literature relevant to the events considered in this paper. Subsection 2.1 provides a summary of the history of the pre-existing IL methods of accounting for credit losses and of the pressure in the wake of the financial and banking crisis of the late 2000s to replace them by more forward-looking methods. Subsection 2.2 provides some background on bank regulation that relates to credit losses. Subsection 2.3 provides a summary of relevant academic literature.

2.1.   *The incurred-loss method of accounting for credit-loss impairment*

At the time of the financial and banking crisis of the late 2000s, the IL method for credit-loss impairment, which required that the recognition of loan losses should be supported by evidence that a loss had been incurred, was established in U.S. GAAP and in IFRS. This subsection provides some background on the IL methods in U.S. GAAP and IFRS that is relevant to the events considered in this paper.

2.1.1.   *U.S. GAAP: Incurred-loss*

The history of IL in U.S. GAAP includes action motivated by the perceived need to constrain discretion that might allow systematic delay in loan-loss recognition and understatement of loss allowances and, subsequently, action motivated by the perceived need to constrain discretion that might allow systematic overstatement of loss allowances. The latter of these appears to have contributed to criticism at the time of the financial and banking crisis of the late 2000s of the lack of timeliness of pre-existing methods of accounting for credit losses.

From 1975, SFAS 5 (FASB 1975) provided guidance on recognition of losses on receivables including loans. It included the following requirement:

An estimated loss from a loss contingency (as defined in paragraph 1) shall be accrued by a charge to income if both of the following conditions are met:
   a. Information available prior to issuance of the financial statements indicates that it is probable that an asset had been impaired or a liability had been incurred at the date of the financial statements. It is implicit in this condition that it must be probable that one or more future events will occur confirming the fact of the loss.
   b. The amount of loss can be reasonably estimated. (FASB 1975, paragraph 8)

Following the savings and loan crisis of the late 1980s, SFAS 5 was criticised for being ambiguous and so flexible that financially weak banks were able to manage earnings upwards by delaying recognition of losses (GAO 1991, GAO 1992). In May 1993, the FASB issued SFAS 114 (FASB 1993a). This was aimed at providing clearer and more consistent guidance on accounting for impairment of loans, other than small homogeneous loans collectively evaluated for impairment, including with respect to issues raised in GAO (1992). The criterion for recognition of impairment in SFAS 114 was consistent with that in SFAS 5, but the more specific guidance might have been expected to reduce the danger referred to by GAO (1992) that discretion might be used inappropriately in order to delay the recognition of loan losses. SFAS 114 (FASB 1993a) included the following reminder aimed at avoiding unduly restrictive interpretation of the IL requirement of FASB (1975):

The term probable is further described in paragraph 84 of Statement 5, which states:
The conditions for accrual in paragraph 8 [of Statement 5] are not inconsistent with the accounting concept of conservatism. Those conditions are not intended to be so rigid that they require virtual certainty before a loss is accrued. They require only that it be probable that an asset has been impaired or a liability has been incurred and that the amount of loss be reasonably estimable. (FASB 1993a, paragraph 10)

Also in May 1993, the FASB issued SFAS 115 (FASB 1993b), which was motivated in part by a perceived need for more consistent guidance on impairment of debt securities. The IL credit-loss impairment requirements of SFAS 5, SFAS 114 and SFAS 115 were included in the pre-FASB (2016) FASB codification topics 450, 310 and 320, respectively. FASB codification topic 310 includes the following with respect to loan impairment:

The following provides an overview of generally accepted accounting principles (GAAP) for loan impairment:
   a. It is usually difficult, even with hindsight, to identify any single event that made a particular loan uncollectible. However, the concept in GAAP is that impairment of receivables shall be recognized when, based on all available information, it is probable that a loss has been incurred based on past events and conditions existing at the date of the financial statements.
   b. Losses shall not be recognized before it is probable that they have been incurred, even though it may be probable based on past experience that losses will be incurred in the future. It is inappropriate to consider possible or expected future trends that may lead to additional losses. (FASB Codification, paragraph 310-10-35-4)

In the years following the issue of SFAS 114 and in contrast to the concern about understatement of losses raised prior to the issue of SFAS 114, concern was expressed by SEC representatives that U.S. banks might be using discretion inappropriately in order to facilitate earnings management through overstatement of loan-loss allowances.[4] In 1998 the SEC questioned the loan-loss accounting of SunTrust Banks Inc. and required it to reduce its loan-loss allowance by \$100 million. During the SunTrust investigation, the SEC also sent letters to a number of U.S. banks questioning their loan-loss allowances (Meyer 1999). These actions were viewed as a warning signal to all U.S. banks that the SEC would not tolerate over-provisioning for loan losses during good times. However, U.S. bank regulators did not believe that the loan-loss allowances of U.S. banks were systematically excessive. They were concerned that the SEC's actions might create a perception that loan-loss allowances would have to be reduced, and claimed that any general downward pressure on allowances could have a serious effect on the safety of the U.S. banking system (Meyer 1999, Rushton 1999). There was concern on the part of U.S. banks that they might be caught in a conflict between the SEC and U.S. bank regulators, with the former requiring lower allowances and the latter requiring higher allowances (Wall and Koch 2000, pp. 1–2). There ensued a debate between the SEC, the FASB and U.S. bank regulators on accounting for credit losses. Then, in July 2001, the SEC and bank regulators stated their joint position on loan-loss allowances in SAB 102[5] and FFIEC (2001), respectively, which required banks to estimate loan-loss allowances in accordance with GAAP with enhanced documentation to support their allowance estimates. The joint guidance of 2001 might be seen as a tightening of IL loan-loss recognition requirements or, at least, as a reaffirmation of the IL principle in U.S. GAAP (Camfferman 2015, p. 8).

Such tightening might be expected to limit loan-loss-related earnings management, but at the cost of reduced timeliness in loan-loss recognition. Evidence in Balla and Rose (2015) and Beck and Narayanamoorthy (2013) suggests that this may have occurred. Balla and Rose (2015) find that, after the guidance of 2001, the relationship between earnings and loan-loss expense weakened, indicating reduced earnings management; however, they also claim that the guidance constrained U.S. banks' early recognition of losses in the years prior to the crisis of the late 2000s. Beck and Narayanamoorthy (2013) report that, after the SAB 102 and FFIEC (2001) guidance became effective, the estimation of banks' loan-loss allowances appeared to become more reliant on past charge-offs and less reliant on current non-accrual loans. This was accompanied by a decline in the informativeness, as proxied by the ability to explain future losses, of the loss allowances of weak banks after SAB 102 and FFIEC (2001) became effective and especially immediately before the financial and banking crisis. The authors suggest two possible reasons for this. First, in the relatively unstable environment faced by weak banks, more forward-looking indicators such as non-accrual loans are likely to be more beneficial than backward-looking indicators such as past charge-offs in enhancing the informativeness of loss allowances. Second, although SAB 102 and FFIEC (2001) may have been effective in constraining overstatement of loss allowances, they could not be expected to be effective in constraining weak banks' management of earnings through delay in the recognition of loan losses.[6]

The perception that effects of the sort indicated by Balla and Rose (2015) and Beck and Narayanamoorthy (2013) were at work prior to the crisis led to a swing, in the aftermath of the financial and banking crisis, away from concern about earnings management and towards concern about timeliness of loss recognition and loss-allowance adequacy. This was reflected in, among other things, the comments made in 2009 by the Comptroller of the Currency, John Dugan, to the effect that, in the prolonged period of benign economic conditions before the late-2000s crisis, a number of banks had felt constrained in their ability to document adequately the judgmental factors that might have allowed them to make provisions that were higher than historical experience would imply.[7]

2.1.2.   *IFRS: Incurred-loss*

In common with the history of IL in U.S. GAAP, the history of IL in IFRS includes action that appears to have been motivated by the perceived need to constrain discretion that might allow earnings management. It also includes some indication of the lack of a clear-cut distinction between IL and EL that we refer to later in this paper.

Prior to the 2003 revision of IAS 39, the word 'incurred' was not used in IAS 39 in connection with impairment relating to credit losses. The requirements of the pre-2003 version of IAS 39 included the following:

A financial asset is impaired if its carrying amount is greater than its estimated recoverable amount. An enterprise should assess at each balance sheet date whether there is any objective evidence that a financial asset or group of assets may be impaired. If any such evidence exists, the enterprise should estimate the recoverable amount of that asset or group of assets and recognise any impairment loss [...] Objective evidence that a financial asset or group of assets is impaired or uncollectable includes information that comes to the attention of the holder of the asset about:
   a. significant financial difficulty of the issuer;
   b. an actual breach of contract, such as a default or delinquency in interest or principal payments;
   c. granting by the lender to the borrower, for economic or legal reasons relating to the borrower's financial difficulty, of a concession that the lender would not otherwise consider;
   d. a high probability of bankruptcy or other financial reorganisation of the issuer;
   e. recognition of an impairment loss on that asset in a prior financial reporting period;
   f. the disappearance of an active market for that financial asset due to financial difficulties; or
   g. a historical pattern of collections of accounts receivable that indicates that the entire face amount of a portfolio of accounts receivable will not be collected.

The disappearance of an active market because an enterprise's securities are no longer publicly traded is not evidence of impairment. A downgrade of an enterprise's credit rating is not, of itself, evidence of impairment, though it may be evidence of impairment when considered with other available information. (IASB 2000, paragraphs 109–110)

Although the term 'incurred' was not used in the credit-loss impairment requirements of the pre-2003 version of IAS 39, the evidence requirements quoted above were similar to those of the 2003 revision of IAS 39, which are commonly regarded as IL.

In a detailed review of events related to the 2003 revision of the credit-loss impairment requirements of IAS 39, Camfferman (2015, p. 4) notes that the practice of making a distinction between IL and EL in the context of accounting for credit losses only started to become common at the time of the deliberations leading up to that 2003 revision.[8] However, the distinguishing features of EL relative to IL in relation to accounting for credit losses were not clear at that time, as was illustrated by the following from the Basis for Conclusions of the 2003 revision of IAS 39:

Some respondents to the Exposure Draft were confused about whether the Exposure Draft reflected an 'incurred loss' model or an 'expected loss' model. (IASB 2003, paragraph BC108)

Camfferman (2015) observes that the IASB's deliberations in relation to the 2003 revision of IAS 39 tended at times towards more forward-looking EL-type features and tended at other times towards strengthening and emphasising the pre-existing loss-event-focused IL-type features of the IAS 39 requirements. The IASB eventually came down on the side of an affirmation of IL. Camfferman (2015) comments as follows that the desirability of convergence with U.S. GAAP and the need to constrain earnings management were influential in leading to that outcome:

The IASB acted under time pressure to improve the standards inherited from the IASC for the first mass adoption of IFRS in 2005, with the result that the wording of the standard as finally approved by the Board, with respect to loan impairment, differed considerably from the proposals on which constituents had been asked to comment. In the end, the importance attached to convergence with U.S. Generally Accepted Accounting Principles (U.S. GAAP) and the prevailing of an anti-abuse perspective on the issue seem to have tilted the Board towards a strict incurred-loss model. (Camfferman 2015, p. 3)

The revised IAS 39 impairment requirements were as follows:

> A financial asset or a group of financial assets is impaired and impairment losses are incurred if, and
> only if, there is objective evidence of impairment as a result of one or more events that occurred after
> the initial recognition of the asset (a 'loss event') and that loss event (or events) has an impact on the
> estimated future cash flows of the financial asset or group of financial assets that can be reliably esti-
> mated. [...] Losses expected as a result of future events, no matter how likely, are not recognised.
> Objective evidence that a financial asset or group of assets is impaired includes observable data
> that comes to the attention of the holder of the asset about the following loss events:
>   a. significant financial difficulty of the issuer or obligor;
>   b. a breach of contract, such as a default or delinquency in interest or principal payments;
>   c. the lender, for economic or legal reasons relating to the borrower's financial difficulty, granting
>   to the borrower a concession that the lender would not otherwise consider;
>   d. it becoming probable that the borrower will enter bankruptcy or other financial reorganisation;
>   e. the disappearance of an active market for that financial asset because of financial difficulties; or
>   f. observable data indicating that there is a measurable decrease in the estimated future cash flows
>   from a group of financial assets since the initial recognition of those assets, although the
>   decrease cannot yet be identified with the individual financial assets in the group, including:
>
>   i.   adverse changes in the payment status of borrowers in the group (e.g., an increased number
>   of delayed payments or an increased number of credit card borrowers who have reached
>   their credit limit and are paying the minimum monthly amount); or
>   ii. national or local economic conditions that correlate with defaults on the assets in the group
>   (e.g., an increase in the unemployment rate in the geographical area of the borrowers, a
>   decrease in property prices for mortgages in the relevant area, a decrease in oil prices for
>   loan assets to oil producers, or adverse changes in industry conditions that affect the bor-
>   rowers in the group). (IASB 2003, paragraph 59)

Significant changes introduced in the 2003 revision of IAS 39, which could be seen as a reaffir-
mation of the restrictions of IL, included a statement that impairment should be based on 'one or
more events that occurred after the initial recognition of the asset (a "loss event")', the explicit
prohibition of recognition of 'losses in respect of future events, no matter how likely' and the
inclusion of more detail on evidence requirements for collective provisioning reflected in the
replacement of sub-paragraph (g) in the pre-2003 version by sub-paragraph (f) in the revised
version.

As with the U.S. history referred to in the previous subsection, events described here contributed to setting the scene for a swing, in the aftermath of the financial and banking crisis, away
from concern about earnings management and towards concern about timeliness of loss recognition and loss-allowance adequacy.

2.1.3. *Indications of differences between U.S. GAAP and IFRS applications of incurred loss*

There is evidence that IL methods as applied in the U.S. gave rise to higher loss allowances on
average, other things equal, than outside the U.S. Our confidential conversations with senior
observers of the development of the FASB and IASB EL methods indicated a widely-held
view that the recognition of loan-losses under the IL approach as applied in the U.S., in particular
for smaller banks, tended to be at the more conservative end (i.e., higher loss allowances) of what
is acceptable under the IL method and, other things equal, more conservative than in countries
using IFRS. A letter written by the American Bankers Association (ABA) in response to the
FASB (2012) exposure draft contained a comment consistent with the view that the hurdle for
recognition of loan impairments may have been lower under the FASB's IL method than under
the IASB's IL method:[9]

Loss events, appear to be defined as an earlier point in time under U.S. accounting practices than under International Financial Reporting Standards (IFRS). Under IFRS, the term "loss event" is defined within IAS 39. [...] In U.S. GAAP, there is generally no discussion of loss events as they relate to loans. However, within bank practices, as guided by banking agencies, the following are normally considered "loss events":

- Borrower loses major source of income. For a consumer, it is normally his/her employment. For a commercial borrower, it is a major customer.
- Overall, financial results put repayment at risk, as evidenced in a commercial loan review.
- Property value deterioration, as evidenced when loan to value ratios exceed 100%.

Thus, U.S. practice would likely refer to IAS 39 "loss events" not as loss events, but as loss *identification* events, which are generally subsequent to loss events. It is indeed a challenge to estimate when a loss event has occurred in the U.S., but there is general agreement that the loss event happens prior to default. Thus, the foundation for defining when a loss is a loss under IFRS naturally leads to later loss recognition than in the U.S.

Related to this, an ABA document of June 2016 noted evidence that, in determining their loss allowances, U.S. banks make substantially greater use than European banks of assumptions that losses are 'incurred but not reported' (IBNR).[10]

As we describe later, differences of the type referred to above between pre-existing practice in the U.S. and elsewhere presented a challenging context for the attempt by the FASB and the IASB to develop a common solution for accounting for credit losses. The barrier created by the difference in pre-existing practice will have been particularly challenging in combination with the interaction between U.S. bank regulation and U.S. GAAP.[11]

2.1.4. *Pressure to adopt expected-loss methods in accounting for credit losses*

We note above the observation in Camfferman (2015) that the IL/EL distinction in relation to accounting for credit losses only started to be made at the time of the 2003 revision of IAS 39 and was not very clear at the time. The discussion in Camfferman (2015) suggests that, even for the purpose of describing years later the events leading up to the 2003 revision, the IL/EL distinction is best conveyed by reference to 'positions on a continuum of approaches that allow greater or lesser scope for early loss recognition' (Camfferman 2015, p. 4): IL tends to be used in connection with backward-looking observable concepts such as 'loss events'; EL tends to be used in connection with forward-looking concepts such as 'recoverable amounts'; EL tends to be used to refer to methods involving the inclusion of expected credit losses in the calculation of the effective interest rate; EL tends to be used to refer to methods that recognise at portfolio level losses that may not yet be individually identified. The fact that it was thought easiest to convey the IL/EL distinction in relation to accounting for credit losses by giving indicative characteristics rather than by giving a definition of the distinction is indicative of lack of clarity in the distinction.

Despite a possible lack of clarity with regard to the IL/EL distinction in the context of accounting for credit losses, the calls in the aftermath of the banking and financial crisis for more timely accounting for credit losses included encouragement to consider EL models. Such encouragement came from the Financial Crisis Advisory Group in a report to standard setters in July 2009:

> In the financial instruments project, the Boards should explore alternatives to the incurred loss model for loan loss provisioning that use more forward-looking information. These alternatives include an expected loss model and a fair value model. (Financial Crisis Advisory Group 2009, p. 7)

From a prudential-regulatory perspective, it came from the Financial Stability Board in a report to G20 leaders in September 2009:

We strongly encourage the IASB and FASB to agree on improved converged standards that will:

- Incorporate a broader range of available credit information than existing provisioning requirements, so as to recognise credit losses in loan portfolios at an earlier stage as part of an effort
  to mitigate procyclicality. We are particularly supportive of continued work on impairment standards based on an expected loss model. (Financial Stability Board 2009, pp. 7–8)

Also from a prudential-regulatory perspective, it came from BCBS in August 2009:

Loan loss provisioning should be robust and based on sound methodologies that reflect expected
credit losses in the banks' existing loan portfolio over the life of the portfolio … The accounting
model for provisioning should allow early identification and recognition of losses by incorporating
a broader range of available credit information than presently included in the incurred loss model
and should result in an earlier identification of credit losses. (BCBS 2009, paragraph 12).

It is easy to understand why, in the aftermath of a financial and banking crisis in which lack of
timeliness in accounting for credit losses had attracted attention, the replacement of a backward-looking restrictive IL method by a more forward-looking EL method would appear attrac-
tive. A rhetorical question asked by a speaker at a European Parliament hearing on IFRS 9
captures the immediately apparent attraction of the concept of EL in the context of accounting
for credit losses: 'who would not want to provide for a loss, which is expected?' (Mike
Ashley, European Parliament, 1 December 2015).[12] Such rhetorical questions sometimes imply
that the answer is not as straightforward as might first appear.

2.2. *Some background on bank regulation that relates to credit losses*

Events described in this paper relate in some ways to the interests of prudential regulators and
therefore to any influence that prudential regulators might be perceived to have had on these
events. In light of this, we provide in this subsection some background information on aspects
of bank regulation that relate to credit losses. Much of bank regulation deals with the determination of the capital that banks are required to hold and with the measurement of the capital
that they actually hold. These are a central focus of the various Basel accords (BCBS 1988,
BCBS 2006, BCBS 2011). For the purposes of this paper, these accords provide a useful indicator
of the interest that bank regulators might have in the issue of accounting for credit losses.

Under the Basel framework, the regulatory capital that a bank is required to hold is set by
reference to the risk attached to its activities and is aimed at covering unexpected losses that,
in light of that risk, might arise. A key principle underlying the measurement of actual regulatory
capital is that it should be measured after deducting appropriate allowances for expected losses,
thereby ensuring that capital is fully available to absorb unexpected losses. This principle has
become blurred where regulatory-capital rules have permitted loss allowances recognised in
banks' financial statements to be treated as part of regulatory capital.[13] In the remainder of this
subsection, we outline elements of the treatment of loan-loss allowances under the various
Basel accords.

The 1988 Basel 1 accord defined capital for bank-supervisory purposes as comprising two
tiers: Tier 1, described as core capital; Tier 2 described as supplementary capital. Under Basel
1, general loss allowances, which along with other loss allowances reduced book equity and
Tier 1 capital by their net-of-tax amount, were included in Tier 2 capital up to a maximum of
1.25% of risk-weighted assets (BCBS 1988, paragraphs 18 and 21).

The Basel 2 framework (BCBS 2004b, BCBS 2006) introduced three 'pillars' which, collectively, were aimed at promoting stronger risk-management practices in the banking industry:
pillar 1 'Minimum Capital Requirements', which deals with the calculation of minimum
capital requirements and with the measurement of regulatory capital, including with regard to

the treatment of expected credit losses in the measurement of regulatory capital; pillar 2 'Supervisory Review Process', which relates to internal-control mechanisms with regard to risk and capital requirements; pillar 3 'Market Discipline', which is aimed at ensuring that disclosure is adequate to inform market participants about risk and capital requirements. Under the Basel 2 framework, credit risk for regulatory-capital purposes would be assessed either under the internal ratings-based (IRB) approach, under which approved banks could use their own internal rating systems to measure credit risk, or under the standardised approach, which would use external credit assessments. In the pre-Basel-2 consultations, when the introduction of up-front recognition of expected losses for regulatory-capital purposes first became a prominent issue, there was some debate about whether expected losses should be dealt with through the determination of required capital (i.e., as an addition to risk-weighted assets, the denominator of a regulatory-capital ratio) or through the measurement of actual capital (i.e., as a deduction from capital, the numerator of a regulatory-capital ratio). After objections to initial proposals to follow the former route, the latter route was eventually chosen (BCBS 2001a,b, BCBS 2003, BCBS 2004a Introduction). The resultant IRB approach in relation to loss allowances (termed here 'provisions') is described as follows in the Basel 2 framework document:

> Banks using the IRB (internal ratings-based) approach [...] must compare (i) the amount of total eligible provisions, as defined in paragraph 380, with (ii) the total expected losses amount as calculated within the IRB approach and defined in paragraph 375. Where the total expected loss amount exceeds total eligible provisions, banks must deduct the difference. Deduction must be on the basis of 50% from Tier 1 and 50% from Tier 2. Where the total expected loss amount is less than total eligible provisions, as explained in paragraphs 380 to 383, banks may recognise the difference in Tier 2 capital up to a maximum of 0.6% of credit risk-weighted assets. (BCBS 2006, paragraph 43)

BCBS (2006, paragraph 43) also stated that, under the IRB approach, the Basel 1 treatment of general loan-loss allowances as part of Tier 2 capital would no longer be permitted. Under the Basel 2 standardised approach, the treatment of loan-loss allowances is as under Basel 1 (BCBS 2006, paragraph 42), whereby general loan-loss allowances are included in Tier 2 capital up to a maximum of 1.25% of risk-weighted assets.[14]

Under the Basel 3 accord, issued in 2010 and revised in 2011 (BCBS 2011), the deduction from capital in respect of a shortfall of the stock of provisions relative to expected losses under the IRB approach should be made entirely within Common Equity Tier 1 capital, which is part of Tier 1 capital (BCBS 2011, paragraph 73). Where the total expected loss amount is less than total eligible provisions, banks may recognise the difference in Tier 2 capital up to a maximum of 0.6% of credit-risk-weighted assets (BCBS 2011, paragraph 61). Under the Basel 3 standardised approach, the treatment of loan-loss allowances is as under Basel 1 (BCBS 2011, paragraph 60).

From the foregoing, it can be seen that, although the loan-loss allowances on banks' balance sheets are over-ridden in some ways by bank-regulators' adjustments to regulatory capital, loan-loss allowances affect regulatory capital. For example, for banks following the Basel standardised approach, the net-of-tax loss allowance recognised in the balance sheet reduces Tier 1 capital directly and the gross-of-tax general allowance increases Tier 2 capital up to a maximum of 1.25% of risk-weighted assets.[15] Furthermore, even for IRB banks, for which a Basel 3 regulatory expected-loss estimate that exceeds the accounting allowance overrides the allowance, movements in the allowance directly affect Tier 1 regulatory capital if the allowance exceeds the regulatory expected-loss estimate (Kruger et al. 2018, p. 116).[16] Also, we note that, although bank regulators typically have the power to write their own rules that over-ride accounting rules in the measurement of regulatory capital, Ryan and Keeley (2013,

p. 69) observed that U.S. bank regulators appeared unwilling to do so in relation to U.S. GAAP as interpreted by the SEC in SAB 102.

2.3.   *Literature review*

The IL methods for accounting for credit losses that were in place under U.S. GAAP and IFRS at the time of the financial and banking crisis of the late 2000s were more heavily weighted towards limiting earnings management and the associated overstatement of loss allowances than towards permitting discretion that might facilitate timely recognition in loss allowances of information about likely credit losses. In part in response to advice from a prudential-regulatory perspective, the crisis prompted a shift in relative emphasis away from the former and towards the latter. This was reflected in the development of new EL-based methods of accounting for credit losses.[17] In this subsection, we review elements of the prior literature that are relevant to these features of the events examined in this paper. We structure our review such as to focus on (i) elements of the literature on earnings management and capital management in relation to banks and (ii) elements of the literature on accounting conservatism and timeliness in relation to banks, including in relation to stability of the financial system. See also Giner and Mora (2018) for further consideration of the issues considered in our review and related issues, in particular in relation to the academic literature on accounting conservatism.

2.3.1.   *Elements of the literature on earnings management and capital management in relation to banks*

The restrictions of the IL method of accounting for credit losses, criticised at the time of the financial and banking crisis of the late 2000s, could be attributed in part to the understandable importance previously attached to the restriction of opportunities for manipulation of credit-loss expense that might be undertaken for earnings-management purposes.

There is a substantial body of evidence that such manipulation has occurred in order to manage either or both of earnings and regulatory capital.[18] Moyer (1990) and Beatty et al. (1995) report evidence of loss-allowance-related regulatory-capital management in the U.S. prior to the implementation of the first Basel accord (Basel 1), when U.S. loan-loss allowances had a greater regulatory-capital-increasing benefit than after implementation of Basel 1.[19] Kim and Kross (1998) and Ahmed et al. (1999) report evidence that such capital management was reduced in the post-Basel period after the regulatory-capital benefit was reduced. Further evidence of loss-allowance-related earnings and/or capital management in the U.S. is reported in Collins et al. (1995), Lobo and Yang (2001), Kanagaretnam et al. (2003), Kanagaretnam et al. (2004) and Liu and Ryan (2006). Huizinga and Laeven (2012) examine U.S. banks' use of accounting discretion during the crisis. They report evidence that such discretion, including with respect to loan-loss expense, was used to overstate book values of financial assets during the crisis. In contrast, Jin et al. (2016) report evidence that U.S. banks' discretion with respect to loan-loss expense prior to the crisis was used primarily for risk-management purposes through provision for future credit losses rather than for earnings-management-related purposes. Evidence of loss-allowance-related earnings and/or regulatory-capital management has also been reported for Japan (Shrieves and Dahl 2003), Australia (Anandarajan et al. 2007) and Spain (Perez et al. 2008). Hasan and Wall (2004) report evidence of loss allowances being used to manage earnings in a large number of countries. A multi-national study by Fonseca and Gonzalez (2008) reports that the use of loan-loss-related earnings smoothing varies predictably across countries in relation to factors including investor protection, disclosure, regulation and the degree of financial development. Another multi-national study by Bouvatier et al. (2014) reports that European banks with more concentrated ownership have used discretionary loan-loss expense to smooth their income, and that this effect is less strong in countries with stronger supervisory regimes that might be expected to limit opportunistic behaviour.

A number of studies focus on the trade-off between (i) constraints on discretion that might be used to manage earnings and (ii) facilitation of timely and informative reported credit-losses. We have already referred to the evidence in Balla and Rose (2015) and in Beck and Narayanamoorthy (2013) that the strengthening of IL-recognition requirements in the U.S. in the early 2000s reduced earnings management but placed constraints on banks' timely recognition of loan losses. In a similar vein, Gebhardt and Novotny-Farkas (2011) find that the IL restriction imposed through the adoption of IAS 39 (IASB 2003) by European banks reduced the extent to which loan losses were used to manage earnings but resulted in less timely loan-loss recognition. They questioned the desirability of restricted discretion under IAS 39 in light of its possible adverse consequences during the financial and banking crisis of the late 2000s.[20] Marton and Runesson (2017) also find evidence that, compared with pre-existing local GAAP, IAS 39 reduced the timeliness of loan-loss expense in the European Union. They find that loan-loss expense under the IAS 39 IL method predicts future credit losses, as measured by charge-offs, to a lesser extent than under local GAAP, consistent with the IL model reducing the timeliness of loss recognition. They find that the comparative advantage of local GAAP is stronger (i) under strict enforcement, (ii) in larger banks, which are likely to benefit from relatively high levels of specialised skills and system support, and (iii) in relatively profitable banks, where incentives to manage earnings may be relatively low. They note that their results suggest that introduction of more discretionary EL methods will need to be supported by appropriate enforcement mechanisms. In relation to post-crisis proposals for more discretionary and forward-looking credit-loss-accounting methods, Bushman and Williams (2012) point to the risk that the benefits from reduced procyclicality arising from such methods may be swamped by losses in transparency. They report evidence that discretion in loan-loss provisioning that is used for timely loss recognition enhances discipline over bank risk-taking but that discretion in loan-loss provisioning that is used for earnings-smoothing purposes dampens that discipline. Acharya and Ryan (2016) argue that, absent banks' exercise of discretion, an EL model should provide earlier warning of economic downturns than the IL model but that FASB (2012) would not suppress much if any volatility because it significantly broadens banks' discretion. Novotny-Farkas (2016) notes that the IFRS 9 EL model should have the beneficial effect of allowing earlier loss recognition and might enhance financial stability if it is implemented properly and consistently, but that the degree of discretion that it allows gives significant scope for earnings management.

The evidence summarised in this subsection indicates that there was some justification for standard setters to focus on restriction of earnings management in the credit-loss accounting methods that they had in place prior to the crisis. It also indicates that there is reason to monitor the effects of the earnings-management opportunities created by the greater discretion permitted by the new EL methods relative to the pre-existing IL methods.

2.3.2. *Elements of the literature on accounting conservatism and timeliness in relation to banks*

During the standard setters' development of their EL methods of accounting for credit losses, a significant issue arose regarding the magnitude of loss allowances. As outlined in Section 1 and described more fully later in the paper, a significant cause of the failure of FASB/IASB convergence on accounting for credit losses was that the IASB's preferred method for the determination of loss allowances was seen by the FASB as insufficiently conservative, in that allowances for credit losses would not be established soon enough, and the FASB's preferred method was seen by the IASB as excessively conservative, in that allowances for credit losses would be established too soon. We now consider elements of the literature that are relevant to this matter. We do so under the headings of 'Conditional and unconditional conservatism' and 'Association between timeliness in recognition of credit losses and stability of the financial system'.

2.3.2.1. *Conditional and unconditional conservatism.* It might be argued that a conservative focus on loss-allowance adequacy, at the potential risk of over-stating those allowances, is beneficial to the extent that it allows the exercise of prudence under conditions of uncertainty, leading to timely recognition of new information about credit losses.[21] The type of news-dependent accounting conservatism envisaged here is sometimes termed 'conditional conservatism' (Ball and Shivakumar 2005, Beaver and Ryan 2005). The beneficial effects of this type of conservatism have been extensively examined in the accounting literature through asymmetric-timeliness measures of the sort pioneered by Basu (1997), which measure the extent to which bad news is recognised in financial statements more quickly than good news. It might also be argued that a conservative focus on loss-allowance adequacy, at the potential risk of over-stating those allowances, is not beneficial to the extent that it might introduce a substantial level of bias that is not only uninformative in itself but might also limit the extent to which movements in loss allowances reflect new information. The type of news-independent accounting conservatism envisaged here contributes to what is sometimes termed 'unconditional conservatism' (Ball and Shivakumar 2005, Beaver and Ryan 2005). As the distinction between conditional conservatism and unconditional conservatism is of some relevance to the events examined in this paper, we review briefly in this subsection some elements of the literature relating to these concepts.

There is much evidence in the general financial-reporting literature of the benefits of conditional conservatism. It has been found to be beneficial in addressing information-asymmetry problems, including through acceleration in the triggering of debt-covenant violations (Zhang 2008), facilitation of access to debt markets thereby alleviating under-investment (Garcia Lara et al. 2016), addressing information requirements of debtholders of near-insolvent companies (Aier et al. 2014) and constraining behaviour by managers that may be detrimental to relatively uninformed outside equity investors (LaFond and Watts 2008). Beneficial effects of timely loss recognition documented in the general financial-reporting literature are also reflected in relation to financial institutions. Nichols et al. (2009) report evidence that, as predicted because of the greater information asymmetry that they face, public banks are more conditionally conservative than private banks. Vyas (2011) reports evidence that market prices of financial institutions reflect exposure to risky assets more quickly in the presence of timelier write-downs of those assets. Lim et al. (2014) report that conditional conservatism on the part of banks is associated with high reputation, enabling among other things the ability to charge higher interest to loan customers. Akins et al. (2017) find that timely loan-loss recognition constrains corruption in relation to banks' lending.

Conditional conservatism can be contrasted with news-independent or unconditional conservatism. Unconditional conservatism typically arises in a number of ways, of which commonly quoted examples are: (i) for long-lived assets, the use of depreciation/amortisation rates that exceed the economic rates; (ii) for internally-generated intangible assets, immediate expensing of the costs of developing those assets. The non-recognition of growth options and of the present value of monopoly returns is sometimes also quoted as an example of unconditional conservatism, but some see this as different in character from the two items referred to above (Ryan 2006, Roychowdhury and Watts 2007). An effect of news-independent unconditional conservatism can be to introduce uninformative bias that restricts the extent to which informationally-valuable news-dependent conditional conservatism can be applied. Ball and Shivakumar (2005, pp. 90–91) refer to this potentially adverse effect in the context of contracting efficiency.[22]

2.3.2.2. *Association between timeliness in recognition of credit losses and stability of the financial system.* Much of the evidence on the benefits of timely recognition of credit losses and resultant loss-allowance adequacy relates to the stability of the financial system, which is of interest to prudential regulators. We consider this body of literature in the context of the consideration of the interest of prudential regulators in the issue of accounting for credit losses.

It has been argued that prudential regulators have an asymmetric loss function because understated loss allowances may contribute to bank failure, with consequent severe costs to bank regulators, whereas overstated allowances are unlikely to impose severe costs on regulators (Benston and Wall 2005). Pressure from taxpayers who may have to meet the financial cost of bank failures is also likely to contribute to this effect (Kane 1997, Wall and Koch 2000, p. 15). Prudential regulators might therefore be expected to be less averse to the overstatement of loss allowances than others with an interest in accounting for credit losses.

Prudential regulators' interest in loss allowances arises both through their role in relation to regulatory capital and through other mechanisms. It is convenient to consider the regulatory-capital-related role of loss allowances in the context of the Basel 2 framework, referred to earlier. As noted previously, in relation to the framework's pillar 1 'Minimum Capital Requirements', loan-loss allowances on banks' balance sheets are an input to the calculation of Tier 1 capital and Tier 2 capital. A number of studies report evidence that suggests that the direct effect of accounting for credit losses on regulatory capital, which could be characterised as a pillar-1-related effect, in combination with an asymmetric loss function could result in a preference on the part of prudential regulators for allowances that might be higher than the strict interpretation of accounting conceptual frameworks might give. Laeven and Majnoni (2003), Bikker and Metzemakers (2005) and Bouvatier and Lepetit (2008) provide consistent evidence that the lack of timeliness in loan-loss recognition under IL methods exacerbates economic downturns. These studies argue that IL methods prevent banks from timely loan-loss recognition in good times and require banks to increase loss allowances substantially in bad times, which hits regulatory capital when it is expensive to raise capital. Beatty and Liao (2011) predict that, in light of likely concerns about regulatory-capital constraints, banks with relatively untimely credit-loss recognition make relatively large reductions in their lending during recessions. Their results support this prediction. Bushman and Williams (2015) report that delayed loss recognition affects the stability of the banking system through the creation of codependence of downside tail risk among banks, with high-delay banks simultaneously facing in bad times financing frictions that will impede their access to new capital.

The directional effect of mechanisms that could be characterised as relating to pillar 2 'Supervisory Review Process' and pillar 3 'Market Discipline' on the preferences of prudential regulators with respect to loss allowances is less clear. In relation to loss allowances, these elements of the Basel framework contribute to the capital adequacy of banks by requiring that high-quality information should inform the determination of loss allowances and should be conveyed to market participants through those loss allowances. Relative to pillar-1-related channels, these channels might be more likely to induce a focus on faithful representation of losses, similar to that of accounting standard-setters, and might be less likely to motivate preferences for potentially overstated allowances. Ryan (2017) considers issues related to this matter. He argues that the effects of differences in methods of accounting for loan losses on regulatory capital ratios are likely to be relatively small: although loan-loss allowances may on average be a substantial proportion of equity (typically in the region of 10%), they are on average a small proportion of total assets (typically in the region of 1%).[23] This suggests that regulatory-capital ratios, which express regulatory capital as a ratio of risk-weighted assets, are likely to be relatively insensitive to proportionate changes in loan-loss allowances. Based in part on such considerations, Ryan (2017) argues that, although there may be some effect through regulatory-capital ratios, the primary effect of banks' loan-loss-accounting requirements on financial stability is less likely to arise directly through the direct regulatory-capital-ratio channel than through the enhancement of the understanding of banks' risks on the part of the banks themselves, market participants and regulators. This argument suggests that accounting for loan losses may affect financial stability more strongly through channels related to the Basel pillars 2 and 3 than through the Basel pillar-1-related direct regulatory-capital-ratio-related channel.

Another mechanism by which the accounting for credit losses can influence stability is through its effect on banks' investing and funding decisions. As noted by Benston and Wall (2005) and Novotny-Farkas (2016), timely recognition of loan losses will reduce earnings and equity, which will themselves discourage risky behaviour with regard to investment and financing.

Although prudential regulators can be expected to share to some extent the preferences of accounting standard setters that loss allowances should faithfully represent losses and although regulatory-capital ratios may not be very sensitive to proportionate changes in loan-loss allowances, there is reason to believe that asymmetric loss functions in combination with direct effects of loss allowances on regulatory capital referred to earlier might give prudential regulators a lower aversion to over-stated loss allowance than accounting standard setters have.

3.   The development since 2009 of the FASB's and the IASB's expected-loss-based methods of accounting for credit-loss impairment

In the aftermath of the financial and banking crisis of the late 2000s, the FASB and the IASB each proceeded with the development of credit-loss impairment methods aimed at achieving more timely recognition of predictable losses.[24] In this section, we outline the development between 2009 and 2016 of the FASB's and IASB's EL methods for accounting for impairment relating to credit losses. We provide a summary and discussion for each of the sets of proposals issued by the standard setters. Our summaries and discussions are based on: (i) our review of FASB and IASB publications; (ii) our review of FASB and IASB meeting records and recordings of meetings; (iii) our confidential conversations with senior observers of the process; (iv) our reading of comment letters written in response to the five proposal documents issued by the FASB and/or the IASB between 2009 and 2013, of which discussion is informed by analysis reported in O'Hanlon et al. (2018).

A representation of the timeline of key outputs is presented in Figure 1, which gives full titles of the outputs. For fuller details of the proposal documents, see the European Parliament paper by O'Hanlon et al. (2015) and the related paper by Hashim et al. (2016).[25]

3.1.   *IASB exposure draft: November 2009 (IASB 2009)*

IASB (2009) aimed to reflect the economics of lending. In particular, it aimed to avoid the problem whereby, under the pre-existing IL method, interest revenue was recognised in full from the origination of a loan but initially-expected losses that are compensated within the interest revenue were not recognised until loss events occur:

> The (IL) approach is internally inconsistent because expected losses are implicit in the initial measurement of the asset, but not taken into account in determining the effective interest rate used for subsequent measurement. This results in a systematic overstatement of interest revenue in the periods before a loss event occurs. In effect, subsequent impairment losses are in part reversals of inappropriate revenue recognition in earlier periods. (IASB 2009, paragraph BC11)

IASB (2009)	Joint FASB/IASB	Three-bucket	IASB (2013a)	IASB (2014a)
Exposure Draft ED/2009/12. Financial Instruments: Amortised Cost and Impairment. →	**Supplementary Document.** FASB/IASB (2011a)	proposals → FASB/IASB (2011b) *Staff Paper. Impairment: Three-bucket approach.*	*Exposure Draft* → *ED/2013/3. Financial Instruments: Expected Credit Losses.*	*IFRS 9: Financial Instruments.* (Effective for annual periods beginning on or after 1 January 2018)
(November 2009)	FASB: *Supplementary Document. Accounting for Financial Instruments and Revisions to the Accounting for Derivative Instruments and Hedging Activities: Impairment.* (31 January 2011)	(Key elements of these proposals were reflected in IASB (2013a) but not in → FASB (2012).)	(March 2013)	(July 2014)
FASB (2010a) *Exposure Draft: Proposed Accounting Standards Update. Accounting for Financial Instruments and Revisions to the Accounting for Derivative Instruments and Hedging Activities.* →	*AND* IASB: *Supplement to ED/2009/12. Financial Instruments: Amortised Cost and Impairment (Financial Instruments: Impairment).*		FASB (2012) *Exposure Draft: Proposed Accounting Standards Update. Financial Instruments: Credit Losses.* →	FASB (2016) *Accounting Standards Update No. 2016-13. Financial Instruments – Credit Losses (Topic 326): Measurement of Credit Losses on Financial Instruments.* (Effective for fiscal years beginning after 15 December 2019 or 15 December 2020 for different types of entity)
(26 May 2010)	(January 2011).	(13 June 2011, plus other papers to mid-2012)	(20 December 2012)	(June 2016)

Figure 1.   Expected loss approaches to credit-loss impairment: documents issued by FASB and/or IASB from 2009 to 2016.

The IASB (2009) method treated the transaction price (amount lent or purchase price) at which financial assets were initially recognised as being the present value of expected future cash inflows as at the initial-recognition date, net of future shortfalls relative to contractual cash flows (credit losses) expected as at that date, discounted at a credit-loss-inclusive integrated effective interest rate (hereinafter, IEIR). The IEIR would be used for accrual of interest revenue. Recognition of initially-expected credit losses would thereby be spread over the expected life of assets. Subsequent revisions to expected cash flows, discounted at the initially-estimated IEIR, would then be recognised in full as they occurred. Figure 2 represents this diagrammatically. Figure 3 includes a numerical illustration of the recognition of initially-expected credit losses under the IASB (2009) proposal. We and many observers with whom we spoke share the view expressed in the IASB's subsequent 2013 exposure draft that 'expected credit losses are most faithfully represented by the proposals in the 2009 ED. Those proposals reflected the economic link between the pricing of financial assets and the expected credit losses at initial recognition' (IASB 2013a, p. 10). Analysis of comment letters reported in O'Hanlon et al. (2018) indicates strong support for the general principle of spreading across time of the recognition of initially-expected credit losses. However, based on the IASB's own assessment of feedback referred to in IASB (2014a, paragraph BCIN.12), analysis of comment letters reported in O'Hanlon et al. (2018) and comments that the authors received from observers, it is evident that the IASB (2009) IEIR method was widely regarded as posing substantial challenges: it would be difficult for preparers to combine interest and credit-loss information; it would be difficult for users to interpret measures that combine interest and credit-loss information. Some comment letters also questioned whether assets are priced by reference to expected losses in the way implied by IASB (2009). Also, some respondents to IASB (2009)[26] and some observers with whom we spoke noted that the smooth recognition of initially-expected credit losses over time in IASB (2009) is inconsistent with the uneven manner in which losses arise over time.

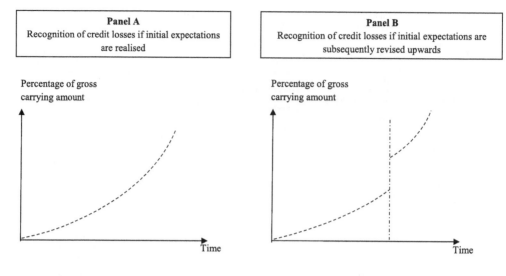

Panel A is based on a diagram from IASB (2013b).

Figure 2.   Recognition of initially-expected credit losses under IASB (2009).

In light of feedback on IASB (2009), the IASB then pursued a path aimed at achieving its objective 'to reflect initial expected credit losses as part of determining the effective interest rate' (FASB/IASB 2011a, paragraph IN5) through a method that was more practicable than that described in IASB (2009), including within its subsequent attempt to develop with the FASB a converged common solution.

3.2.   *FASB exposure draft: 26 May 2010 (FASB 2010a)*

As indicated in its title, the FASB (2010a) exposure draft had a wider scope than IASB (2009), with credit-loss impairment being one of various financial-instrument issues that were addressed. With regard to credit losses, FASB (2010a) proposed that an entity should recognise credit impairment in net income 'when it does not expect to collect all contractual amounts due for originated financial asset(s) and all amounts originally expected to be collected upon acquisition for purchased financial asset(s)' (FASB 2010a, paragraph 38). Significant features of the FASB (2010a) proposals were that losses would no longer need to be 'probable' in order to be recognised and that it should be assumed that economic conditions at the impairment-measurement date would remain unchanged for the remaining life of assets held. An implication of FASB (2010a) was the requirement for full recognition at day 1 (i.e., at the time of initial recognition) of all credit losses expected over the contractual life of financial assets held. This treatment, which could be seen as an extreme form of unconditional conservatism, became a controversial issue later in the process. Figure 3 includes a numerical illustration of recognition of day-1 loss and of why this might be seen as a problem. The FASB (2010a) proposals differed from the IASB (2009) proposals primarily in that, whereas the IASB proposals gave relatively high weight to income-recognition considerations, the FASB proposals gave relatively high weight to balance-sheet-focused allowance-adequacy considerations.[27]

The FASB (2010a) method had much in common with the Current Expected Credit Loss (CECL) method subsequently included in the later FASB (2016) Accounting Standards Update

The IASB (2009) integrated-effective-interest-rate approach

A bank originates at the start of year 1 (designated here 'day 1') a portfolio of loans totalling Currency Units (CU) 1,000.00. It is believed that the fair value of the portfolio at origination is CU 1,000.00.

Panel 1 of the table below gives the contractual cash flows due from the borrowers and the cash flows (net of expected credit losses) that, as at day 1, the bank expects to collect. Cash flows are expected to occur at yearly intervals, with 'Year 1' being one year after 'Day 1', etc. The effective interest rates based on contractual and expected cash flows are 10% and 8%, respectively. Panel 2 of the table gives the movements on the loan account (net book value) as they would be if the cash flows expected as at day-1 were received and were accounted for under the integrated effective interest rate (IEIR) method proposed in IASB (2009).

| | Panel 1 | | | | Panel 2 | | | |
| | Expectations as at day 1 | | | | Based on cash flows expected as at day-1, under the IASB (2009) IEIR method | | | |
	Contractual cash flows	Expected credit losses	Expected cash flows net of credit losses		Brought forward	Interest accrued (at 8%)	Cash	Carried forward
Day 1	-1,000.00		-1,000.00				1,000.00	1,000.00
Year 1	350.00	-5.00	345.00		1,000.00	80.00	-345.00	735.00
Year 2	325.00	-10.00	315.00		735.00	58.80	-315.00	478.80
Year 3	300.00	-16.00	284.00		478.80	38.30	-284.00	233.10
Year 4	275.00	-23.25	251.75		233.10	18.65	-251.75	000.00
Effective interest rate (EIR)	10%		8%					

Day-1 recognition of lifetimes expected losses

This illustration uses the numbers given in the table above.

The fair value of the CU 1,000.00 of the portfolio of loans can be written as the present value of the contractual cash flows discounted at the EIR based on contractual cash flows (10%):
$$350.00/1.10 + 325.00/1.10^2 + 300.00/1.10^3 + 275.00/1.10^4 = CU\ 1,000.00.$$
It can also be written as follows as the expected cash flows discounted at the IEIR based on expected cash flows (8%):
$$345.00/1.08 + 315.00/1.08^2 + 284.00/1.08^3 + 251.75/1.08^4 = CU\ 1,000.00.$$

In illustrating the recognition of lifetime expected losses at day 1, 'loss' is estimated using discounted-cash-flow (DCF). In measuring impairment of financial assets, DCF is required under IASB (2014a) and is permitted, but not required, under FASB (2016). The net book value of the portfolio after subtracting the day-1 loss would be measured as follows by discounting the expected cash flows, net of expected credit losses, at the contractual EIR of 10%:
$$345.00/1.10 + 315.00/1.10^2 + 284.00/1.10^3 + 251.75/1.10^4 = CU\ 959.29.$$

The day-1 loss (expense) and day-1 loss allowance (contra-asset account) to be recognised would be 1,000.00 - 959.29 = CU 40.71. The amount of CU 959.29 could be said to reflect initially-expected credit losses twice: within the cash flows, which are stated net of those initially-expected losses, and within the discount rate of 10%, which includes a premium to compensate for those initially expected losses. If the portfolio were to be written down immediately (at day 1) to CU 959.29, it would be stated at below the fair value of CU 1,000.00.

Note: The situation depicted here is different from one in which a loan is made on favourable terms such that the fair value of the expected recoverable amounts is less than the amount lent. It is uncontroversial that, in such circumstances, the loan should be written down to fair value at day 1.

Figure 3. Numerical illustration of the IASB (2009) integrated-effective-interest-rate approach and of day-1 recognition of lifetime expected losses.

on credit losses in that it removed the 'probable' threshold for loss recognition and in that it required loss-allowances to reflect all contractual amounts not expected to be collected for the remaining life of an asset. Despite its similarity to the eventual CECL EL method, it was not at the time regarded by the FASB as an EL method. This was because, as stated in FASB (2010a, Paragraph BC175):

[…] it would not permit an entity to forecast future events or economic conditions in developing those estimates as would occur in an expected loss model;

and

Under an expected loss model, the Board understands that an entity would recognize a constant rate of credit impairments through the life of the financial asset based on expectations about losses on the date of acquisition or origination, with any changes from initial expected credit impairments recognized in the period of the change.

Although for the reasons given above the FASB did not see the FASB (2010a) method as an EL method, neither did it see it as an IL method. This was 'because recognition of credit impairment would not be based on any triggering event' (FASB 2010a, Paragraph BC174). Despite what the FASB said about EL and IL in relation to the FASB (2010a) method, some respondents to FASB (2010a) interpreted the method as EL and some interpreted it as IL.

Feedback on FASB (2010a) was largely supportive of dropping the requirement that losses should be 'probable' in order to be recognised and was largely unsupportive of the proposal that it should be assumed that economic conditions at the impairment-measurement date would remain unchanged for the remaining life of assets. In light of feedback on FASB (2010a), the FASB pursued a path aimed at achieving an objective 'to ensure that the allowance balance was sufficient to cover all estimated credit losses for the remaining life of an instrument' (FASB/IASB 2011a, paragraph IN6), including through its subsequent attempt with the IASB to develop a converged common solution.

3.3.   *Joint FASB/IASB supplementary document: January 2011 (FASB/IASB 2011a)*

The joint FASB/IASB supplementary document presented an impairment method that the FASB and IASB believed would 'enable them to satisfy at least part of their individual objectives for impairment accounting while achieving a common solution to impairment' (FASB/IASB 2011a, paragraph IN3). Specifically, it was hoped that the supplementary document would satisfy at least part of the primary objective of the IASB 'to reflect initial expected credit losses as part of determining the effective interest rate' and at least part the FASB objective 'to ensure that the allowance balance was sufficient to cover all estimated credit losses for the remaining life of an instrument' (FASB/IASB 2011a, paragraphs IN5-7).

FASB/IASB (2011a) retained the FASB (2010a) elimination of the FASB's 'probable' threshold. Unlike IASB (2009), it proposed that initially-expected credit losses should be decoupled from the effective interest rate. Unlike IASB (2009) and FASB (2010a), it stated clearly that the information set to be used in estimating expected credit losses should include all available information including 'historical data, current economic conditions, and supportable forecasts of future events and economic conditions' (FASB/IASB 2011a, paragraph B5). The requirement to use an information set including supportable forecasts that is substantially broader than permitted by pre-existing IL methods was carried forward with similar wording into all subsequent FASB and IASB exposure drafts and standards on credit losses, together with the elimination of the FASB's 'probable' threshold. The standard setters' converged broadening of the information set permitted to be used for the purpose of recognising credit-loss impairment addresses an important element of the problem with the timeliness of the accounting for credit losses highlighted in the crisis.

Another key proposal in the supplementary document was that, for the purpose of accounting for credit losses, financial assets should be categorised into a 'good book' and a 'bad book'. At each reporting date, the impairment allowance would comprise:

- for assets for which it is appropriate to recognise expected credit losses over time (good book), the higher of: (i) time-proportional expected credit losses (TPA), addressing through spreading of loss recognition over time the IASB's preference to reflect the relationship between expected credit losses and pricing;[28] and (ii) credit losses expected to occur within the foreseeable future period (at least twelve months) (FFP), addressing the FASB's focus on loss-allowance adequacy; TPA can be seen as a spreading approach, which does not involve day-1 losses,[29] and FFP can be seen as an immediate-recognition approach, which does involve day-1 losses;
- for all other assets (bad book), the entire amount of expected credit losses.

Assets would be included in and transferred between the good-book and bad-book categories in accordance with an entity's internal risk-management practices.

The joint FASB/IASB supplementary document elicited substantial numbers of responses from U.S. respondents that could be assumed to be FASB constituents and non-U.S. respondents that could be assumed to be IASB constituents or potential constituents. This permitted direct comparison of responses for the two groups reported in O'Hanlon et al. (2018), for which some statistics are reproduced in Table 1.[30]

These statistics indicate differences between preferences of FASB and IASB constituents that might contribute to barriers to FASB/IASB convergence on accounting for credit losses. Non-U.S. respondents tended to favour good book/bad book categorisation consistent with a preference to recognise initially-expected losses on good-book assets over time, whereas U.S. respondents tended to oppose it. With regard to the good-book allowance, non-U.S. respondents tended to favour an income-statement-focused spreading approach (TPA), whereas U.S. respondents tended to favour a balance-sheet-focused immediate-recognition approach (FFP) that would require day-1 losses.

3.4. *Continued work on seeking convergence: The three-bucket approach*

After receiving feedback on FASB/IASB (2011a), the FASB and the IASB continued in 2011 and 2012 with joint deliberations aimed at developing a possible converged method of accounting for credit-loss impairment. Within these deliberations, the standard setters considered a so-called three-bucket approach (FASB/IASB 2011b) developed from the proposals in the supplementary document. Here, assets would be categorised into one of three buckets:

- Bucket 1: assets that had not been affected by observable events indicating a direct relationship to possible future default, for which there would be partial recognition of expected losses, where options considered included TPA and 12-month expected losses;

Table 1. Responses to comment letters on FASB/IASB (2011a) summarised from O'Hanlon et al. (2018).

Proposed treatment	Positive comment		Negative comment	
	Non-U.S.	U.S.	Non-U.S.	U.S.
Categorisation into good book and bad book	82%	34%	10%	43%
Good-book allowance: TPA	70%	18%	19%	64%
Good-book allowance: FFP	32%	49%	52%	35%

Note: These statistics relate to 111 non-U.S. respondents and 72 U.S. respondents. For each of the six pairs of statistics (non-U.S./U.S.) reported above, the difference between the proportion of non-U.S. respondents commenting in the stated way and the proportion of U.S. respondents commenting in the stated way is significant at the 5% level (two-tailed test).

- Buckets 2 and 3: assets affected by events indicating a direct relationship to future default, with bucket 2 comprising groups of assets for which specific assets in danger of default had not been identified and bucket 3 comprising specific assets for which credit losses are expected to occur or have occurred, for which lifetime expected losses would be recognised.

During their deliberations, the FASB and the IASB eliminated the TPA spreading approach from consideration. They agreed to deliberate a relative method in which all in-scope financial assets would initially be placed in bucket 1, for which the allowance at each date including day 1 would comprise 12-month expected loss, with any assets that suffered significant subsequent deterioration in credit quality relative to credit quality at initial recognition then being moved to lifetime expected loss. In that it involved recognition of 12-month expected losses for bucket-1 assets, this method was similar to the FASB's preferred FFP good-book method and did not explicitly involve spreading in the way that the IASB (2009) IEIR method or the TPA method did. However, the IASB accepted this method, with some conceptual misgivings with regard to day-1 losses, in part because it offered a practicable approximation to the outcomes from the IASB (2009) IEIR method and in part because it was hoped that this might facilitate FASB/IASB convergence.[31]

In August 2012, the FASB indicated that it did not wish to continue to work with the IASB towards development of a method based on the three-bucket categorisation of financial assets into a non-credit-deteriorated category and a credit-deteriorated category with only partial recognition of expected credit losses for the first category, which it termed a 'dual-measurement' approach. After the FASB's August 2012 decision, the FASB and the IASB proceeded to develop their own separate standards while continuing to consult with each other. In subsequent explanation in FASB (2012, paragraph BC11) of its decision to disengage from the three-bucket deliberations with the IASB, the FASB said that application of two different measurement objectives would be confusing for users, would involve a 'cliff effect' as assets were reclassified, would create earnings-management opportunities, and could be seen as involving an undesirable IL-type recognition trigger. Although we are not aware of evidence of a direct connection between the two events, we note that the August 2012 FASB meeting occurred only a few weeks after the publication of an SEC document (SEC 2012) that was viewed by the IASB Chair Hans Hoogervorst as signalling the end of the era of IASB/FASB convergence (McEnroe and Sullivan 2014, p. 18).[32]

The difference between the pre-existing practices of banks in the U.S. and elsewhere with regard to loss-allowances, which would contribute to the eventual failure of the FASB and IASB to achieve a common solution to accounting for credit losses, had been reflected in discussion at a joint FASB/IASB meeting in July 2011.[33] At that meeting, there was both concern from the IASB side that recognition of a 12-month good-book (bucket-1) allowance at initial recognition was excessive and concern from the FASB side that a 12-month good-book allowance was insufficient. At that meeting an IASB member questioned how a day-1 loss on assets originated at fair value could provide useful information to users of financial statements. A FASB representative indicated that the FASB might not wish to adopt a method for accounting for credit losses that reduced allowances: 'I start with the belief that there has to be some change here. Reserves generally have been inadequate in the U.S. banking system'. He said that he had conducted analysis that indicated that a 12-month bucket-1 allowance would have virtually no impact on loss allowances of U.S. commercial banks and might even reduce them. In response, an IASB representative noted that this was a U.S.-bank perspective and would not be expected to hold outside the U.S.

Further illustration of the tensions caused by the differences in pre-existing practice with regard to allowances that had contributed to the failure of the FASB and the IASB to agree a common three-bucket-based solution is given by discussion at an IASB meeting of October

2012.[34] Here reference to allowance levels is linked to concerns of bank regulators. At that meeting, an IASB member referred to the following passage in an IASB feedback-summary paper and requested further information from the IASB staff about the issue referred to:[35]

> The prudential regulators have not expressed a formal opinion on the three-bucket model at this stage. However, their preliminary feedback was mixed. Some, particularly in the U.S., favour a lifetime expected loss model. This is primarily because they fear that the three-bucket approach may actually reduce allowance balances relative to those recognised today. Some were concerned that the three-bucket model, unless more clearly articulated, could enable entities to avoid recognising lifetime expected losses on a timely basis.

An IASB staff member said that this paragraph reflected U.S. bank regulators' concern that, because of the way in which U.S. banks used IBNR-type loss provisioning in their current application of SFAS 5 (FASB 1975), the application of a three-bucket method in the U.S. might result in a reduction of allowance balances relative to their then-current levels. Another IASB staff member then commented as follows:

> That's very U.S.-specific. The feedback we have had from our constituents outside the U.S. is that, based on their analysis of the model [....], there would be an increase in provisions based on the three-bucket model and, in some cases, a very significant increase in provisions. And that is one of the tensions [...] that we have had all the way through this project in that the starting places of the banks in different parts of the world are so different. This puts a lot of pressure on our ability to come to a converged solution.

We note that the concerns of bank regulators referred to above are consistent with the direction that might be predicted based on our discussion in subsection 2.3.2.2.

Allowance-adequacy-related concerns of the FASB with regard the three-bucket proposals were also reflected by a FASB representative at a joint FASB/IASB meeting in July 2013: it had been estimated that the three-bucket approach favoured by the IASB would reduce U.S. allowances by about 15% whereas the FASB preferred 'single-measurement' approach, under which full-contractual-life expected credit losses would be recognised, would increase them by about 40%.[36]

From the above, it can be seen that, by the later stages of the process, the seriousness of the challenge posed by the difference between pre-existing practice with regard to loss-allowances in the U.S. and elsewhere was well recognised. Related to this, it is notable that the FASB and U.S. prudential regulators tended to see pre-existing U.S. GAAP as giving rise to insufficiently timely recognition of credit losses and inadequate loss allowances,[37] and feared that the measures that were proposed by the IASB to improve matters in this regard might make matters worse in the U.S.

We did not note evidence from meeting records that differences between the IASB and the FASB with respect to pre-existing accounting standards or with respect to conceptual reasoning were a major source of the FASB/IASB differences. In relation to this, the FASB and IASB had issued in 2010 identical conceptual framework chapters entitled 'Qualitative characteristics of useful financial information', which referred to matters including 'bias' and 'neutrality' that are highly relevant to this issue (FASB 2010b, IASB 2010). Furthermore, as noted below, an IASB member in the final IASB exposure draft (IASB 2013a) and two FASB members in the final FASB standard (FASB 2016) raised very similar conceptually-based objections to day-1 losses later in the process.

3.5. IASB exposure draft: March 2013 (IASB 2013a) and IFRS 9: July 2014 (IASB 2014a)

The IASB decided at a December 2012 meeting to issue a new exposure draft incorporating a three-bucket approach.[38] This was subsequently issued in March 2013 (IASB 2013a). Discussion at the December 2012 meeting indicated that a major cause of the IASB's objection to the FASB's preferred method was its understanding of the likely magnitude of the FASB's lifetime day-1 losses, which were expected to be substantially larger than the IASB's 12-month day-1 losses. The following comment from the Chair of the IASB at the December 2012 meeting illustrates that IASB members acknowledged the conceptual flaw with the 12-month allowance and associated day-1-loss, and that this feature had initially been accepted by the IASB in part because it might have assisted with convergence with the FASB which was no longer expected to occur as part of the then-current process:[39]

> [...] I do recollect that the whole board had a severe hiccup about this 12-month day-1 loss. We didn't like it because it is conceptually flawed, and we know that, but we were willing to [...] take that, first of all because we were in the process of reaching some kind of convergence with the FASB. Well, that moment has unfortunately passed, but we were where we were and it was not very simple to come up with a simple and better solution for this issue [...] There are conceptual issues. Fortunately, quantitatively our conceptual flaw is a lot smaller than [...] the current FASB proposal [...].

Despite the conceptual concerns with the 12-month day-1 allowance, there did not appear to be any appetite at that stage to re-open consideration of other approaches that would have delayed progress towards the issue of a final standard, and IASB (2013a) was issued on the basis that it was likely to result in the approximate achievement of the aim of IASB (2009) to recognise initially-expected credit losses over time. Assets were described as being in one of three 'stages' with regard to credit deterioration, where stages 1, 2 and 3 corresponded closely to buckets 1, 2, and 3 from the three-bucket proposals. The stages are as follows:

- Stage 1 assets: assets for which credit quality has not deteriorated significantly since initial recognition or that have low credit risk at the reporting date. 12-month expected losses are recognised, including at day 1, and interest is calculated based on the gross carrying amount before deducting the loss allowance;[40]
- Stage 2 assets: assets for which credit quality has deteriorated significantly since initial recognition, unless they have low credit risk at the reporting date, but for which there is no objective evidence of a credit-loss event. Full lifetime expected credit losses are recognised, with interest calculated on the gross carrying amount before deducting the loss allowance;
- Stage 3 assets: assets for which there is objective evidence of impairment. Full lifetime expected credit losses are recognised, with interest calculated on the carrying amount of the asset after deducting the loss allowance.

One board member's concern about the 12-month allowance with its day-1 loss requirement for stage-1 assets was expressed as follows within an alternative view published within IASB (2013a):

> the loss allowance at an amount equal to 12-month expected credit losses would result in a credit loss at initial recognition even when a financial asset is priced on market terms and where, consequently, no economic credit loss exists [...] In no other area of financial reporting is an allowance immediately established to reduce the value of an asset that is purchased or originated on market terms. (IASB 2013a, paragraph AV2)

As reported in O'Hanlon et al. (2018), non-U.S. responses to IASB (2013a) included a substantial amount of negative comment on the day-1-loss requirement, much of which referenced supportively the alternative view published within the exposure draft. There was also some concern about operational practicability of the transfer criterion from the 12-month-loss category to the lifetime-loss category. However a substantial majority of respondents regarded the 12-month loss allowance for stage-1 assets together with transfer to lifetime loss after significant-deterioration in credit quality as an acceptable approach. At an IASB meeting of September 2013, an IASB member noted the apparent contradiction in the fact that a large number of respondents to IASB (2013a) had said that the 12-month allowance was both conceptually unjustified and acceptable.[41]

IFRS 9 (IASB 2014a) incorporated the key proposals of IASB (2013a), including the three stages and the 12-month loss allowance (including at day 1) for stage-1 assets.[42] It noted that the recognition of 12-month expected losses for assets for which credit risk has not increased significantly since initial recognition was a cost–benefit-based operational simplification for dealing with expected losses on good-book assets (IASB 2014a, paragraph BC5.195). It included a requirement that measurement of expected credit losses should reflect a broadened information set that includes 'reasonable and supportable information that is available without undue cost or effort at the reporting date about past events, current conditions and forecasts of future economic conditions' (IASB 2014a, paragraph 5.5.17). No dissenting opinion on the 12-month allowance and its day-1 loss was included in IFRS 9 (IASB 2014a).

It remains to be seen whether day-1-loss becomes a significant problem in years after IASB (2014a) has become effective.

3.6. FASB exposure draft: December 2012 (FASB 2012) and FASB accounting standards update no. 2016-13: June 2016 (FASB 2016)

The FASB (2012) exposure draft was issued in December 2012. It proposed 'only one measurement approach, which is the current estimate of contractual cash flows not expected to be collected on financial assets held at the reporting date' (FASB 2012, p. 5). FASB (2012) was developed into the Accounting Standards Update (FASB 2016) containing the CECL method. This requires that the allowance for expected credit losses is 'a valuation account that is deducted from the amortised cost basis of the financial asset(s) to present the net amount expected to be collected on the financial asset' (FASB 2016, paragraph 326-20-30-1). FASB (2016) included a requirement that measurement of expected credit losses should reflect a broadened information set: 'an entity shall consider available information relevant to assessing the collectibility of cash flows. This information may include internal information, external information, or a combination of both relating to past events, current conditions, and reasonable and supportable forecasts' (FASB 2016, paragraph 326-20-30-7).

Difficulties in achieving a shared understanding between the FASB and financial-statement preparers with regard to what is required by CECL appeared to contribute to the substantial time that elapsed between FASB (2012) and FASB (2016). As reported in O'Hanlon et al. (2018), responses to FASB (2012) indicate that a high proportion of U.S. respondents had concerns about the practicability of estimation and interpretability of allowances covering expected losses over the whole life of assets and with regard to the requirement to recognise such allowances at day 1. In response to feedback reflecting concern about the difficulty of estimating expected losses over the whole contractual life of assets, the FASB acknowledged that it may not have explained the CECL forecasting requirements very well in FASB (2012),[43] and it took steps to allay concern about these. It emphasised in its final standard that:

> for periods beyond which the entity is able to make or obtain reasonable and supportable forecasts of expected credit losses, an entity shall revert to historical loss information. (FASB 2016, paragraph 326-20-30-9)[44]

The day-1-loss feature became a focus of a dissenting opinion by two FASB members. They referred to the belief of some commentators that:

the incremental loss that would be recognized [...] is not based on the economics of the transaction but rather on a prudential desire to have a higher level of loan loss reserves reflected in financial reports to investors. (FASB 2016, pp. 236–237)

Using similar language to that of the IASB (2013a) alternative view, they questioned the conceptual soundness of day-1 loss:

They are unaware of any other area of financial reporting for which a loss and a related valuation allowance are immediately established to reduce the value of a recognized asset that is purchased or originated on market terms. (FASB 2016, p. 237)

It remains to be seen what problems may arise after FASB (2016) has become effective in relation to the requirement to estimate expected losses over the whole life of financial assets held and the requirement to recognise such expected losses in full at day 1.

3.7. *Involvement of regulators in the process*

Subsection 2.1.4 refers to preferences from regulatory-related sources for the development of accounting standards that would give more timely recognition of credit losses. It is useful at this point to comment on the involvement of regulators in the process described in this section. It is evident from our examination of meeting records that financial and banking regulators were consulted throughout the process.[45] As might be expected based on our review in subsection 2.3.2.2 of issues related to timely recognition of losses and the stability of the financial system, regulators tended to prefer relatively conservative approaches. This is exemplified by the reference in subsection 3.4 above to regulators' concern that three-bucket-based allowances might be inadequate. It is also exemplified by a similar concern on the part of prudential regulators reflected in an IASB outreach summary in respect of IASB (2013a).[46] Financial and banking regulators submitted comment letters in respect of all five proposal documents referred to above.[47] In the relatively small number of letters from financial and banking regulators in response to FASB (2012) and IASB (2013a) examined by O'Hanlon et al. (2018), there was substantially less opposition to day-1 loss than from other respondents.[48]

4.   Problems that may arise when the standards become effective: lifetime losses and day-1 losses

The standard setters have moved relatively straightforwardly to a converged broadening of the information set that is permitted to be used in estimating credit losses that can be recognised in financial statements. Instead of the relatively restricted information set permitted by pre-existing IL methods, both standard setters permit the use of an information set that, without the pre-existing FASB 'probable' threshold, includes reasonable and supportable forecasts (IASB 2014a, paragraph 5.5.17, FASB 2016, paragraph 326-20-30-7). This directly addresses a major element of the problem with the lack of timeliness in credit-loss recognition that gave rise to concern in the wake of the financial and banking crisis of the late 2000s. However, this very positive outcome was achieved within a lengthy process that also resulted in what some regard as less desirable outcomes. O'Hanlon et al. (2018) report that comment letters written in response to the standard setters' final exposure drafts suggest two particular issues that may give rise to problems when the standards become effective.

First, the FASB's requirement that loss allowances at each date should recognise all credit losses expected to occur over the whole life of assets gave rise to a high level of concern, in particular with regard to practicability of implementation. An illustration of this type of concern was provided at a FASB roundtable meeting of 4 February 2016. At that meeting, Community Bank representatives expressed strong concern arising from their understanding that the FASB's requirement within the CECL method for estimation of expected losses over the whole life of assets would require them to use complex and costly models that would be of no incremental value within their businesses. As noted above, the FASB has made substantial effort to address the causes of such concern.

Recent literature includes some suggestion that the requirement to recognise full-contractual-life expected losses in a U.S. context may not be as big a problem as it might first appear and may have a beneficial effect. Wu (2016) argues that the level of sales, prepayments and defaults in the U.S. context may mean that the time that loans are expected to remain within lenders' loan books may be substantially shorter than their full contractual life. Although this does not elim-inate the requirement to estimate losses over the full contractual life of loans,[49] it may mean that the task of forecasting such losses is facilitated by the ability to assume that losses beyond a certain point will be minimal. Giner and Mora (2018) argue that a requirement to recognise full-contrac-tual-life expected losses could be beneficial in the U.S. context, in which the originate-to-distribute business model is relatively common. Such a requirement might be expected to achieve the timely recognition of credit losses that are expected to arise years after disposal/distribution and that might not be recognised in a timely manner before disposal/distribution under the IASB's 12-month expected-loss approach. Giner and Mora (2018) argue that the requirement may consequently have the beneficial effect in the U.S. context of discouraging excessively risky lending.

Second, both standard setters have introduced requirements to recognise at day 1 initially-expected losses on assets originated or acquired at fair value.[50] The problem with day-1 loss is illustrated in Figure 3, referred to previously. There are various ways in which this problem can be expressed. Examples are listed below with, in each case, an endnote reference to a comment letter expressing the problem in that way:

1. Writing an asset down to below fair value immediately on initial recognition appears to be inconsistent with the standard setters' conceptual frameworks which require faithful rep-resentation of the phenomena that are purported to be represented.[51,52]
2. In that they are reflected both in the numerator and the denominator of a discounted-cash-flow (DCF) calculation, initially-expected losses are counted twice. See Figure 3. This is similar to the error that might arise if one were to discount a risk-adjusted stream of expected future payoffs using a risk-inclusive discount rate.[53,54]
3. Assuming that the pre-day-1-loss book value of an originated asset is equal to fair value at the origination date, this book value already recognises origination-date expectations regarding the amount and timing of shortfalls relative to contractual cash flows. These expectations should not be recognised again at the origination date.[55]
4. Recognising credit losses at origination but recognising associated credit-premium-inclus-ive interest later does not reflect the economics of the lending transaction.[56]
5. The requirement to write risky loans down to below fair value at the origination date suggests possibilities for earnings management, for example by originating a portfolio of risky loans in one period (in which a day-1 loss would be recognised) in the expectation of disposing of it at fair value in a subsequent period (in which the day-1 loss would be reversed).[57] See subsection 2.3.1 for evidence that banks have used credit losses to manage earnings where opportunities arose.

Furthermore, it was noted as part of the standard-setting process, including in the FASB's summary of feedback on FASB (2012), that day-1 loss may have the adverse economic effect of disincentivising lending.[58]

The standard setters' introduction of the requirement to recognise credit losses at day 1 could be seen as a form of unconditional conservatism, which as noted in subsection 2.3.2.1 can have the adverse effect of restricting the extent to which informationally-valuable news-dependent conditional conservatism can be applied. Compared with other unconditionally conservative treatments, recognition of initially-expected losses at day 1 could be seen as relatively extreme. It appears similar to the application of an extreme form of accelerated depreciation under which all of the depreciation expected to be recognised over the life of an asset is recognised immediately on acquisition.

Although there is a widespread view that the recognition of day-1 losses is not conceptually justified, a number of U.S.-based observers with whom we discussed this issue suggested that recognition of day-1 loss can give reasonable outcomes. Rationales for this view included the following. These rationales were also reflected either in comment letters, to which we provide an endnote reference to an example in each case, or in the academic literature:

1. Losses tend to occur early in the life of a loan.[59] Although they do not typically occur at day 1, day-1 recognition is consistent to some extent with the early incidence of losses. Concerns about whether day 1 or some other time is the right time to recognise losses may sometimes derive from unrealistic beliefs about the accuracy with which the timing of losses can be predicted. This argument holds particularly in the case of large open portfolios.

2. Once a bank makes a loan, it takes on the exposure to the risk of losses inherent in the loan. In the interests of having an appropriately prudently-stated balance sheet at the possible cost of a less informative income statement, it is desirable to recognise losses at the outset.[60] This argument is related to the following argument made by the FASB in its justification of the recognition of losses at origination within a response to a 'frequently asked question':[61]

   > When an entity originates a loan, that entity has increased its exposure to credit losses. Likewise, when a contractual payment is received in full from the borrower, the entity's exposure to credit loss has decreased. The Board believes that recognizing all expected credit losses in the balance sheet causes the income statement to appropriately reflect the economic phenomenon that has occurred – namely, the extent to which an entity has increased or decreased its exposure to credit risk during the period.

3. Related to the previous point, with imperfect information and in particular in good economic times, amounts lent may exceed the fair value of the expected future cash receipts from the loan. A limited element of day-1 loss may help deal with this. This argument has some similarity to an argument by a U.S. bank regulator from the 1990s referred to by Wall and Koch (2000, p. 9): bad loans tend to be made in good times, and it is therefore appropriate to establish loss allowances in good times in order to cover the as-yet-unidentified losses that will subsequently be revealed.

Concern about day-1 loss is raised primarily with reference to the FASB's CECL method, for which expected losses over the full contractual term of financial assets have to be recognised at day 1. The issue also arises with IFRS 9 (IASB 2014a). However, it is important to note that the FASB's rationale for including a day-1 loss allowance was different from that of the IASB. The 'frequently asked question' response quoted above suggests that the FASB believed that reflecting initially-expected losses at day 1, which is easily justified for the purpose of determining banks' capital requirements, is also the conceptually correct thing to do for the purpose of measuring credit-loss expense and loss allowances in financial statements. In contrast, it appears that IASB's introduction of a day-1-loss requirement was not based on a belief that recognition of day-1 loss was conceptually correct. As noted earlier in our subsection 3.5, the IASB's day-1-loss requirement appears to have been introduced because it was believed to provide a practicable approximation to the recognition of initially-expected losses over the life of financial assets and because, at the time at which the IASB had initially decided to accept this approach, it was believed that this might facilitate FASB/IASB convergence.

Overall, it appears difficult to justify day-1 loss on conceptual grounds. One possible justification is that it provides a practicable approximation to the outcomes from a conceptually more justifiable spreading-based approach. Another might be conservatism. However, as indicated above, day-1 loss is an example of unconditional conservatism, which it can be argued creates uninformative bias.

5. Was expected-loss the best route to improvement of accounting for credit losses?

Evidence of the perceived major nature of the change involved in introducing an EL method can be found in the statement in a letter of 13 January 2016 to the FASB Chair from the President and CEO of the ABA that 'The CECL model represents the biggest change – ever – to bank accounting.'[62]

As we have noted above, a notable achievement of the two standard setters was their converged broadening of the information set used to measure credit-loss impairment, such that it includes reasonable and supportable forecasts and is not subject to a 'probable' threshold. Subject to caveats about opportunities that this might create for earnings and capital management, on which prior evidence was reviewed in subsection 2.3.1, this should have a significant beneficial effect with respect to timeliness in the accounting recognition of information about credit losses, which was a major focus of criticism in the aftermath of the financial and banking crisis of the late 2000s.[63] In this subsection, we raise the question of whether the improvement in the timeliness of credit-loss recognition, including through broadening of the information set permitted to be used, could have been achieved more straightforwardly and in a more converged manner through an alternative route to the type of EL route that the standard setters followed.

5.1. *Is there a clearly understood distinction between incurred loss and expected loss?*

Our study of events since 2009 leads us to the view, similar to that reflected in the study by Camfferman (2015) to which we referred previously, that there appears not to be a clear and widely-shared understanding of the distinguishing features of an EL method relative to an IL method in relation to accounting for credit losses. Observations that contribute to this view are as follows:

1. As noted in subsection 3.4 above, FASB documents reported the claim that the principle within the three-bucket EL method for determining whether an asset should be moved to the lifetime-loss category could be seen as introducing an IL trigger. Although some observers with whom we spoke feel that this claim is unfair, it illustrates the potential difficulty in distinguishing between IL methods and EL methods.
2. Some respondents to FASB (2010a) saw the FASB (2010a) method as an EL method, some respondents saw it as an IL method and, as noted in our subsection 3.2, the FASB itself saw it as neither.
3. The rationales for the FASB (2010a) impairment method not being seen by the FASB at the time as an EL method included that it would not spread recognition of initially-

expected losses over time. However, such a feature was also absent from the FASB's own final EL (CECL) method in FASB (2016), which dealt with expected losses through full recognition at each reporting date without any spreading procedure.

4. At the FASB roundtable meeting of 4 February 2016, a Community Bank representative described what he saw as an acceptable more forward-looking adaptation ('tweak') of the pre-existing IL method. FASB representatives commented that the process described by the Community Bank representative was an example of an implementation of the CECL EL method.

Drawing on the above and our reading of comment letters, we have observed a number of views with regard to the distinguishing feature of an EL method relative to an IL method. Some understand that a distinguishing feature of EL is simply that impairment is based on expected cash flows or expected losses. Some understand that a distinguishing feature is that impairment is based on expected cash flows and expected losses where expectations are derived from an information set that can include forecasts of future events and economic conditions. Some understand that a distinguishing feature is that recognition of initially-expected losses is spread over the life of assets. The observation that the term 'expected loss' can mean different things to different people was also noted in a FASB summary of feedback on FASB (2012).[64]

5.2.   *Preferences for a route other than expected loss*

Examination of comment letters on the standard setters' various proposal documents since 2009 indicates that some prominent respondents have continued to express a preference for the retention of an IL approach, typically in a modified form with a broadening of the information set that might be used as a basis for recognition of credit-loss impairment. For example, the Association of Chartered Certified Accountants (ACCA), which is one of the UK's major accounting bodies, said in its comment letter in response to IASB (2013a) that:[65]

> ACCA would prefer to retain the current incurred loss model which is less subjective and does contain a clear principle that can be applied across the piece. An incurred loss model in the new IFRS 9 however should be modified from the present IAS 39 version, by making it clear that losses that have been incurred but have not yet been reported as defaults should be recognised and that losses can occur before debtors actually default on repayments.

Also, the ABA has provided detailed comment along similar lines. In its comment letter of 14 May 2013 on the FASB (2012) exposure draft, the ABA said that, among other things, CECL will: 'require enormous and costly operational change, and potentially wreak havoc with FASB's own conceptual framework of accounting'. The ABA then went on to state its preference for a proposed modified IL model termed the Banking Industry Model (BIM):[66]

> The BIM (initially introduced in 2011) is the best path toward an internationally converged solution that responds to concerns of bankers, bank investors, and banking regulators by:
> - Discontinuing the 'probable loss' notion.
> - Providing appropriate guidance in understanding the loan impairment process, 'loss events,' and 'forward-looking loss events,' as well as additional disclosures to assist users in understanding the processes and comparing them between companies.
> - Recognizing subliminal risks that build during an economic expansion in a transparent fashion.
> - Retaining impairment accounting within the FASB conceptual framework by recognizing impairment only when a loss event is believed to have occurred.
> - Building on current systems and financial metrics, rather than wholesale change.

The BIM referred to above had previously been described in an appendix to the ABA's comment letter of 11 March 2011 in response to the 2011 supplementary document. The ABA introduced its BIM as follows:[67]

> We believe that the fundamental principles inherent in the incurred loss model are sound and have served the industry, regulators and financial statement users effectively by providing a well under-stood framework to determine credit-related allowances. However, over time, the incurred loss model has increasingly been interpreted in a way that has resulted in a significant flaw: allowance cal-culations based on too narrow a view of the credit cycle. History has shown that the credit profile of financial instruments is highly cyclical, typically with a period of benign loss activity that coincides with the expansion and peak of overall economic activity and credit availability, followed by a shorter and more concentrated period of elevated credit losses. Narrow interpretations and application of the incurred loss model result in the compression of this cycle by considering only losses estimated over an abbreviated loss emergence period and restricting the use of market trends and other data that would indicate changes in the probability or severity of loss until such deterioration is observable. The events of the recent financial crisis put a spotlight on this weakness in the application of the incurred loss model, resulting in the criticism noted above. Although we believe the fundamental prin-ciples of the incurred loss model remain sound, some thoughtful and tailored changes are necessary to incorporate the cyclical behavior of financial instruments and lack of transparency around inherent losses prior to the deterioration of the credit environment.

The BIM is then described as comprising two components:

(1) A base component (the 'Base Component') that represents the estimate of expected inherent losses in the portfolio that are reasonably predictable;
(2) A credit risk adjustment component (the 'CRA') that represents additional credit losses that are not yet reflected in current credit risk metrics used to estimate the Base Com-ponent but are estimated using macro-level factors and are expected to emerge with more transparency as the credit cycle unfolds.'

The second item is similar to items denoted 'incurred but not reported' in IAS 39 (IASB 2003, paragraph AG90). The preference referred to above for a broader application of the IL method is echoed in comment letters on FASB (2012) and IASB (2013a) examined by O'Hanlon et al. (2018).[68] The claim that the IL method was being applied in an insufficiently conservative manner prior to the crisis is reminiscent of the point that was made in SFAS 114 (FASB 1993a, paragraph 10) and quoted in our subsection 2.1.1 about the desirability of avoiding insuf-ficiently conservative application of SFAS 5 (FASB 1975).

5.3. *An alternative way of approaching the improvement of accounting for credit losses?*

In this subsection, we raise the question of whether the EL route was the best route to follow for the purpose of improving the accounting for credit losses.

We first offer our own view of how the terms 'incurred' and 'expected' might relate to each other in the context of accounting for credit losses:

i. Any method of accounting for credit losses must use a current (as at the loss-rec-ognition date) information set of some sort;
ii. Any method of accounting for credit losses operates in a setting in which financial assets were originally recognised at a transaction price (amount lent or purchase price) that can normally be expected to have reflected expectations at the initial-recognition date of future shortfalls relative to contractual cash inflows;

    iii. The information set referred to in (i) is used, explicitly or implicitly, to make estimates of ***expected*** future cash flows (or shortfalls relative to contractual or previously expected amounts) and risk in relation to a financial asset or financial assets;

    iv. These estimates are used, explicitly or implicitly, to arrive at an appropriate carrying value for a financial asset or financial assets;

    v. The appropriate carrying value is then compared with the pre-existing carrying value of the asset or assets to establish what loss if any has been ***incurred*** and should be recognised as an impairment within a loss allowance.

In this representation, in which the terms 'expected' and 'incurred' both appear, IL/EL is not a key distinguishing feature. We believe that more meaningful distinguishing features are as follows:

1. *(In item (i)) The information set that is permitted to be used.* This could be a restricted information set comprising events and evidence of the sort permitted within pre-existing so-called IL methods, for which the link to estimates is relatively direct and provides relatively precise estimates of impairment. Alternatively, it could be a broader information set comprising events and evidence of the sort permitted within pre-existing so-called IL methods *plus* reasonable and supportable impairment-measurement-date forecasts of subsequent events and economic conditions, for which the link to estimates is relatively less direct and may provide estimates of impairment that are relatively less precise and that are relatively vulnerable to earnings management.

2. *(In item (ii)) The treatment of initially-expected shortfalls relative to contractual cash inflows.* The initial carrying value of any financial asset (amount lent or purchase price) will reflect expectations at the initial-recognition date of future shortfalls relative to contractual cash inflows. All impairment methods, whether they are described as IL or EL or anything else, have to deal in some way with such initially-expected shortfalls (initially-expected losses). One possible approach to dealing with this issue would be to recognise the initially-expected shortfalls at the time of the initial recognition of the asset. A second possible approach would be to spread the initially-expected shortfalls across the life of the asset alongside the accrual of interest. Both of these approaches have been proposed within EL methods in recent years. The first was adopted within FASB (2016) and, for a subset of the initially-expected shortfalls, in IASB (2014a). However, although it may be consistent with the way in which bank regulators require expected losses on exposures to be reflected for the purpose of determining banks' capital requirements, this approach is not easily justified for the purpose of measuring credit-loss expense and loss allowances in financial statements. The second was proposed in IASB (2009) but was not adopted, mainly due to claimed implementation problems. A third possible approach, which is the traditional approach adopted within IL methods, is to recognise such initially-expected shortfalls during the life of the assets, alongside shortfalls that were not initially expected, as part of impairments triggered when specified conditions, such as the occurrence of 'loss events', are met. The problem with this third approach, as was noted in motivating the IASB (2009) IEIR-based proposal (IASB 2009, paragraph BC11), is that the restrictive nature of the specified conditions might result in credit-premium-inclusive interest revenue being recognised in advance of the associated initially-expected shortfalls.

The problem with IL methods referred to above brings us back to the information set that is permitted to be used as the basis for the accounting recognition of credit losses. A broadening of the information set within an IL framework, to include reasonable and supportable forecasts of future events and economic conditions and with fuller use of the pre-existing 'incurred but not reported' concept, might have addressed both the need for new information on credit losses to be recognised in a more timely manner and the need for initially-expected losses to be recognised significantly earlier than under pre-existing practice. A broadening of the information set within an IL framework could reasonably be expected to reduce substantially the mismatch between the timing of the recognition of initially-expected losses and the recognition of associated credit-premium-inclusive interest revenue that the IASB (2009) spreading approach was aimed at addressing. Such a route would present accounting standard setters with a challenge in balancing the desirability of a broader and more forward-looking permitted information set against the desirability of restriction on earnings management. However, such a challenge also exists with the EL methods that have been developed. Also, as illustrated in subsection 2.3.1, earnings management by banks is an extensively researched issue and is likely to be familiar territory for accounting standard setters and accountants.

At least, such an approach would have avoided conceptually-questionable day-1-loss which, because the FASB and IASB could not agree on the degree of conservatism to be applied in recognising losses at day 1, was an important contributor to the failure of the FASB and the IASB to achieve convergence on accounting for credit losses.

It is helpful to consider now what might have been the main contributory factor to the requirements for day-1 losses in the final FASB and IASB standards. The fact that IASB (2009) was issued in the immediate aftermath of the crisis and proposed an EL method without day-1 losses suggests that neither political and regulatory pressure for increased loss allowances in the immediate aftermath of the crisis nor the choice of an EL route itself was a main contributory factor. We believe that the main contributory factor was the choice to adopt the particular type of EL approach that was eventually adopted. We make the following distinction between EL approaches:

1. *Spreading-based approaches.* Methods that aim to achieve the suitably timely recognition over time of initially-expected losses, for example through the IASB (2009) IEIR method or the FASB/IASB (2011a) TPA method, plus immediate recognition of changes in expectations about expected losses.
2. *Immediate-recognition-based approaches.* Methods that aim to achieve the recognition at each reporting date of expected future losses. This category includes the FASB (2016) CECL method. The IASB (2014a) method also falls into this category, although its use of a 12-month good-book loss allowance is aimed at approximating the distribution of income across time that would occur under spreading-based approaches.

A key difference between the two categories is that the first does not give rise to day-1 losses but the second does. The key factor leading to day-1 losses appears to have been the choice, after spreading-based EL approaches had been eliminated from consideration during the three-bucket deliberations, to follow immediate-recognition-based EL approaches of the type that prudential regulators might be comfortable with. As observed above, an alternative path that could have been taken at this point was exploration of broader-information-set-based and more-responsive IL-type approaches that could have approximated the outcomes of an EL spreading approach without leading to day-1 losses.

6. Conclusion

In the wake of the financial and banking crisis of the late 2000s, the FASB and the IASB moved quickly to improve the timeliness of the accounting recognition of credit losses, including through an attempt to reach a converged common solution. With regard to accounting for credit losses, the crisis appeared to have prompted a shift in relative concern away from the need to constrain earnings management and towards the need to facilitate timeliness of loss recognition and loss-allowance adequacy. With the encouragement of the Financial Stability Board (2009), BCBS (2009) and the Financial Crisis Advisory Group (2009), the accounting standard setters followed a route based on the concept of EL, which in relation to credit losses had originally become prominent for the purpose of setting banks' capital requirements. Following the EL route, the standard setters arrived relatively straightforwardly at a converged broadening of the information set to be used for the purpose of estimating credit losses to be recognised in financial statements, such that it would include reasonable and supportable forecasts. We believe that this directly addresses to a significant degree problems with the timeliness of the accounting for credit losses that were highlighted in the crisis. However, the standard setters encountered significant difficulties in their attempts to address the recognition of initially-expected losses, and their failure to agree on this issue contributed importantly to their failure to achieve convergence on accounting for credit losses. After the standard setters eliminated from consideration EL methods that would spread the recognition of initially-expected losses over time such that they were recognised alongside credit-premium-inclusive interest revenue without day-1 losses, they were left with EL methods requiring the recognition of expected losses at each reporting date including day 1. The recognition of day-1 losses, which is easily justified for the purpose of determining banks' capital requirements, is not easily justified for the purpose of measuring credit-loss expense and loss allowances in financial statements, as exemplified by an informed commentator body's observation that proposals might wreak havoc with the FASB's conceptual framework, an alternative view from an IASB member and a dissenting opinion from two FASB members. Furthermore, the issue of day-1 losses acted in combination with differing preferences with regard to conservatism on the part of the IASB and the FASB, with the latter's more conservative preference for day-1 recognition of full-contractual-life expected losses appearing to be motivated in part by existing practice that had been subject to prudential-regulatory-related influence, to contribute significantly to the failure of FASB/IASB convergence. With the benefit of hindsight, it appears to us possible that positive outcomes might have been achieved in a more straightforward and converged manner if, after the elimination from consideration of a spreading-based EL approach, the standard setters had explored broader-information-set-based and more-responsive IL-type approaches that could have approximated the outcomes of an EL spreading approach without leading to day-1 losses.

In conversations with some observers, we reflected on whether the EL methods that have now been developed would have been more effective than the IL method in mitigating the effects of the financial and banking crisis. From these conversations, it appears to be widely believed that, although a less restrictive method might have had some beneficial effect, it is unlikely that any ex-ante acceptable method of accounting for credit-loss impairment would have substantially mitigated the consequences of a shock of the magnitude that occurred in the crisis. This view was also reflected in some comment letters.[69] We note that the financial and banking crisis of the late 2000s started in the U.S., where loss recognition tended to occur earlier than elsewhere, which suggests the limited impact that differences in methods of accounting for credit losses might have with regard to crisis prevention.[70]

Issues relating to whether a less radical route might have been advisable are expressed well in a comment letter on FASB/IASB (2011a) submitted by Sandler O'Neill Partners, a U.S. investment-banking firm:[71]

> The incurred-loss impairment models in use during the financial crisis were criticized for (i) not recognizing losses soon enough, (ii) not incorporating information forward-looking enough to encompass

the lifetime of assets and complete economic cycles, and (iii) not providing a uniform approach to the impairment of similar assets.

The problems of the recent financial crisis did not result from an inability to reserve for probable credit losses proactively enough. Rather, [...] the fundamental failure was underwriting [...].

To be clear, any bank capable of apprehending the magnitude of expected losses for the worst-performing assets during the financial crisis simply would not have originated or acquired those assets. Thus, the crux of the problem was not an incurred- versus expected-loss approach to reserves but, rather, that the financial system was awash in too many assets for which no reserve methodology would have been adequate. For the best banks, incurred-loss reserving worked just fine, and for the worst banks no impairment methodology would have helped because the fundamental failure was one of underwriting, not reserving.

There is a legal maxim that 'hard cases make bad law.' It posits that difficult or unusual facts provide a poor basis for a law or rule of general application that must cover a wider range of less extreme circumstances [...].

Targeted improvements to existing impairment methodology are far preferable to its overreaching replacement [...].

It may be worthwhile to consider whether the events considered in this paper are an example of accounting standard setters, faced with exceptional economic events that prompted important questions about accounting but were not to a significant degree caused by accounting or preventable by accounting, taking a radical route instead of another less radical route that might have achieved substantial benefit at substantially lower cost.

Disclosure statement

No potential conflict of interest was reported by the authors.

Funding

This work was supported by ICAEW Charitable Trusts [grant number 5-453].

Notes

1. See the FASB/IASB press release dated 20 October 2008, available from: http://www.fasb.org/news/nr102008.shtml [Accessed 18 August 2017].
2. For example, Hashim et al. (2016) report that loans typically account for 60% to 70% of banks' total assets. Ryan (2017) observes that 'the allowance for loan losses (which reduces loans outstanding) and the provision for loan losses (which reduces net income) are by far the most important and judgmental accrual estimates for most banks'.
3. Throughout this paper, references to a method being perceived as conceptually strong denote that the method is perceived as faithfully representing the economic substance of activities. This is consistent with the way in which the term 'conceptual' is used in many of the comment letters examined by O'Hanlon et al. (2018) in their study of responses to the various proposals on accounting for credit losses issued by the IASB and/or the FASB between 2009 and 2013.
4. See transcripts of remarks made by the SEC's Chief Accountant, Michael Sutton, in November 1997 (available from: https://www.sec.gov/news/speech/speecharchive/1997/spch195.txt) and by the SEC's Chairman, Arthur Levitt, in September 1998 (available from: https://www.sec.gov/news/speech/speecharchive/1998/spch220.txt) [Both accessed 10 April 2018].
5. SAB 102 is available from: https://www.sec.gov/interps/account/sab102.htm [Accessed 10 April 2018].
6. In a discussion of Beck and Narayanmoorthy (2013), Ryan and Keeley (2013) argue that SAB 102 did not express any preference for historical loss information in making allowance estimates, but acknowledge that the SAB requirements for the application of consistency and discipline may have delayed banks' recognition of losses on heterogeneous loans.

7. Available from: https://www.occ.treas.gov/news-issuances/speeches/2009/pub-speech-2009-16.pdf [Accessed 10 April 2018].
8. Prior to and during the deliberations leading up to the 2003 revision of IAS 39, the treatment of expected losses under the internal-ratings-based (IRB) approach to be introduced in Basel 2 (BCBS 2004b) was being considered by BCBS (BCBS 2001a,b, 2003, 2004a).
9. Comment letters on FASB (2012) are available from: http://www.fasb.org/jsp/FASB/CommentLetter_ C/CommentLetterPage&cid=1218220137090&project_id=2012-260 [Accessed 18 August 2017].
10. Available from: https://www.aba.com/Advocacy/Issues/Documents/CECL-backgrounder.pdf [Accessed 24 April 2018]. As noted in IAS 39 (IASB 2003, paragraph AG90), IBNR denotes loss events of which a lender is unaware as at a reporting date but that can be assumed to have occurred prior to that reporting date, but not loss events expected to occur after that reporting date.
11. Hodder and Hopkins (2014) refer to the requirement that regulatory accounting principles must be consistent with or no less stringent than GAAP. IASB (2014a, paragraph BC5.116) notes that 'the interaction between the role of prudential regulation and loss allowances is historically stronger in the U.S.'. A speaker at a European Parliament hearing on IFRS 9 commented that ' … the whole history of U.S. GAAP accounting for loan losses is steeped in what the prudential regulators in the U.S. have required […]' (Mike Ashley, European Parliament, 1 December 2015).
12. A document containing the contribution by this speaker is available from: http://www.europarl.europa. eu/cmsdata/93535/Statement%20Ashley%20EN.pdf [Accessed 18 August 2017].
13. Ng and Roychowdhury (2014) examine the association between loan-loss allowances included in Tier 2 capital and bank failure. Their examination suggests that this element of Tier 2 capital does not behave like an element of capital that acts as a buffer against failure risk.
14. Some banks that used the IRB approach also used the standardised approach for some business units, and their Tier 2 regulatory capital therefore continued to include some general loan-loss allowances.
15. Practice in the U.S. is to treat the whole loss allowance as a general allowance for the purpose of calculating Tier 2 capital under the Basel standardised approach. For reference to this, see OCC (1998, p. 4).
16. U.S. IRB banks are required to satisfy the capital requirements of both the IRB approach and the standardised approach. (For a reference to this, see the Federal Register, Friday October 11, 2013, p. 62,021. This is available from: https://www.gpo.gov/fdsys/pkg/FR-2013-10-11/pdf/FR-2013-10-11.pdf [Accessed 20 April 2018].)
17. Issues related to the trade-off between restricting earnings management and permitting discretion are sometimes considered in relation to a trade-off between 'relevance' and 'reliability'. In light of the fact that 'reliability' has now been removed as a qualitative characteristic from the IASB and FASB conceptual frameworks, we do not structure our review around this trade-off. 'Relevance' and 'reliability' were included as qualitative characteristics in the pre-2010 conceptual frameworks of the IASB and the FASB (FASB 1980, IASB 2001). The FASB and IASB 2010 conceptual frameworks removed the term 'reliability' from their qualitative characteristics on the ground that the term was ambiguous in the context of conceptual frameworks (FASB 2010b paragraphs BC3.20-BC3.24, IASB 2010, paragraphs BC3.20-BC3.24). This ambiguity had been noted by Ball (2006, p. 9). It is also noted in the IASB's 2018 Conceptual Framework (IASB 2018, paragraph BC2.29).
18. The directional effects of loan-loss expense on earnings and regulatory capital are not necessarily the same. Loan-loss expense that decreases net-of-tax earnings and decreases shareholders' equity can increase regulatory capital if gross-of-tax loss allowances are included in regulatory capital.
19. Prior to implementation in the U.S. in 1989 of the Basel 1 accord, loss allowances were included in primary capital. Subsequent to the implementation of Basel 1, which saw the introduction of a split of capital into Tier 1 and Tier 2, general loss allowances up to 1.25% of risk-weighted assets could be included in Tier 2 capital. The Basel 1 accord, issued in 1988, was implemented by the U.S. bank regulatory and supervisory agencies in 1989. (For a reference to this, see the Federal Register, Friday December 7, 2007, p. 69,289, footnote 3. This is available from: https://www.gpo.gov/fdsys/pkg/FR-2007-12-07/pdf/FR-2007-12-07.pdf [Accessed 12 April 2018].)
20. O'Hanlon (2013) finds no evidence that accounting for credit losses by U.K. banks became less timely after the move from the evidence requirements of pre-existing U.K. GAAP to those of IAS 39. However, it should be noted that accounting for credit losses under U.K. GAAP was already in accordance with incurred-loss and that the effect of the adoption of IAS 39 on accounting for credit losses in the U.K. was therefore likely to be less pronounced than in some other countries.
21. The concept of 'prudence' featured in the pre-2010 conceptual frameworks of the FASB and the IASB, with the term 'conservatism' being used interchangeably with 'prudence' in the FASB framework. In

both cases, it was emphasised that 'prudence' denoted the exercise of caution under conditions of uncertainty and should not lead to the systematic understatement of net asset values. The 2010 FASB and IASB conceptual frameworks, the term 'prudence' was removed because of the possibility that it might be incorrectly interpreted as encouraging downward bias in net asset values, which would be inconsistent with neutrality (FASB 2010b, paragraphs BC3.27-BC3.28, IASB 2010, paragraphs BC3.27-BC3.28). In 2018, the IASB issued a revised conceptual framework. This reinstated the concept of 'prudence', again stating that the term is intended to denote the exercise of caution under conditions of uncertainty and not the systematic understatement of net asset values (IASB 2018, paragraph 2.16).

22. For fuller discussion of conditional and unconditional conservatism in the general financial-reporting literature, see Watts (2003a), Watts (2003b), Beaver and Ryan (2005) and Ryan (2006).

23. Evidence in Lee and Rose (2010) for U.S. bank holding companies for 2000–2009, from which Ryan (2017) quotes some figures, indicates that the average ratios of loan-loss allowance to equity, equity to total assets and loan-loss allowance to total assets are in the region of 10%, 10% and 1%, respectively. These magnitudes are similar to those reported by Hashim et al. (2016, pp. 255–256) for 2007–2014 for U.S. banks and for banks in developed markets outside the U.S.

24. The early stages of this activity took place against the background of proposals under which most financial instruments would be measured at fair value (IASB 2008, FASB 2010a). However, there was strong opposition to the proposed significant increase in the use of fair value, particularly for loans. Subsequent stages of development of new impairment methods took place in the expectation that a large proportion of financial assets, including loans, would continue to be measured at amortised cost.

25. The European Parliament paper by O'Hanlon et al. (2015) was written before the FASB standard (FASB 2016) was finalised.

26. See, for example, the letter from the Cigna Corporation in respect of IASB (2009): 'This proposed model that reports level investment returns implies consistent, level investment risk, which does not reflect actual performance or events. Credit risk changes over time for individual instruments and financial statement reporting should not inadvertently mask such changes.' Comment letters on IASB (2009) are available from: http://archive.ifrs.org/Current-Projects/IASB-Projects/Financial-Instruments-A-Replacement-of-IAS-39-Financial-Instruments-Recognitio/Impairment/ED/Comment-Letters/Pages/Comment-letters.aspx [Accessed 24 April 2018].

27. Some found it surprising that the FASB (2010a) proposals on credit-loss impairment differed so much from the IASB (2009) proposals, particularly in light of the aim at the time that the FASB and the IASB should work together on accounting for financial instruments. See the comment letter from the American Insurance Association (page 1). Comment letters on FASB (2010a) are available from: http://www.fasb.org/jsp/FASB/CommentLetter_C/CommentLetterPage&cid=1218220137090&project_id=1810-100 [Accessed 18 August 2017]. In relation to this point, IASB (2009) had noted that 'It is not uncommon for the boards to deliberate separately on joint projects and then subsequently to reconcile any differences in their technical decisions' (IASB 2009, paragraph IN13).

28. The TPA allowance would be equal to all credit losses expected for the remaining portfolio life multiplied by the portfolio's age as a proportion of its expected life.

29. IASB (2013a) noted that the TPA spreading method differs from the IASB (2009) spreading method in that it spreads across time both the recognition of initially-expected losses and the recognition of subsequent changes in expectations about losses: 'The SD (supplementary document) attempted to reflect the relationship between expected credit losses and interest revenue using the TPA. The TPA reflects this relationship through the allocation of expected credit losses over time, "adjusting" the contractual interest. However, it does this through a short-cut, and therefore the result does not represent the economics as faithfully as the 2009 ED (exposure draft) did. Because the TPA allocates over time both the initial expected credit losses and the subsequent changes in lifetime expected credit losses, the measurement results in an understatement of changes in expected credit losses until the entity recognises lifetime expected credit losses.' (IASB 2013a, paragraph BC35).

30. O'Hanlon et al. (2018) categorised a total of 183 respondents to FASB/IASB (2011a) as being either non-U.S. respondents that could be assumed to be IASB constituents or potential constituents (111 (61%)) or U.S. respondents that could be assumed to be FASB constituents (72 (39%)). Some respondents (international accounting firms, international associations, international bank-regulatory organisations and other international regulatory organisations) were included in neither of these categories for the purpose of the statistics reported here.

31. See the comment by the Chair of the IASB at a meeting of December 2012, which we quote in our subsection 3.5.
32. After August 2012, the IASB and the FASB continued to work towards convergence in some areas. For example, they issued a joint proposal on Leasing in 2013 (FASB 2013, IASB 2013c), although the FASB and the IASB eventually produced different standards in this area, and they issued a converged standard on Revenue Recognition in 2014 (FASB 2014, IASB 2014c). It therefore appears likely that, although the FASB's disengagement from the three-bucket deliberations may have been related to a broader move away from convergence in general, this in itself would not have stopped the attempts to achieve a converged common solution on credit-loss impairment. It appears likely that the dominant factor was the boards' inability to agree on the substance of the proposals.
33. Recording available from: http://media.ifrs.org/2011/IASB/July/Impairment_session2.mp3 [Accessed 18 August 2017].
34. Recording available from: http://media.ifrs.org/AP4Impairment18102012.mp3 [Accessed 18 August 2017].
35. See paragraph 32 in agenda paper 5A, available from: http://archive.ifrs.org/Meetings/MeetingDocs/IASB/2012/October/Impairment-1012-05A.pdf [Accessed 18 August 2017].
36. Recording available from: http://media.ifrs.org/2013/IASB/July/Impairment_AR5_PM.mp3 [Accessed 18 August 2017].
37. Because the magnitude of loss allowances is affected by practice with regard to charge-offs as well as by the timeliness with which credit-loss expense is recognised, more timely recognition of credit losses does not necessarily lead to higher loss allowances. See Liu and Ryan (2006) for evidence that charge-offs may be used to obscure the effect on loss allowances of the management of credit-loss expense. For a given charge-off practice and other things equal, more timely recognition of credit losses would give rise to larger allowances.
38. Recording available from: http://media.ifrs.org/2012/IASBMeetings/December/ImpairmentAR5141212.mp3 [Accessed 18 August 2017].
39. Recording available from: http://media.ifrs.org/2012/IASBMeetings/December/ImpairmentAR5141212.mp3 [Accessed 18 August 2017].
40. IASB (2013a) defined 12-month expected credit losses for a loan for which credit risk has not increased significantly since initial recognition to be the product of (i) the gross carrying amount of the loan, (ii) the proportion of the gross carrying amount of the loan expected to be lost if the loan defaults (loss given default) and (iii) the probability of default over the next 12 months (IASB 2013a, paragraphs IE2-IE3).
41. Recording available from: http://media.ifrs.org/2013/IASB/September/Impairment_AR5_Session1.mp3 [Accessed 18 August 2017].
42. The three-stage terminology from IASB (2013a) is not used in the standard itself, but is used in an IASB summary document (IASB 2014b, p. 18).
43. See, for example, paragraph 6 in the document available from: http://archive.ifrs.org/Meetings/MeetingDocs/IASB/2013/July/5D-Impairment.pdf [Accessed 18 August 2017].
44. This point was stressed in communications with stakeholders, including at the FASB roundtable meeting of 4 February 2016 attended by representatives of Community Banks at which the representatives expressed serious concern about the forecasting requirements of CECL.
45. For references to such activities, see:
     • IASB March 2010 – available from: http://archive.ifrs.org/Current-Projects/IASB-Projects/Financial-Instruments-A-Replacement-of-IAS-39-Financial-Instruments-Recognitio/Impairment/Meeting-Summaries/Documents/FI_0310b13Aobs.pdf (paragraphs 9 and 10) [Accessed 1 December 2017];
     • FASB/IASB April 2011 – available from: http://archive.ifrs.org/Current-Projects/IASB-Projects/Financial-Instruments-A-Replacement-of-IAS-39-Financial-Instruments-Recognitio/Impairment/Meeting-Summaries/Documents/FI0411b04Eobs.pdf (paragraphs 2 and 52–54) [Accessed 1 December 2017];
     • IASB October 2012 – available from: http://archive.ifrs.org/Meetings/MeetingDocs/IASB/2012/October/Impairment-1012-05A.pdf (paragraph 32)) [Accessed 1 December 2017];
     • IASB July 2013 – available from: http://archive.ifrs.org/Meetings/MeetingDocs/IASB/2013/July/05A-Impairment.pdf (paragraphs 33–37), [Accessed 1 December 2017].
46. Available from: http://archive.ifrs.org/Meetings/MeetingDocs/IASB/2013/July/05A-Impairment.pdf (paragraph 35) [Accessed 1 December 2017].

47. Of the 1,588 comment letters examined by O'Hanlon et al. (2018), 47 (3%) were from financial and banking regulators.
48. Of the total of 510 letters in response to FASB (2012) and IASB (2013a) examined by O'Hanlon et al. (2018), 14 (3%) were from financial and/or banking regulatory bodies.
49. See question 23 in a document published by the American Bankers' Association, available from: https://www.aba.com/Advocacy/Issues/Documents/CECL-backgrounder.pdf [Accessed 26 April 2018].
50. It should be noted that the situation described here differs from one in which a loan might be made on terms favourable to the borrower such that the fair value of the expected recoverable amount is less than the amount lent. In such a situation, it would be uncontroversial that the loan should be written down to fair value at day 1.
51. For conceptual framework documents, see FASB (2010b) and IASB (2010).
52. See, for example, the letter from the Illinois CPA Society commenting on FASB (2012): 'We believe the fundamental premise on which the Proposed ASU rests is at odds with the Conceptual Framework. [...] By requiring banks to recognize a provision for current expected credit losses for at-market loans at inception the Proposed ASU would require banks to recognize expected credit losses twice – once through the initial pricing of the loan and again through the separate day one loss allowance. This results in financial statements that do not faithfully represent the economic phenomenon of the issuance of an at-market loan, whereby neither party has realized an economic gain or loss.' Comment letters on FASB (2012) are available from: http://www.fasb.org/jsp/FASB/CommentLetter_C/CommentLetterPage&cid=1218220137090&project_id=2012-260 [Accessed 18 August 2017].
53. A discounted-cash-flow (DCF) approach is only one of various methods by which loss allowances may be determined under the FASB's CECL method.
54. See, for example, the letter from Duff and Phelps LLC commenting on FASB (2012): 'One theoretical flaw in the model is that the discount rate applied to the expected credit losses (effective interest rate) already takes into account the credit risk priced in by the lender at origination and would have the effect of double-counting the initial estimate of credit losses.' Comment letters on FASB (2012) are available from: http://www.fasb.org/jsp/FASB/CommentLetter_C/CommentLetterPage&cid=1218220137090&project_id=2012-260 [Accessed 18 August 2017].
55. See, for example, the letter from UDVA commenting on FASB/IASB (2011a). With respect to the proposal for day-1 recognition of foreseeable-future-period (FFP) losses, this respondent says that this treatment is '[...] inconsistent with initial recognition of financial instruments at fair value as the transaction price (fair value in an arm's length transaction) already reflects the expected losses.' Comment letters on FASB/IASB (2011a) are available from: http://www.fasb.org/jsp/FASB/CommentLetter_C/CommentLetterPage&cid=1218220137090&project_id=2011-150 [Accessed 18 August 2017].
56. See, for example, the letter from the Canadian Bankers Association commenting on FASB (2012): 'We do not believe that recognizing all interest earned over the life of the loan and total lifetime expected credit losses at inception is an appropriate reflection of the economics of the loan transaction.' Comment letters on FASB (2012) are available from: http://www.fasb.org/jsp/FASB/CommentLetter_C/CommentLetterPage&cid=1218220137090&project_id=2012-260 [Accessed 18 August 2017].
57. See, for example, the letter from Cisco Systems, Inc. commenting on FASB (2012): 'Recognition of ECL (expected credit losses) at inception would contribute to significant income statement volatility and provides an avenue for potential earnings management. For example, under the Proposal, we would record a credit loss at the time of purchase of a financial instrument that is not driven by an economic event. Subsequently, if we sold the same financial instrument in a different reporting period, we may record a gain even though there is not a change in credit risk.' Comment letters on FASB (2012) are available from: http://www.fasb.org/jsp/FASB/CommentLetter_C/CommentLetterPage&cid=1218220137090&project_id=2012-260 [Accessed 18 August 2017].
58. See paragraph B21 in the document available from: http://archive.ifrs.org/Meetings/MeetingDocs/IASB/2013/July/5D-Impairment.pdf [Accessed 18 August 2017].
59. See, for example, the letter from the Federal Financial Institution Regulatory Agencies in respect of FASB (2012): 'We have observed that credit losses typically emerge relatively early in the life of loans and do not occur ratably over a financial instrument's life.' Comment letters on FASB (2012) are available from: http://www.fasb.org/jsp/FASB/CommentLetter_C/CommentLetterPage&cid=1218220137090&project_id=2012-260 [Accessed 18 August 2017].
60. See, for example, the letter from Carlson Capital LP in respect of FASB (2010a): 'Our long-held view is that there is an inherent risk of loss from the moment every dollar is lent.' Comment letters on FASB (2010a) are available from: http://www.fasb.org/jsp/FASB/CommentLetter_C/CommentLetterPage&cid=1218220137090&project_id=1810-100 [Accessed 18 August 2017].

61. This passage is from the response to question 3 in a FASB 'Frequently Asked Questions' document available from: http://www.fasb.org/cs/BlobServer?blobkey=id&blobwhere=1175826417092&blobheader=application/pdf&blobcol=urldata&blobtable=MungoBlobs [Accessed 18 August 2017].
62. Available from: https://www.aba.com/Advocacy/LetterstoCongress/Documents/RussellGolden-FASB-011316.pdf [Accessed 26 April 2018].
63. IASB (2014a, paragraph BCE.93 (d)) notes the benefit of the broadened information set in making credit-loss impairment more forward-looking.
64. See paragraph A6 in the document available from: http://archive.ifrs.org/Meetings/MeetingDocs/IASB/2013/July/5D-Impairment.pdf [Accessed 18 August 2017].
65. Comment letters on IASB (2013a) are available from: http://archive.ifrs.org/Current-Projects/IASB-Projects/Financial-Instruments-A-Replacement-of-IAS-39-Financial-Instruments-Recognitio/Impairment/Exposure-Draft-March-2013/Comment-letters/Pages/Comment-letters.aspx [Accessed 18 August 2017].
66. Comment letters on FASB (2012) are available from: http://www.fasb.org/jsp/FASB/CommentLetter_C/CommentLetterPage&cid=1218820137090&project_id=2012-260 [Accessed 18 August 2017].
67. Comment letters on FASB/IASB (2011a) are available from: http://www.fasb.org/jsp/FASB/CommentLetter_C/CommentLetterPage&cid=1218820137090&project_id=2011-15011-150 [Accessed 18 August 2017].
68. O'Hanlon et al. (2018, p. 23) report that a substantial number of US respondents to the 2012 FASB exposure draft and some non-U.S. respondents to the 2013 IASB exposure draft expressed preference for a modified and less restrictive IL-based approach over an EL-based approach.
69. See, for example, the letter from BDO in respect of IASB (2009): 'We are not convinced that an expected loss model would have done anything to identify the onset of the global financial crisis at an earlier stage, or reduce the extent of the impairment losses that were reported after the onset of the global financial crisis.' Comment letters on IASB (2009) are available from: http://archive.ifrs.org/Current-Projects/IASB-Projects/Financial-Instruments-A-Replacement-of-IAS-39-Financial-Instruments-Recognitio/Impairment/ED/Comment-Letters/Pages/Comment-letters.aspx [Accessed 24 April 2018].
70. We did not see any evidence that the standard setters themselves saw any contradiction in the fact that the crisis had started in the U.S., where loss recognition tended to occur earlier than elsewhere.
71. Comment letters on FASB/IASB (2011a) are available from: http://www.fasb.org/jsp/FASB/CommentLetter_C/CommentLetterPage&cid=1218820137090&project_id=2011-150 [Accessed 18 August 2017].

References

Acharya, V.V. and Ryan, S.G., 2016. Banks' financial reporting and financial system stability. *Journal of Accounting Research*, 54 (2), 277–340.
Ahmed, A.S., Takeda, C., and Thomas, S., 1999. Bank loan loss provisions: a re-examination of capital management, earnings management and signaling effects. *Journal of Accounting and Economics*, 28 (1), 1–25.
Aier, J.K., Chen, L., and Pevzner, M., 2014. Debtholders' demand for conservatism: evidence from changes in directors' fiduciary duties. *Journal of Accounting Research*, 52 (5), 993–1027.
Akins, B., Dou, Y., and Ng, J., 2017. Corruption in bank lending: The role of timely loan loss recognition. *Journal of Accounting and Economics*, 63 (2–3), 454–478.
Anandarajan, A., Hasan, I., and McCarthy, C., 2007. Use of loan loss provisions for capital, earnings management and signalling by Australian banks. *Accounting and Finance*, 47 (3), 357–379.
Ball, R., 2006. International Financial Reporting Standards (IFRS): pros and cons for investors. *Accounting and Business Research*, 36 (Sup 1), 5–27.
Ball, R. and Shivakumar, L., 2005. Earnings quality in UK private firms: comparative loss recognition timeliness. *Journal of Accounting and Economics*, 39 (1), 83–128.
Balla, E. and Rose, M.J., 2015. Loan loss provisions, accounting constraints, and bank ownership structure. *Journal of Economics and Business*, 78 (March-April), 92–117.
Basu, S., 1997. The conservatism principle and the asymmetric timeliness of earnings. *Journal of Accounting and Economics*, 24 (1), 3–37.
BCBS, 1988. *International Convergence of Capital Measurement and Capital Standards*. July 1988. Basel: Bank for International Settlements.

BCBS, 2001a. *Consultative Document: The New Basel Capital Accord*. January 2001. Basel: Bank for International Settlements.

BCBS, 2001b. *Working Paper on the IRB Treatment of Expected Losses and Future Margin Income*. July 2001. Basel: Bank for International Settlements.

BCBS, 2003. *Consultative Document: The New Basel Capital Accord*. April 2003. Basel: Bank for International Settlements.

BCBS, 2004a. *Modifications to the Capital Treatment for Expected and Unexpected Credit Losses in the New Basel Accord*. January 2004. Basel: Bank for International Settlements.

BCBS, 2004b. *International Convergence of Capital Measurement and Capital Standards: A Revised Framework*. June 2004. Basel: Bank for International Settlements.

BCBS, 2006. *International Convergence of Capital Measurement and Capital Standards: A Revised Framework – Comprehensive Version*. June 2006. Basel: Bank for International Settlements.

BCBS, 2009. *Guiding Principles for the Replacement of IAS 39*. August 2009. Basel: Bank for International Settlements.

BCBS, 2011. *Basel III: A Global Regulatory Framework for More Resilient Banks and Banking Systems*. June 2011. Basel: Bank for International Settlements.

Beatty, A. and Liao, S., 2011. Do delays in expected loss recognition affect banks' willingness to lend? *Journal of Accounting and Economics*, 52 (1), 1–20.

Beatty, A., Chamberlain, S.L., and Magliolo, J., 1995. Managing financial reports of commercial banks: the influence of taxes, regulatory capital, and earnings. *Journal of Accounting Research*, 33 (2), 231–261.

Beaver, W.H. and Ryan, S.G., 2005. Conditional and unconditional conservatism: concepts and modelling. *Review of Accounting Studies*, 10 (2–3), 269–309.

Beck, P.J. and Narayanamoorthy, G.S., 2013. Did the SEC impact banks' loan loss reserve policies and their informativeness? *Journal of Accounting and Economics*, 56 (2–3), 42–65.

Benston, G.J. and Wall, L.D., 2005. How should banks account for loan losses? *Journal of Accounting and Public Policy*, 24 (2), 81–100.

Bikker, J.A. and Metzemakers, P.A.J., 2005. Bank provisioning behaviour and procyclicality. *Journal of International Financial Markets, Institutions and Money*, 15 (2), 141–157.

Bouvatier, V. and Lepetit, L., 2008. Banks' procyclical behavior: does provisioning matter? *Journal of International Financial Markets, Institutions and Money*, 18 (5), 513–526.

Bouvatier, V., Lepetit, L., and Strobel, F., 2014. Bank income smoothing, ownership concentration and the regulatory environment. *Journal of Banking and Finance*, 41 (April), 253–270.

Bushman, R.M. and Williams, C.D., 2012. Accounting discretion, loan loss provisioning, and discipline of banks' risk-taking. *Journal of Accounting and Economics*, 54 (1), 1–18.

Bushman, R.M. and Williams, C.D., 2015. Delayed expected loss recognition and the risk profile of banks. *Journal of Accounting Research*, 53 (3), 511–553.

Camfferman, K., 2015. The emergence of the 'incurred-loss' model for credit losses in IAS 39. *Accounting in Europe*, 12 (1), 1–35.

Collins, J.H., Shackelford, D.A. and Wahlen, J.M., 1995. Bank differences in the coordination of regulatory capital, earnings, and taxes. *Journal of Accounting Research*, 33 (2), 263–291.

FASB, 1975. *Statement of Financial Accounting Standards No. 5: Accounting for Contingencies (SFAS 5)*. March 1975. Norwalk, CT: Financial Accounting Standards Board.

FASB, 1980. *Statement of Financial Accounting Concepts No. 2 Qualitative Characteristics of Accounting Information*. May 1980. Norwalk, CT: Financial Accounting Standards Board.

FASB, 1993a. *Statement of Financial Accounting Standards No. 114: Accounting by Creditors for Impairment of a Loan (SFAS 114)*. May 1993. Norwalk, CT: Financial Accounting Standards Board.

FASB, 1993b. *Statement of Financial Accounting Standards No. 115: Accounting for Certain Investments in Debt and Equity Securities (SFAS 115)*. May 1993. Norwalk, CT: Financial Accounting Standards Board.

FASB, 2010a. *Exposure Draft: Proposed Accounting Standards Update. Accounting for Financial Instruments and Revisions to the Accounting for Derivative Instruments and Hedging Activities*. 26 May 2010. Norwalk, CT: Financial Accounting Standards Board.

FASB, 2010b. *Statement of Financial Accounting Concepts No. 8. Conceptual Framework for Financial Reporting*. September 2010. Norwalk, CT: Financial Accounting Standards Board.

FASB, 2012. *Exposure Draft: Proposed Accounting Standards Update. Financial Instruments: Credit Losses*. 20 December 2012. Norwalk, CT: Financial Accounting Standards Board.

FASB, 2013. *Exposure Draft: Proposed Accounting Standards Update (Revised). Leases.* 16 May 2013. Norwalk, CT: Financial Accounting Standards Board.

FASB, 2014. *Accounting Standards Update No. 2014-09. Revenue from Contracts with Customers (Topic 606).* May 2014. Norwalk, CT: Financial Accounting Standards Board.

FASB, 2016. *Accounting Standards Update No. 2016-13. Financial Instruments – Credit Losses (Topic 326): Measurement of Credit Losses on Financial Instruments.* June 2016. Norwalk, CT: Financial Accounting Standards Board.

FASB/IASB, 2011a. *Supplementary Document. Accounting for Financial Instruments and Revisions to the Accounting for Derivative Instruments and Hedging Activities: Impairment.* 31 January 2011. Norwalk, CT: Financial Accounting Standards Board; AND *Supplement to ED/2009/12. Financial Instruments: Amortised Cost and Impairment (Financial Instruments: Impairment).* January 2011. London: International Accounting Standards Board.

FASB/IASB, 2011b. *Staff Paper. Impairment: Three-Bucket Approach – IASB/FASB Meeting in week commencing 13 June 2011, Agenda Reference 8.* Available from: http://archive.ifrs.org/Current-Projects/IASB-Projects/Financial-Instruments-A-Replacement-of-IAS-39-Financial-Instruments-Recognitio/Impairment/Meeting-Summaries/Documents/FI0611b08obs.pdf [Accessed 18 August 2017].

FFIEC, 2001. *Policy Statement on Allowance for Loan and Lease Losses Methodologies and Documentation for Banks and Savings Institutions.* July 2001. Washington, DC: Federal Financial Institutions Examination Council.

Financial Crisis Advisory Group, 2009. *Report of the Financial Crisis Advisory Group.* 28 July 2009. London and Norwalk, CT: Financial Crisis Advisory Group.

Financial Stability Board, 2009. *Improving Financial Regulation: Report of the Financial Stability Board to G20 Leaders.* 25 September 2009. Basel: Financial Stability Board.

Fonseca, A.R. and González, F., 2008. Cross-country determinants of bank income smoothing by managing loan-loss provisions. *Journal of Banking and Finance,* 32 (February), 217–228.

GAO, 1991. *Failed Banks: Accounting and Auditing Reforms Urgently Needed.* April 1991. Washington, DC: United States General Accounting Office.

GAO, 1992. *Flexible Accounting Rules Lead to Inflated Financial Reports.* June 1992. Washington, DC: United States General Accounting Office.

Garcia Lara, J.M., Garcia Osma, B., and Penalva, F., 2016. Accounting conservatism and firm investment efficiency. *Journal of Accounting and Economics,* 61 (1), 221–238.

Gebhardt, G. and Novotny-Farkas, Z., 2011. Mandatory IFRS adoption and accounting quality of European banks. *Journal of Business Finance and Accounting,* 38 (3–4), 289–333.

Giner, B. and Mora, A., 2018. Bank loan loss accounting and its contracting effects: the new expected loss models. Working Paper, University of Valencia.

Hasan, I. and Wall, L.D., 2004. Determinants of the loan loss allowance: some cross-country comparisons. *The Financial Review,* 39 (1), 129–152.

Hashim, N., Li, W. and O'Hanlon, J., 2016. Expected-loss-based accounting for impairment of financial instruments: The FASB and IASB proposals 2009–2016. *Accounting in Europe,* 13 (2), 229–267.

Hodder, L.D. and Hopkins, P.E., 2014. Agency problems, accounting slack, and banks' response to proposed reporting of loan fair values. *Accounting, Organizations and Society* 39 (2), 117–133.

Huizinga, H. and Laeven, L., 2012. Bank valuation and accounting discretion during a financial crisis. *Journal of Financial Economics,* 106 (3), 614–634.

IASB, 2000. *International Accounting Standard 39 – Financial Instruments: Recognition and Measurement.* October 2000. London: International Accounting Standards Board.

IASB, 2001. *Framework for the Preparation and Presentation of Financial Statements.* April 2001. London: International Accounting Standards Board.

IASB, 2003. *International Accounting Standard 39 – Financial Instruments: Recognition and Measurement.* December 2003. London: International Accounting Standards Board.

IASB, 2008. *Reducing Complexity in Reporting Financial Instruments.* March 2008. London: International Accounting Standards Board.

IASB, 2009. *Exposure Draft ED/2009/12. Financial Instruments: Amortised Cost and Impairment.* November 2009. London: International Accounting Standards Board.

IASB, 2010. *The Conceptual Framework for Financial Reporting.* September 2010. London: International Accounting Standards Board.

IASB, 2013a. *Exposure Draft ED/2013/3 Financial Instruments: Expected Credit Losses.* March 2013. London: International Accounting Standards Board.

IASB, 2013b. *Snapshot: Financial Instruments – Expected Credit Losses.* March 2013. London: International Accounting Standards Board.

IASB, 2013c. *Exposure Draft ED/2013/6 Leases.* May 2013. London: International Accounting Standards Board.

IASB, 2014a. *IFRS 9 Financial Instruments.* July 2014. London: International Accounting Standards Board.

IASB, 2014b. *Project Summary. IFRS 9 Financial Instruments.* July 2014. Available from: http://archive.ifrs.org/Current-Projects/IASB-Projects/Financial-Instruments-A-Replacement-of-IAS-39-Financial-Instruments-Recognitio/Documents/IFRS-9-Project-Summary-July-2014.pdf [Accessed 18 August 2017].

IASB, 2014c. *IFRS 15 Revenue from Contracts with Customers.* May 2014. London: International Accounting Standards Board.

IASB, 2018. *Conceptual Framework for Financial Reporting.* March 2018. London: International Accounting Standards Board.

Jin, J., Kanagaretnam, K., and Lobo, G., 2016. Discretion in bank loan loss allowance, risk taking and earnings management. *Accounting and Finance*, 58 (1), 1–23.

Kanagaretnam, K., Lobo, G.J., and Mathieu, R., 2003. Managerial incentives for income smoothing through bank loan loss provisions. *Review of Quantitative Finance and Accounting*, 20 (1), 63–80.

Kanagaretnam, K., Lobo, G.J., and Yang, D.-H., 2004. Joint tests of signaling and income smoothing through bank loan loss provisions. *Contemporary Accounting Research*, 21 (4), 843–884.

Kane, E.J., 1997. Ethical foundations of financial regulation. *Journal of Financial Services Research*, 12 (1), 51–74.

Kim, M.-S. and Kross, W., 1998. The impact of the 1989 change in bank capital standards on loan loss provisions and loan write-offs. *Journal of Accounting and Economics*, 25 (1), 69–99.

Kruger, S., Rosch, D., and Scheule, H., 2018. The impact of loan loss provisioning on bank capital requirements. *Journal of Financial Stability*, 36 (June), 114–129.

Laeven, L. and Majnoni, G., 2003. Loan loss provisioning and economic slowdowns: too much, too late? *Journal of Financial Intermediation*, 12 (2), 178–197.

LaFond, R. and Watts, R.L., 2008. The information role of conservatism. *The Accounting Review*, 83 (2), 447–478.

Lee, S. and Rose J., 2010. Profits and balance sheet developments at U.S. commercial banks in 2009. *Federal Reserve Bulletin 96.*

Lim, C.Y., Lee, E., Kausar, A., and Walker, M., 2014. Bank accounting conservatism and bank loan pricing, *Journal of Accounting and Public Policy*, 33 (3), 260–278.

Liu, C.-C. and Ryan, S.G., 2006. Income smoothing over the business cycle: changes in banks' coordinated management of provisions for loan losses and loan charge-offs from the pre-1990 bust to the 1990s boom. *The Accounting Review*, 81 (2), 421–441.

Lobo, G.J. and Yang, D.-H., 2001. Bank managers' heterogeneous decisions on discretionary loan loss provisions. *Review of Quantitative Finance and Accounting*, 16 (3), 223–250.

Marton, J. and Runesson, E., 2017. The predictive ability of loan loss provisions in banks – effects of accounting standards, enforcement and incentives. *The British Accounting Review*, 49 (2), 162–180.

McEnroe, J. and Sullivan, M., 2014. Convergence movement – have there been benefits to the convergence process? *CPA Journal*, January, 15–19.

Meyer, L., 1999. *Testimony of Governor Laurence H. Meyer: Loan-loss Reserves Before the Subcommittee on Financial Institutions and Consumer Credit, Committee on Banking and Financial Services, U.S. House of Representatives.* June 1999. Available from: https://www.federalreserve.gov/boarddocs/testimony/1999/19990616.htm [Accessed 24 April 2018].

Moyer, S.E., 1990. Capital adequacy ratio regulations and accounting choices in commercial banks. *Journal of Accounting and Economics*, 13 (2), 123–154.

Ng, J. and Roychowdhury, S., 2014. Do loan loss reserves behave like capital? Evidence from recent bank failures, *Review of Accounting Studies*, 19 (3), 1234–1279.

Nichols, C.D., Wahlen, J.M., and Wieland, M.M., 2009. Publicly traded versus privately held: implications for conditional conservatism in bank accounting. *Review of Accounting Studies*, 14 (1), 88–122.

Novotny-Farkas, Z., 2016. The interaction of the IFRS 9 expected loss approach with supervisory rules and implications for financial stability. *Accounting in Europe*, 13 (2), 197–227.

OCC, 1998. *Allowance for Loan and Lease Losses.* May 1998. Washington, DC: Office of the Comptroller of the Currency.

O'Hanlon, J., 2013. Did loan-loss provisioning by UK banks become less timely after implementation of IAS 39? *Accounting and Business Research*, 43 (3), 225–258.

O'Hanlon, J., Hashim N. and Li, W., 2015. *Expected-Loss-Based Accounting for the Impairment of Financial Instruments: the FASB and IASB IFRS 9 Approaches*. Brussels: European Parliament, ref: IP/A/ECON/2015-14/PE 563.463. Available from: http://www.europarl.europa.eu/cmsdata/93530/IPOL_STU(2015)563463_EN.pdf [Accessed 28 September 2018].

O'Hanlon, J., Hashim N., and Li, W., 2018. *Research Briefing – Accounting for Credit Losses: The Development of IFRS 9 and CECL*. London: Institute of Chartered Accountants Charitable Trusts.

Pérez, D., Salas-Fumás, V., and Saurina, J., 2008. Earnings and capital management in alternative loan loss provision regulatory regimes. *European Accounting Review*, 17 (3), 423–445.

Roychowdhury, S. and Watts, R.L., 2007. Asymmetric timeliness of earnings, market-to-book and conservatism in financial reporting. *Journal of Accounting and Economics*, 44 (1–2), 2–31.

Rushton, E., 1999. *Opening Statement of Emory W. Rushton Concerning Loan Loss Reserves Before the Subcommittee on Financial Institutions*. June, 1999. Washington, DC: Committee on Banking and Financial Services.

Ryan, S.G., 2006. Identifying conditional conservatism. *European Accounting Review*, 15 (4), 511–525.

Ryan, S., 2017. Is banks' current regulatory capital adequacy the mechanism by which their accounting requirements affect financial stability? Working Paper, New York University.

Ryan, S.G. and Keeley, J.H., 2013. Discussion of "Did the SEC impact banks' loan loss reserve policies and their informativeness?" *Journal of Accounting and Economics*, 56 (2–3), 66–78.

SEC, 2012. *Work Plan for the Consideration of Incorporating International Financial Reporting Standards Into the Financial Reporting System for U.S. Issuers Final Staff Report*. 13 July 2012. Washington, DC: Securities and Exchange Commission.

Shrieves, R.E. and Dahl, D., 2003. Discretionary accounting and the behavior of Japanese banks under financial duress. *Journal of Banking & Finance*, 27 (3), 1219–1243.

Vyas, D., 2011. The timeliness of accounting write-downs by U.S. financial institutions during the financial crisis of 2007–2008. *Journal of Accounting Research*, 49 (3), 823–860.

Wall, L. and Koch, T., 2000. Bank loan-loss accounting: A review of theoretical and empirical evidence. *Economic Review – Federal Reserve Bank of Atlanta*, 85 (2), 1–19.

Watts, R.L., 2003a. Conservatism in accounting part I: explanations and implications. *Accounting Horizons*, 17 (3), 207–221.

Watts, R.L., 2003b. Conservatism in accounting part II: evidence and research opportunities. *Accounting Horizons*, 17 (4), 287–301.

Wu, D., 2016. Practical issues in the Current Expected Credit Loss (CECL) model: effective loan life and forward-looking information. Working Paper, Office of the Comptroller of the Currency.

Zhang, J., 2008. The contracting benefits of accounting conservatism to lenders and borrowers. *Journal of Accounting and Economics*, 45 (1), 27–54.

Bank loan loss accounting and its contracting effects: the new expected loss models

BEGOÑA GINER and ARACELI MORA

As a result of the recent financial crisis, several key institutions urged the IASB and the FASB to re-evaluate their models for loan loss accounting and use more forward-looking information. The paper examines the principal features of the new expected loss approach, taking into account the tensions between accounting and prudential objectives with respect to credit losses. We discuss the rationales for the change introduced by IFRS 9 and explore the differences between the IASB and the FASB models. Based on the notions of accounting conservatism and earnings management, we discuss the potential consequences of the new models. While both the FASB and the IASB model are more conservative than the incurred loss approach, each portrays a different type of conservatism, whose ability to provide information will depend on the bank's business model. We also argue that the differences in business models that prevail in different jurisdictions might help to explain the existence of two expected loss models. Besides, we identify new avenues for further research within the financial sector.

1. Introduction

Banks are vital for financial stability. Due to the nature of their assets (i.e. mainly loans[1]) and their financial structure (i.e. highly leveraged and financed largely via deposits) they have specific information asymmetry problems with stakeholders different to those they may have with shareholders. Loans are often illiquid and managers are allowed to exercise high discretion in their valuation and in the estimation of losses. In this paper, we examine the nature and the potential effects of the new accounting treatment for credit losses introduced by IFRS 9 *Financial Instruments*.

Since the beginning of the financial crisis, criticisms have been raised against the International Accounting Standards Board (IASB) and the US Financial Accounting Standards Board (FASB) accounting standards for the impairment model under the amortised cost measurement criterion. The issue with the incurred loss model, in place at that time, was that impairment losses could only be recognised when there was evidence that they existed, while there was a view that earlier recognition of loan losses could have potentially reduced the cyclical moves in the crisis (EFRAG 2009). Thus, after the request of the G7 to examine the factors that contributed to procyclicality, the Financial Stability Forum, predecessor of the Financial Stability Board (FSB), specifically referred to the impact of loan losses in the crisis (FSF 2009). At the G20 London Summit in April 2009, the FSF called on both the IASB and the FASB to reconsider the incurred loss model, and incorporate a broader range of available credit information to measure loan losses in the interest of financial stability. The G20 welcomed the recommendation and explicitly asked standard setters to work with regulators and supervisors[2] to improve standards on valuation and provisioning, with the aim of achieving a single set of high quality accounting standards; they also requested FSB to monitor the progresses (G20 2009). Along the same lines, in its July 2009 report, the Financial Crisis Advisory Group (FCAG)[3] highlighted the delayed recognition of losses associated with loans and other financial instruments as one of the primary weaknesses in accounting standards and their application. In its view the incurred loss model did not properly reflect the underlying economics of lending activity and credit impairment was captured too late. Consequently, FCAG (2009) strongly urged FASB and IASB to re-evaluate their models for loan loss accounting, the 'incurred loss model', and explore alternatives that would use more forward-looking information. As an immediate response, the two Boards set about developing new standards that could address the problems identified. Thus, loan loss accounting was the subject of a joint project that tried to develop an 'expected loss model' for recognising impairment. However, despite the efforts made to achieve a common proposal, some significant differences remained, and the final models differ.

Trombetta et al. (2012) argue that academic research can help us understand the possible effects of accounting standards, and that the existing body of research is a valuable tool to be exploited. With this in mind, this paper aims to provide a theoretical basis to explain the causes and consequences of the change in the accounting paradigm regarding loan impairment models. It outlines the traditional controversy surrounding accounting for loan losses between accounting standard setters and bank prudential institutions, which, in consistency with Zeff (2012)'s arguments, considerably increased after the crisis, to the point that prudential bodies forced the change in the standards. Notwithstanding, it is argued that a change from the incurred to the expected loss model might have been induced by information asymmetry problems specific to banks. Particularly, based on the finance literature, it is stated that moral hazard problems between managers and lenders might explain the consideration of more forward-looking information in the new models, while adverse selection between managers and securitised loan buyers provides likely explanations for the differences between the IASB and the FASB models. Based on the accounting literature, this paper also analyses the potential consequences of these changes on accounting quality in terms of the increase in conservatism (both conditional and unconditional), induced by the standards, as well as the effect on contracting efficiency and earnings management.

Among other aspects, we conclude that providing risk information on loans is a way of increasing market discipline. Hence, it explains the change to an expected loss model, while limiting adverse selection with buyers of securitised loans could also have been critical for the final decisions of the two accounting standard setters. It is our view that the difference in bank business models between jurisdictions – namely the United States (US) and the European Union (EU) – , and the strength of the prudential institutions have played a key role in the final decisions.

Nevertheless, we argue that providing this information through accounting earnings recognition is not the only way to reduce these information asymmetry problems, and might even have some undesirable consequences.

From this review, we also identify some areas for further academic research which should help to better understand the causes and consequences of the application of the new expected loss models.

We discuss next the different views on loan impairment, with special emphasis on the new models introduced by the FASB and the IASB. In section three, we focus on information asymmetry as a key theoretical driver of the loan loss accounting models. In section four we discuss conservatism and its link with earnings management as a key to understanding the loan loss accounting models. Finally, section five concludes and offers suggestions for future research.

2.   Different loan loss models

2.1.   *Backward-looking vs forward-looking information in estimating loan losses*

The confusion over the terminology used adds to the difficulties in understanding the different positions about the recognition of loan impairment.[4] Besides, given the different criteria that exist to estimate the 'allowance' (following either the FASB or the IASB accounting standards) and the 'provision' (following prudential rules), it should come as no surprise that the amounts will ultimately differ.

2.1.1.   *The incurred loss model vs the economic approach*

As stated in the accounting standards in force when the financial crisis unfolded – Financial Accounting Statement (FAS) 5 and 114, and International Accounting Standard (IAS) 39 – under the incurred loss model, loan impairment focuses on losses expected to result from events that have already happened. It considers the expected losses derived from past and present events (i.e. the incurred losses), and explicitly excludes the expected effect of future events (based on forward-looking information). A key question is: Which part of the expected loss should be treated as an expense in the reporting period? To that end a 'triggering event' should be identified. However, as pointed out by Camfferman (2015), the distinction between incurred and expected loss models is not so obvious. Furthermore, making a sharp distinction between them is a relatively new phenomenon.

The incurred loss model adopts a narrower view of loan impairment than the one followed in other accounting standards, as they consider the recoverable amount of the asset.[5] In fact, under the 'economic perspective' followed to recognise such impairments, expected future events do indeed matter. The value of the asset is the present value of its expected net cash flows including expected losses – no matter if they derive from events that have already happened or are based on forward-looking information – which makes up the economic value. At origination expected losses are implicit when pricing the loans (i.e. to calculate the charged interest rate). If this forward-looking approach were applied to loan losses, it would imply 'matching' the interest income with the cost of the credit risk. Changes in cash flow expectations and defaults during an accounting period would be recorded as loan loss expenses (or revenues). Benston and Wall (2005) analytically show that this 'economic approach' clearly would be superior to the traditional incurred loss model if measurement were reliable and cost effective. This condition is normally satisfied when there is an efficient, liquid market, though this is not generally the case when dealing with loans. Hence, the incurred loss model as applied to loans could be seen as a 'restrictive' solution that, given the information asymmetry on these assets, limits earnings management.

Comparing an incurred loss model (recognising losses based on past events) with a more forward-looking information model (taking expected future losses into account), asset values coincide when default is probable, but at any other moment they differ. That said, the incurred loss model is clearly more reliable and less subject to potential earnings manipulation, which is perhaps a reason for its generalised adoption in the accounting standards. However, that model has often been used in a very 'tolerant' manner not only in the past,[6] but before and during the financial crisis. Thus, Cohen et al. (2014) show that US banks managed earnings thorough discretionary loan losses during the crisis; and those that behave more aggressively prior to 2007, exhibited substantially higher market risk once the crisis began. Morris et al. (2016) confirm that US banks used loan losses to smooth reported earnings, and in subperiod 2006–2008 discretion appears to have been used to accrue additional expenses, which is 'inconsistent with the incurred loss model' (p. 177). Notwithstanding, during the crisis, the incurred loss model was criticised by some stakeholders (mainly bank regulators and supervisors) as its backward-looking approach might have led to a 'too-little-too-late' recognition of losses, delaying the report of bad news, inducing bank lending, and consequently promoting cyclicality (Cohen and Edwards 2017).

2.1.2.   *The financial reporting view vs the prudential view*

The debate on whether to include more or less forward-looking information when estimating loan losses rests on the conflicting goals between accounting standard setters on the one side and prudential institutions on the other. In brief, the former aims at providing information to investors, while the second attempts to achieve financial stability. From the investors' viewpoint, maximising the use of forward-looking information could be seen as highly desirable. However, when dealing with recognition and measurement, accounting standard setters tend to avoid that type of information if the resulting figures could face concerns about not being a faithful representation of the phenomena being captured in the financial statements (as stated in the IASB Conceptual Framework).

According to the prudential perspective, banks must maintain sufficient capital to absorb unexpected losses and sufficient loan loss provisions to cover all kinds of expected losses (Laeven and Majnoni 2003). Hence, the prudential view of 'expected losses' includes forward-looking information and tends to adopt an extremely conservative view. Bank regulators use accounting numbers as an input, and adjust them for regulatory-capital purposes. However, ideally from that prudential perspective, loan loss allowances in the balance sheet should converge with regulatory provisions and cover future losses, in line with the objective of financial stability. That said, given the ability of bank regulators to adjust accounting numbers and the existence of regulatory reporting, accounting standard setters are reluctant to deviate from its main objective which is to provide accurate information to market participants (Acharya and Ryan 2016).

Prudential models have sometimes been used for accounting purposes. In particular, the allowance has been employed as a countercyclical mechanism by requiring banks to build up a fund during good times (large impairments even if there are no signs of any problems), which might be depleted in downturns (low impairments when problems occur); this system smooths reported accounting profits over time. The 'dynamic provisioning' introduced by the Bank of Spain in 2000 is a good example of this practice. This impairment model is based on the rationale that the allowance for impairment and the prudential provision are equivalent. This allowance/provision has two components, 'generic' and 'specific.' The generic also called dynamic component is a countercyclical mechanism. It aims to create a buffer during a boom period (when the component is acting as an additional loss) against future losses (when this component is acting as an income), and its main consequence is earnings smoothing through the cycle. Although some authors are supportive of using such dynamic provisioning as an accounting model for impairment (Bouvatier and Lepetit 2008; Pérez et al. 2008; Poveda 2000), most auditors, practitioners, and accounting scholars are strongly opposed (Acharya and Ryan 2016; Barth and Landsman 2010; FEE-EFRAG 2009; Laux 2012)

Among the accounting profession there is a consensus on the inappropriateness of using the prudential perspective for accounting purposes. As Wall and Koch (2000) note, the use of loan loss provisions as equivalent to impairment is not just inappropriate from an accounting perspective but is also ineffective with respect to bank safety. By recording a large loss, the capacity of banks to attend liabilities in the future does not directly change, although it is true that the reduction in net income could influence the dividend policy and risk exposure. Loan loss accounting will have an effect on financial stability only to the extent it has an influence on the bank's decisions on investment, funding and dividends policy (Novotny-Farkas 2016). The recognition of losses may also have a beneficial impact if it obliges banks to increase capital due to regulatory constraints. Having said that, bank prudential regulators have the ability to change capital requirement rules, or prevent banks from declaring dividends to shareholders, which has a cash flow impact without interfering with reported earnings. Thus, they could require banks to create specific reserves once accounting earnings have been obtained.

The interference of prudential rules with loan loss accounting has always been a matter of concern. As pointed out by Gray and Clarke (2004), during the boom period that followed the financial crises of the 1980s and 1990s, bank prudential regulators in many countries asked for 'larger' loan loss impairments. In the US, even though FAS 5 and 114 were in force imposing the incurred loss model, banks' accounting practices were affected by prudential regulators' claims; thus excessive impairments (more than incurred) were charged in the income statement.[7] As a response, the US SEC criticised banks' behaviour (Levitt 1998; Sutton 1997), 'perhaps, implicitly stating that some banks' practices entailed earnings management – resulting in the use of the term "secret reserves" reappearing' (Gray and Clarke 2004: 323). As Wall and Koch (2000) argue, the general view regarding these secret reserves is that they are used to smooth income over time. In 2001 the US SEC issued a new guidance (SAB 102) designed to 'improve financial reporting quality' by clarifying the application of the incurred loss model.

In Europe, before the introduction of IFRS in 2005, recording expected loan losses in accounting earnings was common practice (Gebhardt and Novotny-Farkas 2011). Moreover, in some countries, prudential rules were followed to estimate impairments to be charged in the income statement. However, when in 2003 the IASB revised IAS 39, certain requirements established in the US Generally Accepted Accounting Principles (GAAP) were considered to clarify the incurred loss impairment model and avoid the excessive recognition of losses (Camfferman 2015).

As a consequence of the recent financial crisis, the debate regarding the interpretation of expected losses arose again.[8] There was a concern, mostly among prudential regulators, that the stronger reliability of an incurred loss model was achieved at the expense of relevance by delaying the recognition of bad news, and even, in some cases, overstating the values of the lowest quality loans, which also increased accounting profits.[9] In particular, accounting write-downs were generally less timely than the devaluation implied by credit indices (Vyas 2011), and consequently, price-to-book ratios were abnormally low (Papa and Peters 2014). It is not clear, however, if the problem lies in the loan loss accounting model or in the very restrictive way it was implemented. Hence it could be the case that, as pointed by the IASB Chairman, the 'too-little-too-late' problem could have been avoided, at least partly, if the incurred loss model had been applied much more vigorously (Hoogervorst 2012).

Beyer et al. (2010) posit that in market-based economies, accounting information fulfils two main roles, valuation and stewardship (or contracting). The valuation role matches with the main objective stated in the FASB and IASB frameworks, which is to provide information for investors to predict future cash flows. The contractual role is more in line with bank regulators, who expect accounting standards help them to achieve their goal of financial stability. The question of whether both perspectives are (or should be) aligned is a matter of judgment, but according to the IFRS Foundation (2015) by bringing transparency, accountability and efficiency to the financial markets the accounting standards will also contribute to *long-term* [emphasis added] financial stability.[10] Nevertheless, the more general view is that the different missions are in conflict, and particularly in the event of a financial and economic crisis such conflict results in political pressure on standard setters (Zeff 2012). Similarly, Lambert (2010) draws a distinction between using information either to predict future cash flows or to influence future cash flows. The latter is closely related to the idea of using information to avoid moral hazard problems. Although accounting standards might play a role in designing the information set for such purpose, this is not the objective of either the FASB or the IASB. Other stakeholders, most importantly bank regulators, who may require such information, could do so through their own procedures without interfering with accounting standards for other purposes to avoid unnecessary conflicts.[11]

While during the boom period, at the end of the century, the dispute between standard setters and prudential bodies ended with a stricter application of the accounting standards, on this occasion the standards have been changed. To some degree, the new standards could be seen as more oriented towards a contractual perspective than to an informative one. It is likely that the different economic scenarios in both periods help to explain the different outcomes as discussed below.

2.2.   The two expected loss models: IASB vs FASB

As mentioned in the introduction, the G20, the FSB, and its predecessor the FSF, among others, pressurised the IASB and the FASB to develop new impairment models. This pressure, plus the advice of FCAG, led the Boards to begin deliberations about loan loss accounting in 2009, as part of the changes in their respective standards on financial instruments. After a deep debate and several drafts, their final standards on impairment were issued in 2014 and 2016 respectively; IFRS 9 has been in force since 2018, while the US standard will be implemented in 2020 and 2021 (depending on the type of entity).[12]

The IASB proposed the first exposure draft of the expected loss model, which tried to capture the economic substance of lending transactions (IASB 2009). Its primary objective was to consider all future cash flows including expected credit losses based on past, current, and future conditions when calculating the present value and determining the 'adjusted effective interest rate'. Following this approach, all-life expected losses must be estimated as well as their allocation over the expected life. Hence, it imposed a 'matching' between revenues, which are based on the interest rate charged to the loans, and losses (defaults) of a loan portfolio. Provided credit losses occur as expected, compared with an incurred loss model, this economic approach would normally mean lower net income in the early periods and higher net income after losses have been incurred.[13] This approach received criticisms not only from preparers (mainly because of difficulties in estimating the time allocation of expected losses), but also from prudential institutions. In their view, when credit losses are concentrated in the early part of the asset's life, incurred losses could be higher than the allowance formed to date.

A year later FASB issued its first exposure draft (FASB 2010). It aimed to ensure that the allowance is sufficient to cover all estimated credit losses for the remaining life of a portfolio, therefore it required 'day-1' losses for all-life expected losses.[14] Prudential institutions preferred this solution to the IASB approach, since the allowance at the end of the reporting period would be more aligned with the provision estimated following prudential regulation.[15] Example 1 in the Appendix provides a simplified case to illustrate the difference between these approaches.

Given the pressure of constituents to achieve a common solution, in 2011 both Boards jointly issued a Supplementary Document (SD) that attempted to develop a solution that could satisfy both views (FASB 2011; IASB 2011). Nevertheless, discrepancies remained, and the subsequent drafts issued by the FASB (2012) and the IASB (2013) followed different models, although both included day-1 losses. Consequently, both models have been criticised due to the undervaluation of loans at origination date. Indeed, the economic value does not change at purchase or origination due to expected losses, what changes is the effective interest rate. Finally, a year later, the IASB published IFRS 9: *Financial Instruments* (IASB 2014), including the impairment model with some minor changes with respect to its 2013 draft. The FASB issued Accounting Standards Update 2016–13: *Financial Instruments–Credit Losses (Topic 326)* in June 2016 (FASB 2016).[16] However, given the materiality of the issue and the problems that the lack of convergence may generate, the possibility of re-emerging pressures for convergence should not be ruled out, as Hashim et al. (2016) suggest. We highlight below some aspects that characterise the two final standards and devote the next sections to develop their theoretical underpinning.

The IASB model uses two measurement bases. For assets for which credit risk has not increased significantly since initial recognition, the allowance reducing their contractual value is an amount equal to '12-month expected credit losses'[17] (stage 1), while for assets whose credit risk has increased significantly,[18] the allowance is an amount equal to 'all-life expected credit losses' (stages 2 and 3).[19] Thus, under this 'deterioration approach' the allowance balance increases (due to the recognition of additional losses) when the credit quality deteriorates. Contrary to this dual approach, the FASB requires an allowance equal to all-life expected losses from origination and for all assets.[20] On the basis that initial estimates of losses are taken into account to price the loans (i.e. the interest rate charged), the issue is whether initially expected losses should be recognised as impairment loss in the income statement immediately (FASB model[21]) or over time (as in the IASB model). The Appendix provides the very simplified example 2 that illustrates the major differences between the two models.

Both models have been criticised for having conceptual weaknesses, but the underestimation of the economic value is probably the most significant one from a conceptual viewpoint.[22] Besides, in the standard development process, both the constituents of FASB and IASB expressed concerns about day-1 loss (O'Hanlon et al. 2017). As discussed in the fourth section, this undervaluation implies both models are perceived as unconditionally conservative solutions. The FASB model recognises all expected losses at origination, so firms will only record losses (or profits) later on, if there is a change in the estimations. However, there will be no distinction in the income statement between these losses and those derived from an increase in the loan portfolio. As for the IASB model, firms will also be affected by the initial undervaluation though to a lesser extent; and, unlike the FASB model, firms will be able to show impairment in the income statement when a loan deteriorates. Due to the novelty of these models it is not easy to predict the likely impact of their implementation, but we concur with Hashim et al. (2016) that the FASB model's outcome is more difficult to foresee. This is due to the combination of the FASB requirement to record all expected losses on day-1 with 'its stipulation that forecasts over the contractual term of financial assets are not required where forecasts are not supportable' (Hashim et al. 2016: 262).

Next section provides the theoretical background which might explain the final outcomes of these standards.

3. Loan losses and information asymmetry

The core issue of agency theory applied to a contractual relationship is the asymmetric information distribution, which can cause contracting problems, namely adverse selection and moral hazard (Akerlof 1970; Jensen and Meckling 1976; Ross 1973). Adverse selection occurs when there is asymmetric information prior to a deal between a buyer (investor) and a seller (issuer). After entering in a contract, moral hazard occurs when a party benefits from not providing full information to the other party by not suffering the consequences of the taken risk. Ex-ante as well as ex-post problems severely affect the behaviour of banks; therefore, they can help to explain the prudential institutions' preferences for loan impairment and their pressure on accounting standard setters. However, as highlighted by Beatty and Liao (2014), in general the empirical accounting literature has ignored those bank-specific agency problems that accompany the information asymmetry.

Banks are regulated institutions mainly because they are vital for financial stability. Indeed, the shock waves caused by a banking crisis may affect the entire economy (King and Levine 1993). Due to both the nature of banks' assets and the financial structure of banks, information asymmetry problems deserve special attention when explaining banks' behaviour. Furthermore, unlike other industries, problems in the banking sector not only (not even mainly) refer to equity investors, since there are other relevant stakeholders, namely lenders (mostly depositors) and bank regulators, who should be considered. However, even though lenders' information problems are at the heart of the microeconomic theory of banks, most of the pre-crisis research has focused on the perspective of equity investors rather than on the one of lenders (Beatty and Liao 2014). Those problems lead to negative economic consequences either at the economy level (the market is in danger due to adverse selection) or at the firm level (moral hazard will normally produce agency costs in a principal/agent relationship). Within this scenario, the role of signalling, and more concretely of accounting information becomes a central debate.

Next, we analyze the use of accounting information as a potential way to solve the information asymmetry problems in banks. We focus on providers of liquidity other than equity investors and on buyers of securitised loans. Besides, we consider the interference of banks' authorities in pursuing financial stability.

3.1. *The manager-lender relationship and moral hazard*

The main investments in banks are loans that have little upward potential but a considerable downside risk, and are characterised by having an illiquid market. As a result, bank managers do not only make investment decisions (and might be involved in suboptimal risk taking from the lenders' viewpoint), but they can also exercise high discretion in their valuation. Hence, the bank's risks are not perfectly observable (Acharya and Ryan 2016). Furthermore, banks distinguish themselves by having much higher leverage than non-financial firms, making their capital structure unique (Sundaresan and Wang 2016). Particularly, banks' liabilities include deposits provided by a great part of the population, which in turn can lead governments to intervene as discussed below. Another characteristic element in banks' financial structure is the relatively small proportion of debt securities.

If banks do not pay attention to the interests of depositors (that is, of society as a whole), then market discipline becomes necessary to prevent bank managers from taking excessive risks. In essence, this mechanism allows investors in bank liabilities – such as (uninsured) deposits and subordinated debt – to 'punish' banks for taking too many risks and, therefore, demand higher returns from those liabilities. In the absence of agency problems, if bank risk choices were observable and deposits were uninsured, there would be perfect market discipline (Blum 2002).

However, as argued by Nier and Baumann (2006), the effectiveness of market discipline is contingent on three aspects, namely: (i) governmental support, (ii) type of funding, and (iii) available risk information. Next, we briefly discuss how each of them works.

First, explicit or implicit government guarantees may limit the yield response of bank liabilities to changes in the bank's default risk. Concerns about the consequences of bank difficulties have led countries to provide deposit insurance which, in the case of a bank's failure, ultimately forces central banks – and, to a certain extent, taxpayers – to cover such losses. Although deposit insurance provides security to depositors and can attract them, it has been questioned for increasing moral hazard problems, since it does not deter managers from making excessive risk investments (Hellmann et al. 2000). Therefore, the lower the degree to which the bank is financed by insured liabilities (that is, to the extent that investors are at risk), the more expensive the default risk. Similarly, the 'too-big-to-fail' protection makes firms believe they can receive the benefits of risk taking, while the government will bear the cost of failure (Cordella and Yeyati 2003; Dam and Koetter 2012; Gorton and Huang 2004). Consequently, it also decreases incentives to avoid moral hazard, and may systematically encourage major institutions to take more risks than optimal. Furthermore, investors may believe they will not suffer losses, even if the institution fails, and they will have less incentives to monitor the institution's risks and apply market discipline (Mishkin 2006).

Second, in the finance literature, it has been widely debated whether funding through debt securities provides market discipline and helps solve agency problems with depositors, or, on the contrary, can even increase them (Rixtel et al. 2015). The subordinated debt securities have been considered, mainly in Europe, as a market signal of banks' viability (Evanoff et al. 2011). However, Belkhir (2013) shows that subordinated debt provides market discipline only when those debtholders have better access to information. Moreover, when outside investors hold subordinated debt, the risk-shifting behaviour of banks tends to become more prominent.

The third aspect affecting the effectiveness of market discipline is the degree of observability of the bank's risk choices, which depends on the information available. In circumstances where deposits are mainly insured, and debt securities (including subordinated debt) are in the hands of uninformed investors, information on the bank's risks becomes a key instrument for altering bank managers' behaviour and reduce moral hazard (Acharya and Ryan 2016; Christensen et al. 2016).

Prudential institutions exercise a monitoring role in the economy, but also try to induce banks to invest wisely and avoid excessive leverage. For this, they use several measures, such as monitoring of risk management systems and capital requirements. Although these measures could be effective in reducing moral hazard, they can be circumvented, for instance by selling potential non-performing loans and transferring the risk to these investors. When buyers do not have the necessary information to understand the risks they assume, this is a source of adverse selection as we discuss below.

3.2.   *The role of the business model and adverse selection*

The change in the banks' business model from the traditional 'originate-to-hold' model to a more sophisticated 'originate-to-distribute' approach has been pointed out as a factor that contributed to the last financial crisis in the US (Purnanandam 2011). The basis of the traditional originate-to-hold model is that banks tend to hold the loans in their balance sheet till maturity. According to Diamond (1984) and Holmström and Tirole (1993), among others, banks add value to the financial system due to their comparative advantage in monitoring borrowers, and in providing information on credit risks. Nevertheless, as Bord and Santos (2012) state, in order to carry out this task properly, banks must hold the loans they originate. With the originate-to-distribute model, either at the time of origination or in the following years, banks distribute the loans by selling them in the secondary loan market mainly by securitisation. Hence, banks can originate loans, earn their fees, and then distribute them to other investors in a large opaque manner (Berndt and Gupta 2009), and not bear the credit risk of these loans. Under these circumstances, incentives to screen loan applicants and to monitor borrowers decrease, while incentives to follow riskier investment practices increase, making the information asymmetry problems more significant (Ayadi et al. 2011).

When the risk taker understands the risks, sharing risks should contribute to financial stability; but, under the originate-to-distribute model, the bank's superior information raises concerns about adverse selection from the perspective of the buyer of the loans. While the bank could be selling the loan for legitimate motives, including improving capital requirements – since this practice would reduce risk-weighted assets, as suggested by Beatty and Liao (2014) – , managers have unobservable private information that they may not want to transfer to buyers. In a perfect market, this situation should lead to a break-down of the secondary loan market due to the classic 'lemons' problem, but in an imperfect market this does not happen, and some advocate a stricter regulation to avoid the adverse selection problem (Berndt and Gupta 2009). A key part of such regulation should be devoted to increasing transparency about investment risks. We highlight that to some extent accounting standards fulfill such role, as they require detailed information in the notes related to the carrying amount of securitised loans (including allowance, delinquency and impairments of the period), as well as the fair value calculation.[23]

Prior to the financial crisis, the business models of European and US banks were very different. From 1997 to 2007 the secondary syndicated loan market in the US grew exponentially, and although in the EU the securitisation market also grew consistently for almost a decade, it did so on a much smaller scale.[24]After the financial crisis, European securitisation markets have plummeted and have never fully recovered, but the US market, which almost entirely collapsed in 2008–2009, has rebounded more quickly.[25] As Tang (2016: 4) states,

> before the crisis in the United States, structural flaws of securitisation were exploited by the excessive freedom given to credit (in particular mortgage) distributors. However, EU issuers overall retained a bigger part of the portfolio of the loans that they securitised than their US counterparts, to the point where originate-to-distribute practices were almost non-existent in the European Union.

Besides, US banks could create very complex structures for their securitizations; that complexity limited investors' understanding of such products and increased the risks attached to them.[26] 'By contrast, overly complex structures were rare in the EU, because issuers and investors had less incentives and freedom to engage in such transactions' (Tang 2016: 4).

Before ending this section, we discuss below how the different impairment models could affect banks with different business models. To some extent, we understand this could also help explain the decisions made by the two standard setters, as well as why prudential institutions were more successful in their pressure to record day-1 losses in the US. We insist that an incurred loss model does not provide any information of potential future losses in the allowances, and there are no allowances when loans originate.

Comparing the two expected loss models for banks that engage in originate-to-distribute loans, if the losses are only expected in the long term, they are likely not to be recorded in the IASB model, while they will be recorded under the FASB solution. Moreover, if there is a requirement to record day-1 losses for all-life expected losses when the loan originates, the incentives to invest in risky loans would be reduced. Therefore, financial reporting requirements can yield ex-ante decision-making changes to firms, and in particular to banks (Acharya and Ryan 2016). This could also be a way of transferring risk information to the buyers, reducing adverse selection problems, and conveying some market discipline when pricing those loans. Nevertheless, excessive allowance at initial recognition is a source of earnings management. To the extent that the origininate-to-distribute loan model is significantly more widespread in the US than in the rest of the world – and was considered a key point of the last crisis – , one can understand the interest shown by prudential regulators in the more conservative FASB solution. Moreover, it seems that this concern has dominated over others in that jurisdiction, which is not surprising given that earnings management is not a problem unless banks maintain the loans for a long period. That said, disclosing risk information using other channels, different from the general-purpose financial statements, is another avenue to communicate information to third parties that could have been considered.

For originate-to-hold loans, earnings management becomes a major issue, however. Between the initial recognition of all-life expected losses, as required by the FASB model, and the time they are incurred, loans remain undervalued and the allowances can be easily managed. This is what prudential bodies prefer when using allowances as a tool for financial stability, but this is not the solution that fits with the objectives of accounting standard setters analysed in sub-section 2.1.2. In order to better meet its purpose, the IASB has adopted a deterioration approach that allows for information about the loan's performance to be considered. Under this model, day-1 losses have an arbitrary limit (the next 12 months), which, in comparison with the FASB model, reduces the possibility of earnings management and allows a better match of the cost of credit risk with the interest income during the expected life of the loan portfolio. We concur with Hashim et al. (2016: 258) that, depending on the circumstances, 'this provides opportunities for communication of information that a uniform approach would not give'.

We are not aware of any previous literature that explicitly links the business model with the decision to issue a specific loan-loss model, but we believe it played an important role and could have been key to preventing the convergence between IASB and FASB. Nevertheless, it seems that this was not an explicit argument used by constituents that responded throughout due process (O'Hanlon et al. 2017).

4. Loan loss accounting and conservatism

As mentioned earlier, providing information on the quality and creditworthiness of loans is a way to reduce the problems arising from information asymmetry. The decision on how this information should be transferred seems to be a special subject of controversy, and, in particular, loan loss recognition becomes a key issue in this discussion. To the extent that the latter affects accounting earnings, in this section we examine the accounting literature on a relevant property of such earnings, conservatism, which will help to analyze the potential consequences of the changes in the loan loss model. But, first, we distinguish between two types of conservatism.

4.1. *Conditional vs unconditional conservatism*

Although conservatism has always played a prominent role in financial reporting, there has been an historical ambivalence in its definition (Ball and Shivakumar 2005). It was defined in the Statement of Financial Accounting Concept (SFAC) 2 as 'a prudent reaction to uncertainty to try to ensure that uncertainty and risks inherent in business situations are adequately considered' (FASB 1980, CON2-6). Despite the provision above, SFAC 2 prevents justifying the intentional understatement of net assets because such a practice may lead to overstated earnings in future periods. The predecessor of the IASB, the International Accounting Standards Committee (IASC), followed the same thinking in its Conceptual Framework, but instead of using the term conservatism referred to prudence, and indicated that the exercise of prudence does not allow the creation of hidden reserves (IASC 1989). In 2010, the FASB and the IASB issued partial revisions of their frameworks. Under the chairmanship of Sir David Tweedie, the IASB eliminated the prudence notion as an ingredient of the qualitative characteristic of reliability (now called faithful representation). The next Chairman, Hans Hoogervorst, explained the removal to avoid misunderstandings about the concept, since it allowed the creation of hidden reserves and cookie-jar accounting, and because the US GAAP did not have a definition of prudence. Moreover, he also argued that despite the elimination, prudence remained deeply engrained in the standards (Hoogervorst 2012). However, the change was not well received, and due to strong opposition, the IASB reinstated the explicit reference to prudence in the new Conceptual Framework, issued in March 2018 (IASB 2018a).[27]

To clarify the interpretation of prudence in accounting, as well as its relation with earnings management, it is convenient to distinguish between two types of conservatism – conditional and unconditional. The distinction is relatively recent, since it was only made in the academic literature at the beginning of this century; as Ball and Shivakumar (2005) argue, the confusion between both types might explain the ambivalence in the conservatism notion mentioned earlier. In our view this differentiation is extremely pertinent when analysing an incurred vs an expected loss impairment model, and when comparing the new models of FASB and IASB. As terms and definitions are conventions and are not always consistent throughout the literature, we clarify next the terms we are going to use for the purpose of our analysis. The expressions unconditional and conditional conservatism are related to a specific notion of 'news', which is information about how the asset in place is 'actually performing' (excluding expectations about future performance).[28]

Based on that, unconditional conservatism conveys the idea that the conservative accounting choice is made before there is information on how well the investment 'has actually performed', so it is not related to news about the actual performance of the asset; it is also called ex -ante, news-unrelated, or balance sheet conservatism. In brief, it mainly refers to assets that appear on the balance sheet below their actual value. As Beaver and Ryan (2005) explain, unconditional conservatism deals with aspects of the accounting process determined at the inception of assets (and liabilities). Unconditional conservatism involves a pre-commitment to understate the book value of assets, which can be driven by accounting standards and accounting practices. Some examples are the immediate expensing of internally developed intangibles, the use of an accounting depreciation more accelerated than the economic one, and the recognition of impairment beyond the economic impairment. Although unconditional conservatism results in understated net assets, considering the entire life of an investment, it does not necessarily result in understated net income; leaving uncertainty aside, unconditional conservatism would only alter the timing of the charge. In other words, if the asset performs as expected, and there are no changes in circumstances, total income will not be affected. Therefore, as Mora and Walker (2015) sustain, the effect of unconditional conservatism is that investment income is lower at the beginning of the life of a project and higher later.

In contrast, conditional conservatism, also called ex-post, news-driven, or earnings conservatism, implies faster recognition of bad news in accounting earnings vis-à-vis good news. If an accounting standard requires a higher degree of verification for recognising good news about the actual performance of an asset than bad news, this will result in an asymmetry, and the system is said to be conditionally conservative. Leaving constant the degree of verification to recognise good news, a reduction in the degree to recognise bad news about the actual performance of the asset will increase the level of conditional conservatism. Regarding loan impairments, widening the indicators or events (which occurred after initial recognition) that can be considered signs of deterioration will anticipate the recognition of bad news, so it will produce more conditional conservative accounting. However, if impairment is not based on market values, or those market values are not referred to liquid markets (as it happens with loans), managers' discretion will play a significant role in the valuation process.

As Basu (2005: 313) points out, 'the key distinction between unconditional conservatism and conditional conservatism is that the former only utilises information known at the inception of the asset's life; whereas conditional conservatism utilises, and hence reveals, information when it is received in future periods.' Focusing on loans, the recognition of a loss based on the expectation of potential future losses, when there are not (yet) visible signs that the asset is underperforming is considered an unconditionally conservative practice. It happens when day-1 losses are recorded, and as a consequence the asset is undervalued until the moment the loss is incurred. As suggested by Pope and Walker (2003) and Basu (2005), modelled by Beaver and Ryan (2005), and empirically tested by García Lara and Mora (2004), unconditional conservatism reduces subsequent conditional conservatism, and the higher the first the greater the impact on the second.

Prior literature shows that the drivers of both types of conservatism tend to differ. As Watts (2003) highlights, contracting is the main determinant of the demand for conditional conservatism. In relation to difficult-to-verify information, as is the case of loan impairment, this demand is particularly strong given that lenders' claims are more sensitive to bad news than to good news. Besides, conditional conservatism plays an important disciplinary role in constraining risky investments and earnings management, as shown in the empirical studies. Thus, Nichols et al. (2009) evidence a greater demand for conditional conservatism to constrain managerial opportunism associated with information asymmetries in US public banks, compared with private ones. Lim et al. (2014) find that the timely recognition of losses is associated with good lending decisions, namely higher spreads, which is consistent with the governance role of conditional conservatism. Some evidence suggests that covenants and conditional conservatism in private debt contracting are positively associated, and act as complements when information asymmetry is high (Callen et al. 2016). Furthermore, those supporting the view that accounting standards should pay more attention to the information needs of lenders argue that the demand for conditional conservatism should be seen as a prime candidate for consideration, or at least should not be ignored (Ball et al. 2015); this is particularly relevant for financial entities. Leaving aside the effectiveness, or otherwise, of banks in applying the current accounting rules, it could also be argued that the delayed recognition of losses on bank assets potentially deprives the market of timely information, and reduces the effectiveness of market discipline (Barth and Landsman 2010).

Unlike other sectors, in the banking industry there is a strong demand for unconditional conservatism, mainly coming from bank regulators and supervisors. Focusing on loan impairment rules, Benston and Wall (2005) argue that prudential institutions have an asymmetric loss function. For them, overstated loan values may increase the probability of failure, which would not only affect public opinion regarding their supervisory function, but might even force taxpayers to cover such losses. On the contrary, understated loans impose no such costs. Thus, prudential bodies would prefer loans be valued at the lower end of reasonable estimates.

Empirical evidence on unconditional conservatism is scarce, but some papers, mostly based on the shareholders' perspective, have found that an unconditional bias of unknown magnitude facilitates earnings management (Penman and Zhang 2002), which could be prejudicial for current shareholders. Jackson and Liu (2010)'s conclusions, though referred to unregulated firms, are useful to appreciate how unconditional conservatism in impairments facilitates earnings management. Additionally, to the extent that, as a consequence of the understated loan values, credit to consumers is restricted, regulators could face criticism for policies that restrict economic growth.

From a different perspective, there is some evidence focused on banks, on the potential beneficial impact of large allowances (unconditional conservatism) on lending behaviour (Beatty and

Liao 2011; Jin et al. 2018), and on the lower probability of bank failure (Kanagaretnam et al. 2014). In other words, on procyclicality and financial stability, which are the main concerns of prudential bodies.

In summary, it can be argued that both the accounting theory and the empirical evidence are consistent with a potential positive role of conditional conservatism to restrict the problems arising from the information asymmetry on loan risks. As for unconditional conservatism, there is no evidence on contracting efficiency, although the literature suggests that it increases the scope for earnings management. However, some results suggest that unconditional conservatism could be useful for the banking industry. Thus, from the financial stability perspective, and leaving aside other considerations, both forms of conservatism appear to have useful attributes.

Before concluding this subsection, we want to highlight that the final level of both types of conservatism will be driven by a combination of the required conservatism in the standards and the subjectivity implicit in the standards; Lawrence et al. (2013) refer to these aspects as non-discretionary and discretionary conservatism, respectively. Both conditional and unconditional conservatism are determined endogenously by the regulators' incentives and the firms' accounting discretion. Furthermore, they are unlikely to be independent of the environmental forces that cause regulators to mandate changes in accounting methods (Basu 2005; Sivakumar and Waymire 2003). In our subsequent analysis that refers to loan impairments, we focus exclusively on the conservatism induced by the standard (non-discretionary), and the terms conditional and unconditional conservatism are used in the manner indicated above, so our statements should be interpreted based on these definitions.

4.2.   *Conservatism and the loan impairment models*

Based on the above discussions, it can be argued that a priori the incurred loss model is not unconditionally conservative. It does not allow losses to be recognised before the asset performs and the indicators of underperforming are visible (triggering event); furthermore, the recognition of losses based on estimations of future performance is expressly prohibited.

On the contrary, the new FASB model induces pure unconditional conservatism, as all-life expected losses are recognised on day-1. Such losses are not related with news about the actual performance of the asset, but with estimations about the future, and are recognised before any objective evidence of underperformance. If there was no error in estimating future losses (i.e. under the hypothetical assumption that the losses occur as expected on day-1), this unconditional conservatism prevents subsequent conditional conservatism, since the deterioration of the loan will not be recognised when it happens (it was already recognised on day-1). Any impact on accounting earnings related to loan impairment after initial recognition will be caused by a change in the estimates of future performance, where positive and negative changes are treated equally in the standard. This means that there is no conditional conservatism induced by the standard per se.

The IASB model is partly unconditionally conservative, as day-1 losses are recognised although to a lesser extent than in the FASB model. At the same time, also in relative terms, it is more conditionally conservative than the incurred loss model because it requires a lower degree of verification for recognising bad news about the actual performance of the asset. In other words, to appreciate underperformance, this model considers more indicators than the incurred loss model, as the notion of 'significant deterioration' is less strict than the requirement of a 'triggering event' imposed in IAS 39. Thus, when there is a significant deterioration of credit risk, which shows that the performance of the asset has worsened, losses have to be recognised in the income statement and transferred from the 12-month category (stage 1) to the lifetime category (stage 2), producing a 'cliff' effect.

Example 3 in the Appendix illustrates the major difference between the incurred and the expected loss models in terms of unconditional conservatism, and the interrelation with earnings management, assuming a theoretical case in which all happens according to expectations. Under those circumstances, the uniform FASB solution will not be able to record any loss when it happens, but the IASB deterioration approach can capture the increase in credit risk when it occurs, and even earlier than an incurred model.

As pointed out by Mora and Walker (2015), it is important to keep in mind that the unconditional conservatism embedded in a standard can lead to earnings management only if subsequent reversals are possible. And this is precisely the case of the new expected loss models, since day-1 losses can be reversed. Therefore, unlike the incurred loss model, in these new models, earnings management could be a more relevant issue. In addition, compared to the incurred loss model, both the FASB model and the IASB model offer greater discretion (although the latter to a lesser extent), which a priori might allow more conservative practices beyond those imposed by the standards. That said, relatively little attention has been paid in the empirical literature to the role of accounting standards per se in the level of conservative practices and their relation with earnings management, both in general and in the banking industry in particular. There is some evidence related to the incurred loss model, however.

As mentioned earlier, even when the incurred loss model was required by the US accounting standards, banks still recognised larger impairments than incurred. To avoid the excessive loan loss allowances, the 1993 Federal Depository Insurance Corporation Improvement Act (FDICIA) and the SAB 102 regulation (SEC 2001) were issued. Altamuro and Beatty (2010) and Beck and Narayanamoorthy (2013) find that after their implementation there was a lower level of allowances, less earnings management, and an improvement in reporting quality; in other words, if properly applied, the incurred loss model reduces unconditional conservatism and consequently earnings management.[29]

Evidence on conditional conservatism induced by the incurred loss model is not conclusive. In Europe, Gebhardt and Novotny-Farkas (2011) analyze the introduction of the incurred loss model through IAS 39, and conclude that EU banks (including UK banks) incorporate credit losses in a less timely manner after its adoption, consistent with a reduction in conditional conservatism. On the contrary, O'Hanlon (2013) shows that the less forward-looking approach followed by IAS 39 (with stricter evidence requirements compared with the prior UK model) did not result in less timely loss recognition. Gebhardt and Novotny-Farkas (2011) evidence that the reduction in impairments, and the lower earnings management, was less significant in countries with powerful prudential supervisors. Furthermore, García-Osma et al. (2019) show that this effect is moderated by the supervisors' political independence, since it is independence that constrains opportunistic income smoothing. Bushman and Williams (2012) analyze banks across 27 countries during the 1995–2006 period, in which the incurred loss model was in use; they document that using forward-looking information about loan impairments can have either beneficial or negative consequences, depending on how managers use their discretion. Accordingly, the authors conclude that an expected loss model designed to smooth earnings dampens discipline over risk-taking, consistent with a decrease in transparency. In contrast, when the model tries to reflect timely recognition of future losses, risk-taking discipline is enhanced.

After the implementation of the new standards, it will be possible to analyze if the new expected loss models help to reduce the information asymmetry with lenders and loan buyers. As discussed in subsection 3.1, giving information about loan risks is a key aspect to achieve market discipline, and adopting an unconditional conservative practice (for example recognising day-1 losses) might be a way of doing so. Although, due to the discretionary component, the two standards may facilitate earnings management, it is not easy to anticipate how big this problem will be in practice. In addition, although the problem seems to be greater the more unconditionally conservative the model is – suggesting that the FASB model could be more problematic – it is also true that the longer the period the loan remains under the bank's control, the greater the possibility of earnings management – and a priori this is longer in the EU than in the US. Therefore, knowing the final effect of the combination of different circumstances in different jurisdiction is a matter of empirical analysis.

Given the above, we understand that the FASB model appears more suitable for the originate-to-distribute loans that for those originated to hold. Leaving aside that there will be less time for earnings management, by recognising all-life expected losses on day-1, managers give their private estimations about future performance to loan buyers. On the contrary, the IASB model does not offer as much information on day-1, which could be considered an issue for orig-inate-to-distribute loans, since they might be sold before having signs of underperformance. From the prudential perspective, providing risk information to potential loan buyers through an allowance that covers all life expected losses at origination is likely to be a 'good' solution, as it could increase market discipline. That said, there is opacity about the estimation of such losses, and, depending on how informed the investors are about the quality of the loans they buy, banks could report immediate gains after selling. Hence, in Hashim et al. (2016: 258)'s view 'this may create incentives for lenders to run down loan books to realise accounting gains on under-valued assets'. This could be also considered as an opportunistic earnings manage-ment practice, which is known in the academic literature as 'real earnings management'.

We conclude this section with two comments of the two accounting standards setters, which we believe help to understand the influence of bank regulators in their respective final standards. In the Basis for Conclusions of the US standard, the FASB states 'the interaction between the role of prudential regulators and loss allowances determined for financial reporting purposes is histori-cally stronger in the United States' (FASB 2016, BC 129). In the process of drafting IFRS 9, the IASB criticised the recognition of all-life losses on day-1, due to its inconsistency with the econ-omics of the asset, and noted that this was a preference for some 'interested parties', which we believe refers to prudential regulators (IASB 2013).[30]

5.   Concluding comments and future research

In this study, we discuss the different views that accounting standard setters and prudential reg-ulators have on loan loss models to understand the change in the IASB and FASB standards after the 2008 financial crisis. Both standards have abandoned the incurred approach to adopt an expected loss approach, which, in line with the prudential regulators' preference, considers forward-looking information when recognising loan impairments. Even though the prior incurred loss models were similar, the new solutions are significantly different. Thus, FASB recognises all life expected losses from the origination of loans, but IASB recognises only part of those losses at inception, while the rest is recognised when there is a 'significant deterioration'. We provide explanations for the lack of agreement between the two standard setters. Furthermore, we discuss the potential implications of the FASB and IASB new standards,

We conclude that the changes in the standards are consistent with the objective of reducing the asymmetry problems related with the unique characteristics of banks' assets (basically loans) and their financial structure (mostly deposits). Thus, moral hazard with lenders justifies the change from the incurred to the expected approach, while adverse selection with buyers of securitised loans could explain the position of FASB. We also conclude that the changes in the standards have been induced by bank prudential regulators in order to discipline banks' lending behaviour in the interest of financial stability, being this influence much more significant in the US.

The lack of convergence between IASB and FASB is consistent with the widespread use of the 'originate-to-distribute' business model in the US (since loans are sold shortly after origination), compared with the most common 'originate-to-hold' model in the rest of the world. Under an incurred loss model, banks could sell a loan before recognising any impairment, since this required a specific 'triggering event'. However, this will not happen with either of the two new models, but particularly with the FASB model, since all-life expected losses will be reported from origination. Indeed, by providing information about all expected losses in day 1, the information asymmetry between bank managers and potential loan buyers is reduced. We argue that the role played by this specific adverse selection problem during the crisis, particularly in the US, forced a solution close to that preferred by prudential institutions.

As a consequence of the use of forward-looking information, we expect an increase in conservatism. To understand the implications of conservative practices, it is important to distinguish between two types of conservatism, conditional and unconditional. On the one hand, in contrast to the incurred loss model, the two new expected loss models are unconditionally conservative, since both require the recognition of losses at the inception of loans (day 1 losses), but the FASB solution is even more so. To the extent that impairment losses can be reversed, earnings management becomes an issue, and the longer the loan investments remains in the bank's balance sheet, the larger the problem. And, on the other hand, only the IASB model is conditionally conservative, and more so than the incurred loss model, since its deterioration approach widens the indicators of impairment. Thus, by imposing less conditions to admit there has been an increase in loan impairments, losses will be recognised earlier.

As discussed throughout this paper, it is widely documented for non-financial entities that conditional conservatism has, on balance, a beneficial net effect on both market and contracting efficiency (e.g. Ball et al. 2015). On the contrary, unconditional conservatism facilitates earnings management (e.g. Jackson and Liu 2010), unless reversals through accruals are not allowed, which is not the case in the new standards. This could undermine the quality of accounting information, and thereby reduce its contracting efficiency.

We acknowledge that, in the banking industry, an unconditionally conservative policy is a way to transfer loan-risk information. It reduces information asymmetry problems with specific stakeholders (lenders and buyers of securitised loans). However, it is also true that accounting earnings are not the only way to provide information about future losses; and from the capital market users' perspective, the recognition of future losses based on managers' estimations can negatively affect transparency if it facilitates earnings management. We admit that the hidden reserves created through unconditionally conservative practices can contribute to bank stability during recessions, avoiding or delaying bank failures. But, this would only be the case if these unconditionally conservative accounting practices were actually leading to more prudent investment, financing, and dividend-paying policies.

Before concluding, we identify some fruitful areas for future research regarding both conservatism and earnings management in the banking industry. The two new expected loss models are more conservative than the incurred loss model in a non-discretionary way (induced by the standards). But also the use of forward-looking information increases managers' discretion, and consequently the possibility of being more conservative in practice (this is in a discretionary way). This increases the opportunities of obtaining additional empirical evidence on how the banks' accounting numbers in terms of (un)conditional conservatism shift, as well as the relationship between the level of conservatism and the institutional and entity characteristics.

Also, this scenario, in which unconditional conservatism (day 1 losses) is required, provides new opportunities for earnings management research. A priori, earnings management is more likely under the FASB than under the IASB standard. However, the originate-to-distribute business model is more common in the US than in the EU, which to a certain extent reduces the problem (loans will stay during a much shorter period in the balance sheet). Consequently, it is an empirical question under which jurisdiction, and under which model, earnings management is more of a serious issue.

Despite, as it has been argued, the divergence between the FASB and the IASB impairment models might be related to the bank business models that prevail in their jurisdictions, neither of the two standard setters has considered the possibility of two different impairment models, depending on the management intent (to securitise or not the loans after origination). Consequently, this is a unique scenario to research the impact of the new models, since for the same business model (whether originate-to-hold or originate-to-distribute), banks will employ a different impairment model depending on the jurisdiction in which they are established.

Regarding the consequences of the new FASB and IASB models, it is also expected that their implementation will cause a major change in the way banks approach and manage credit risk. The recognition of losses earlier than with the incurred loss model will impose a different discipline on lending. This could affect not only loan pricing but also other conditions of the debt contracts, especially covenants. The relation between such covenants and accounting conservatism (both conditional and unconditional) has been mainly analysed in the literature from the perspective of the borrowers, and not from the one of lenders. The new expected loss models, with a priori higher level of conservatism in the financial statements of the lenders could have an impact in the design and monitoring of the covenants. The earlier recognition of losses on investments in the banks' financial statements could affect the abandonment policy; this could facilitate more efficient risk management, but could also promote early abandonment, and, therefore, restrict investments in potentially efficient projects.

Furthermore, it is frequent that banks rely on loan syndications as a means to diversify their risk. The estimation of day-1 losses that both the IASB and the FASB model require, and the discretion implicit in the significant deterioration notion introduced by the IASB, generate opportunities for research on how they influence risk sharing, as well as on the different levels of conservative practices in the members of the syndicate. To the extent that they may differ, it will be more difficult for lenders to agree to the establishment of covenants and subsequent renegotiations with the borrower. Given that these aspects are related to syndicate size (Saavedra 2018), it is an empirical question to find out if the new loan impairment model affects syndicate size and the design of covenants.

Another avenue of research to pursue is the study of the impact that the new FASB and IASB models have on the financial system in terms of procyclicality. It is important to bear in mind that the main motivation to change from an incurred loss model to the new expected loss models was that the former had negative effects on financial stability. At least, this was the complaint from financial regulators and supervisors (FSF 2009), who blamed incurred loss models of contributing to unstable markets. Therefore, it is relevant to study whether the new models have a positive impact on financial stability by reducing procyclicality, without harming transparency. There is some tentative research in this area that, based on simulation, concludes that the effectiveness of the new standards will depend not only on how banks implement them, but on the contribution or interference of central banks, supervisors, and other stakeholders (Cohen and Edwards 2017).

Finally, another additional topic that researchers could pursue derives from the current situation in which governments have become important debtholders. In fact, as a consequence of the financial crisis, some banks have received governmental resources. Therefore, governments should be seen as new stakeholders, whose particular interests could affect accounting practices. The influence of this governmental intervention to reduce moral hazard through accounting practices constitutes, in our view, a promising area for further research.

Funding

This work was supported by Spanish Ministry of Economy and Competitiveness: [Grant Number ECO2013-48208-P].

Notes

1. According to Papa and Peters (2014), the mean (median) carrying value of bank loans worldwide was 48% (52%) of total assets during the period 2004 to 2013.
2. Despite regulators and supervisors perform different roles, making the rules and ensuring their application respectively, they share the same interests regarding accounting information on loan risks. Hence, in this paper, we refer to both of them as prudential institutions or prudential bodies.
3. The FCAG was established in 2008 by the IASB and the FASB to advise the two Boards about standard-setting implications of the global financial crisis and potential changes to the global regulatory environment.
4. It is common in the literature to use some accounting and prudential terms such as provisions and allowances as synonymous, although they are not. Here, we employ the terms based on those used in the present accounting standards and prudential rules. 'Impairment' is defined as the loss recognized in the income statement in the reporting period; 'allowance' is the accumulated impairment that appears in the balance sheet at the end of the reporting period. The term 'provision' is used in the prudential bank regulation, and refers to the portion of the loan which may not be recovered according to the prudential regulation parameters. From a contemporary accounting perspective, the term 'provision' refers to a type of liability, although this has not been always the case. Furthermore, in accounting parlance it is still common to use 'loan loss provision' to refer to 'loan loss allowance'.
5. Thus, for example, IAS 36 requires recording an impairment when the carrying amount of an asset is higher than its fair value and value in use, which implies estimating the present value of expected future cash flows. The recoverable amount is the largest of both figures.
6. The literature confirms income smoothing using loan losses during the 1980s and 1990s in the US (Wahlen 1994, Collins et al. 1995, Lobo and Yang 2001, Beatty et al. 2002, Gunther and Moore 2003, Kanagaretnam et al. 2003, 2004). Shrieves and Dahl (2003) show how Japanese banks used loan loss allowances to smooth reported income. Hassan and Wall (2003) and Bikker and Metzemakers (2005) also find such behavior in cross-country comparisons; the latter finds that entities create larger allowances in good times when earnings are large, suggesting income smoothing. This countercyclical behavior is in line with the prudential view that we discuss in the next subsection.
7. In 1998, SunTrust Banks made a cumulative reduction of about $100 million of the loan loss allowance corresponding to the years 1994 through 1996 following an inquiry by the US SEC. As Wall and Koch (2000) argue, this incident illustrates the conflict between bank regulators and the US SEC at that time.
8. A good illustration of this debate can be seen in Dugan (2009), a prudential supervisor who argued for larger provisions charged in the income statement during good times. He complained about managers and auditors for not doing so due to the accounting standards in place at that time (the incurred loss model).
9. When the expected probability of default is low in the first years but increases substantially over time (which appears highly probable), the loan or portfolio would appear very profitable in the early years while reflecting large losses in later periods. Considering that when pricing loans, managers take into account the expected losses, the contractual interest rate of low-quality loans could be even higher than the normal or expected rate, leading to the counter intuitive result that 'lower quality loans' would lead to higher earnings in the first years. Although it could be argued that the effect is nonmaterial if the portfolio is stable over time, this might not always be the case, as for example in periods of growth.
10. The Basis for Conclusions of the Conceptual Framework (IASB 2018b: para BC1 23 to para BC1-26) summarize the conflicting views about whether or not to include financial stability as an additional objective, as well as the final decision not to do so. 'The Board also noted that providing financial information that is relevant and faithfully represents what it purports to represent can improve users' confidence in the information, and thus contribute to promoting financial stability' (para BC1-26).
11. We recognize that some stakeholders would prefer that accounting standards were closer to the type of objectives embodied in prudential regulation. In this line of argument, Maystadt (2013, p. 9) suggested that the EC should add a new criterion to decide on the endorsement of IFRS, 'the accounting standards adopted should not endanger financial stability'.

12. For an exhaustive analysis of the whole process leading to the new standards, see Hashim et al. (2016).
13. Under this approach the allowance is gradually formed from the difference between the adjusted interest rate and the contractual interest rate.
14. Although at this stage the draft excluded forecasts of losses based on future conditions, they were included afterwards.
15. The comment letters of the Basel Committee to the subsequent documents issued by the two standard setters – PASU (FASB 2012) and ED 2013/3 (IASB 2013) – are very useful to understand the regulators' view:

> As supervisors, we attach the utmost importance to the adequacy of the balance sheet allowance for credit losses … Impairment recognition and measurement should be based on sound methodologies that reflect expected credit losses over the remaining life of a bank's existing portfolios at the reporting date; The new standard should require earlier provisioning than under the incurred loss approach.

> Available at: http://www.ifrs.org/Current-Projects/IASB-Projects/Financial-Instruments-A-Replacement-of-IAS-39-Financial-Instruments-Recognitio/Impairment/Exposure-Draft-March-2013/Comment-letters/Pages/Comment-letters.aspx (accessed 04.03.17).

16. Mr Schroeder, FASB Vice-Chairman, and Board member Mr Smith voted against the final US standard due to the day-1 loss requirement. They employed similar arguments to those used by Mr Cooper, IASB member, who voted against the earlier ED/2013/3 (IASB 2013), as explained in footnote 22.
17. The expression '12-month expected credit losses' is defined in IFRS 9 Appendix A (IASB 2014) as a portion of life time expected losses that result from default events that are possible within 12 months, weighted by the probability of that default occurring. It is exemplified within the Implementation Guidance of IFRS 9.
18. The 'significant deterioration' requirement does not necessarily mean 'objective evidence of impairment' as required in IAS 39. 'If reasonable and supportable forward-looking information is available without undue cost or effort, an entity cannot rely solely on past due information when determining whether credit risk has increased significantly since initial recognition' (IASB 2014: 5.5.11). In other words, IFRS 9 eliminates the threshold, this is the 'triggering event', included in IAS 39.
19. To calculate the interest, a distinction is made between those loans with significant deterioration (stage 2) and those clearly impaired (stage 3); for the first type, the gross value is used, while for the second one, the net value is used. Consequently, this model is also known as the '3-bucket approach'.
20. The Staff Paper prepared for the IASB meeting where the comment letters to ED/2013/3 were analyzed provides the following comments about lifetime expected credit losses (ECL):

> Most respondents consider a lifetime ECL model to totally disregard the economic link between the pricing of a financial instrument and its credit quality, thereby diminishing the relevance of financial reporting. The majority of users of financial statements stated that it is important to maintain the economic link between pricing and credit quality at initial recognition. They are concerned that the FASB model distorts this economic link by exacerbating the double-counting of expected credit losses incorporated in the pricing of financial instruments compared to the IASB model (IFRS Foundation 2013, para 20).

21. The standard does not impose using a discounted cash flow method to estimate expected credit losses (FASB 2016: 326–20–30–3). Therefore, if time value of money is not considered, or if the contractual interest is used, the longer the asset life, the larger the undervaluation will be.
22. In his alternative view expressed in ED/2013/3, IASB member, Mr Cooper – who was in favour of the economic approach in ED/2009/12 (IASB 2009) – states the following:

> The problem with a lifetime expected loss being equal to the present value of contractual cash flows that are not expected to be collected is that the calculation is incomplete … the expected credit losses must be offset at the date of origination or purchase by the expected additional interest revenue (through part of the credit spread) (IASB 2013: AV10, 144).

23. Details on securitization accounting can be seen in Deloitte (2014).
24. According to the European Central Bank (2008), this loan market remained smaller in Europe than in the US, and was relatively more focused on collateralized debt obligations (CDO). Before the crisis, the total issuance volume in the US was five times higher than in Europe; in particular, 50% of US mortgages were funded via securitization in 2007 compared with 13% in Europe.

25. The 2016 working document of the Committee on Economic and Monetary Affairs of the European Parliament (Rapporteur: Paul Tang) provides an analysis of the securitization in the EU compared with the US. It states that in 2014 the volume of securitization in the EU was 74% lower than in 2008, in which it had a maximum € 819 billion; in contrast, the US market that in 2008 was at its minimum level of € 916 billion, in 2014 was five times larger than the EU market (Tang 2016).
26. Although credit rating agencies could have contributed to solve the asymmetry problem, they did not. Thus, instead of controlling these practices, US credit rating agencies gave triple-A ratings; ratings in Europe did not turn out to be quite as wrong as in the US (Tang 2016).
27. The reintroduction of prudence is justified in the Basis for Conclusions of ED/2015/3 as a mechanism to 'help preparers, auditors and regulators to counter a natural bias that management may have towards optimism' (IASB 2015: BC2.9), which we consider implies admitting that it is a means to address the problem of moral hazard in the preparation of the financial statements. However, in the opinion of Barker and McGeachin (2015) something else is missing in the framework that helps to link it with the multiple examples of conservatism in the standards.
28. However, as the reviewer has pointed out, if the definition of news were expanded to include information (expectations) on future performance, the value of the assets would be lower, and from this angle a broader notion of conditional conservatism could be established.
29. However, in the discussion on Beck and Narayanamoorthy (2013), Ryan and Keeley (2013) argue that other factors influenced the results, such as the favorable economic conditions in the post-SAB 102/ pre-financial crisis period.
30. Thus, the Basis for Conclusions of ED/2013/3 state

> The IASB is aware that some interested parties favour a lifetime expected credit loss approach, … Under such an approach, the recognition of initial lifetime expected credit losses is triggered by the initial recognition of a financial asset rather than by the deterioration in credit quality since initial recognition. The IASB does not believe that this is appropriate because it would result in financial assets being recognized at a carrying amount significantly below fair value on initial recognition and would therefore be inconsistent with the economics of the asset. (IASB 2013: BC172, 133)

> Furthermore, in his dissenting view, Mr Cooper sustains 'a 12 month period is without conceptual foundation and that the recognition of this loss allowance would result in financial reporting that fails to reflect the economics of lending activities' (IASB 2013: AV1, 142).

Disclosure statement

No potential conflict of interest was reported by the authors.

References

Acharya, V.V. and Ryan, S.G., 2016. Banks' financial reporting and financial system stability. *Journal of Accounting Research*, 54 (2), 277–340.
Akerlof, G.A., 1970. The market for "lemons": quality uncertainty and the market mechanism. *The Quarterly Journal of Economics*, 84 (3), 488–500.
Altamuro, J. and Beatty, A., 2010. How does internal control regulation affect financial reporting?. *Journal of Accounting and Economics*, 49, 58–74.
Ayadi, R., Arback, E., and Groen, W.P., 2011. *Business models in European banking, A pre and post crisis screening*, Centre of European Policy Studies, Brussels.
Ball, R., Li, X., and Shivakumar, L., 2015. Contractibility and transparency of financial statement information prepared under IFRS: evidence from debt contracts around IFRS adoption. *Journal of Accounting and Economics*, 53 (5), 915–963.
Ball, R. and Shivakumar, L., 2005. Earnings quality in UK private firms: comparative loss recognition timeliness. *Journal of Accounting and Economics*, 39, 83–128.
Barker, R. and McGeachin, A., 2015. An analysis of concepts and evidence on the question of whether IFRS should be conservative. *Abacus*, 51 (2), 169–207.
Barth, M.E. and Landsman, W.E., 2010. How did financial reporting contribute to the financial crisis? *European Accounting Review*, 19 (3), 399–423.

Basu, S., 2005. Discussion of 'conditional and unconditional conservatism: concepts and modelling'. *Review of Accounting Studies*, 10 (2/3), 311–321.

Beatty, A.L., Ke, B., and Petroni, R.K., 2002. Earnings management to avoid earnings declines across publicly and privately held banks. *The Accounting Review*, 77 (3), 547–570.

Beatty, A. and Liao, S., 2011. Do delays in expected loss recognition affect banks' willingness to lend? *Journal of Accounting and Economics*, 52 (1), 1–20.

Beatty A. and Liao, S., 2014. Financial accounting in the banking industry: a review of the empirical literature. *Journal of Accounting and Economics*, 58, 339–383.

Beaver, W.H. and Ryan, S.G., 2005. Conditional and unconditional conservatism: concepts and modeling. *Review of Accounting Studies*, 10, 269–309.

Beck, P. and Narayanamoorthy, G., 2013. Did the SEC impact banks' loan loss reserve policies and their informativeness? *Journal of Accounting and Economics*, 56, 42–65.

Belkhir, M., 2013. Do subordinated debt holders discipline bank risk-taking? Evidence from risk management decisions. *Journal of Financial Stability*, 9, 705–719.

Benston G. and Wall, G., 2005. How should banks account for loan losses? *Federal Reserve Bank of Atlanta Economic Review* 90 (4), 19–38.

Berndt A. and Gupta, A., 2009. Moral hazard and adverse selection in the originate-to-distribute model of bank credit. *Journal of Monetary Economics*, 56 (5), 725–743.

Beyer, A., Cohen, D.A., Lys, T.Z., and Walther, B.R., 2010. The financial reporting environment: review of the recent literature. *Journal of Accounting and Economics*, 50, 296–343.

Bikker, J.A. and Metzemakers, P.A.J., 2005. Bank provisioning behavior and procyclicality. *Journal of International Financial Markets, Institutions and Money*, 15, 141–157.

Blum, J.M., 2002. Subordinated debt, market discipline, and banks' risk taking. *Journal of Banking and Finance*, 26 (7), 1427–1441.

Bord, V. and Santos, J., 2012. *The rise of the originate-to-distribute model and the role of banks in financial intermediation*, FRBNY Economic Policy Review, July.

Bouvatier, V. and Lepetit, L., 2008. Banks' procyclical behavior: does provisioning matter? *Journal of International Financial Markets, Institutions and Money*, 18 (5), 513–526.

Bushman, R.M. and Williams, C.D., 2012. Accounting discretion, loan loss provisioning, and discipline of banks' risk-taking. *Journal of Accounting and Economics*, 54, 1–18.

Callen, J.L., Dou, Y., Xin, B., and Chen, F., 2016. Accounting conservatism and performance covenants: a signaling approach. *Contemporary Accounting Research*, 33 (3), 961–988.

Camfferman, K., 2015. The emergence of the 'incurred-loss' model for credit losses in IAS 39. *Accounting in Europe*, 12 (1), 1–35.

Christensen, H., Nikolaev, V., and Wittenberg-Moerman, R., 2016. Accounting information in financial contracting: the Incomplete contract theory perspective. *Journal of Accounting Research*, 54 (2), 397–435.

Cohen, L.J., Cornett, M.M., Marcus, A.J., and Tehranian, H., 2014. Bank earnings management and tail risk during the financial crisis. *Journal of Money, Credit and Banking*, 46 (1), 171–197.

Cohen, B.H. and Edwards, G.A., 2017. The new era of expected credit loss provisioning. *BIS Quarterly Review*, March, 39–56.

Collins, J.H., Shackelford, D.A., and Wahlen, J.M., 1995. Bank differences in the coordination of regulatory capital, earnings, and taxes. *Journal of Accounting Research*, 33 (2), 263–291.

Cordella, T. and Yeyati, E.L., 2003. Bank bailouts: moral hazard vs. value effect. *Journal of Financial Intermediation*, 12, 300–330.

Dam, L. and Koetter, M., 2012. Bank bailouts and moral hazard: evidence from Germany. *Review of Financial Studies*, 25 (8), 2343–2380.

Deloitte, 2014. Securitization accounting 9th edition, January. Available from: https://www2.deloitte.com/content/dam/Deloitte/lu/Documents/financial-services/us-aers-securitization-accounting-011914-final.pdf.

Diamond, D.W., 1984. Financial intermediation and delegated monitoring, *Review of Economic Studies*, 51 (3), 393–414.

Dugan, J.C., 2009. *Loan loss provisioning and pro-cyclicality, remarks before the Institute of International Bankers*. March 2nd. Available from: https://www.occ.gov/news-issuances/speeches/2009/pub-speech-2009-16.pdf [Accessed 4 March 2017].

European Central Bank, 2008. *The incentive structure of the 'originate and distribute' model*. December. Available from: https://www.ecb.europa.eu/pub/pdf/other/incentivestructureoriginatedistributemodel200812en.pdf?ed4e24fdaf559694a836c7f5f1128a5c [Accessed 4 March 2017].

European Financial Reporting Advisory Group (EFRAG). 2009. Impairment of Financial Assets: The expected loss model. December. Available from: https://www.accountancyeurope.eu/wp-content/uploads/EFRAG_FEE_Paper_Impairment_of_Financial_Assets_-_The_Expected_Loss_Model_09129122009231030.pdf [Accessed 30 December 2018].

Evanoff, D., Jagtiani, J., and Nakata, T., 2011. Enhancing market discipline in banking: the role of subordinated debt in financial regulatory reform, *Journal of Economics and Business*, 63 (1), 1–22.

Federation of European Accountants-European Financial Reporting Advisory Group (FEE-EFRAG). 2009. *Impairment of financial assets. The expected loss model, December*. Available from: http://www.efrag.org/Assets/Download?assetUrl=%2Fsites%2Fwebpublishing%2FSiteAssets%2FEFRAG_FEE_Paper-The_Expected_Loss_Model_Final%2520-%2520web.pdf [Accessed 4 March 2017].

Financial Accounting Standards Board (FASB), 1980. *Statement of Financial Accounting Concept (SFAC) 2. Qualitative characteristics of accounting information*. FASB. Norwalk, CT.

Financial Accounting Standards Board (FASB), 2010. *Accounting for Financial Instruments and Revisions to the Accounting for Derivative Instruments and Hedging Activities*. FASB. Norwalk, CT.

Financial Accounting Standards Board (FASB), 2011. *Supplementary Document. Financial Instruments – Impairment*. FASB. Norwalk, CT.

Financial Accounting Standards Board (FASB), 2012. *Proposed Accounting Standards Update. Financial Instruments – Credit Losses* (Subtopic 825–15). FASB. Norwalk, CT.

Financial Accounting Standards Board (FASB), 2016. *Financial Instruments—Credit Losses (Topic 326). Accounting Standards Update*. No. 2016–13. June. FASB. Norwalk, CT.

Financial Advisory Crisis Advisory Group (FCAG), 2009. *Report of the Financial Crisis Advisory Group*. July. Available from: http://www.ifrs.org/Features/Documents/FCAGReportJuly2009.pdf [Accessed 4 March 2017].

Financial Stability Forum (FSF), 2009. *Report of the Financial Stability Forum on Addressing Procyclicality in the Financial System*. Available from: http://www.fsb.org/wp-content/uploads/r_0904a.pdf [Accessed 4 March 2017].

G20 Leaders, 2009. *London Summit – Leaders' Statement*. April 2nd. Available from: https://www.imf.org/external/np/sec/pr/2009/pdf/g20_040209.pdf [Accessed 4 March 2017].

García Lara, J.M. and Mora, A., 2004. Balance sheet versus earnings conservatism in Europe. *European Accounting Review*, 13 (2), 261–292.

García Osma, B., Mora, A. and Porcuna-Enguix, L. 2019. Prudential supervisors´ independence and income smoothing in European banks. *Journal of Banking and Finance*, 102, 156–176.

Gebhardt, G. and Novotny-Farkas, Z., 2011. Mandatory IFRS adoption and accounting quality of European Banks. *Journal of Business Finance and Accounting*, 38 (3-4), 289–333.

Gorton, G. and Huang, L., 2004. Liquidity, efficiency, and bank bailouts. *American Economic Review*, 94, 455–483.

Gray, L.P. and Clarke, F.L., 2004. A methodology for calculating the allowance for loan losses in commercial banks. *Abacus*, 40 (3), 321–341.

Gunther, J.W. and Moore, R.R., 2003. Loss underreporting and the auditing role of bank exams. *Journal of Financial Intermediation*, 12, 153–177.

Hashim, N., Li, W., and O'Hanlon, J., 2016. Expected-loss-based accounting for impairment of financial instruments: the FASB and IASB Proposals 2009–2016. *Accounting in Europe*, 13 (2), 229–267.

Hassan, I. and Wall, L.D., 2003. *Determinants of the Loan Loss Allowance: Some Cross-Country Comparisons*. Bank of Finland Discussion Papers, 33.

Hellmann, T.F., Murdock, K.C. and Stiglitz, J.E., 2000. Liberalization, moral hazard in banking and prudential regulation: are capital requirements enough? *American Economic Review*, 90 (1), 147–165.

Holmström, B. and Tirole, J., 1993. Market liquidity and performance monitoring. *Journal of Political Economy*, 101 (4), 678–709.

Hoogervorst, H., 2012. *What and What Not to Expect of the Expected Loss Model*, 3rd ECB Conference on Accounting, Frankfurt, 4 June. Available from: http://www.ifrs.org/Alerts/Conference/Documents/ECB462012.pdf [Accessed 4 March 2017].

International Accounting Standards Board (IASB), 2009. *Exposure Draft ED/2009/12: Financial Instruments – Amortised Cost and Impairment*. IASB. London.

International Accounting Standards Board (IASB), 2011. *Supplement to Exposure Draft ED/2009/12 Financial Instruments – Amortised Cost and Impairment*. IASB, London.

International Accounting Standards Board (IASB), 2013. *Exposure Draft ED/2013/3 Financial Instruments – Expected Credit Losses*, IASB. London.

International Accounting Standards Board (IASB), 2014. *IFRS 9: Financial Instruments*. IASB. London.

International Accounting Standards Board (IASB), 2015. *Exposure Draft ED/2015/3 Conceptual Framework for Financial Reporting. Basis for Conclusions*. IASB. London.

International Accounting Standards Board (IASB), 2018a. *Conceptual Framework for Financial Reporting*. IASB. London.

International Accounting Standards Board (IASB), 2018b. *Conceptual Framework for Financial Reporting. Basis for Conclusions*. IASB. London.

International Accounting Standards Committee (IASC), 1989. *Framework for the Preparation of Financial Statements*. IASC. London.

International Financial Reporting Standard (IFRS) Foundation, 2013. *Staff Paper on Financial Instruments: Impairment*. Available from: http://www.ifrs.org/Meetings/MeetingDocs/IASB/2013/July/05C-Impairment.pdf [Accessed 4 March 2017].

International Financial Reporting Standards (IFRS) Foundation, 2015. *Working in the Public Interest: The IFRS Foundation and the IASB*. Available from: https://www.ifrs.org/about-us/the-public-interest/ [Accessed 30 December 2018].

Jackson, S. and Liu, X., 2010. The allowance for uncollectible accounts, conservatism, and earnings management. *Journal of Accounting Research*, 48 (3), 565–601.

Jensen, M.C. and Meckling, W.H., 1976. Theory of the firm: managerial behavior, agency costs and ownership structure. *Journal of Financial Economics*, 3 (4), 305–360.

Jin, J., Kanagaretnam, K., and Lobo, G.J., 2018. Discretion in bank loan loss allowance, risk taking and earnings management. *Accounting & Finance*, 58, 171–193.

Kanagaretnam, K, Justin, J., and Lobo, G.J., 2014. *Bank Accounting Conservatism, Risk Taking and Earnings Management*. Working Paper. EAA congress. Tallin.

Kanagaretnam, K., Lobo, G.J., and Mathieu, R., 2003. Managerial incentives for income smoothing through bank loan loss provisions. *Review of Quantitative Finance and Accounting*, 20 (1), 63–80.

Kanagaretnam, K., Lobo, G.J., and Yang, D.H., 2004. Joint tests of signaling and income smoothing through bank loan loss provisions. *Contemporary Accounting Research*, 21 (4), 843–884.

King, R.G. and Levine, R., 1993. Finance and growth: Schumpeter might be right. *The Quarterly Journal of Economics*, 108 (3), 717–737.

Laeven, L. and Majnoni, G., 2003. Loan loss provisioning and economic slowdowns: too much too late? *Journal of Financial Intermediation*, 12 (2), 178–197.

Lambert, R., 2010. Discussion on implications for GAAP from an analysis of positive research in accounting. *Journal of Accounting and Economics*, 50, 287–295.

Laux, C., 2012. Financial instruments, financial reporting, and financial stability. *Accounting and Business Research*, 42 (3), 239–260.

Lawrence, A., Sloan, R., and Sun, Y., 2013. Non-discretionary conservatism: evidence and implications. *Journal of Accounting and Economics*, 56, 112–133.

Levitt, A. 1998. *The 'Numbers Game,'* September 28. Speech delivered at New York University Center for Law and Business. Available from: https://www.sec.gov/news/speech/speecharchive/1998/spch220.txt [Accessed 4 March 2017].

Lim, C.Y., Lee, E., Kausar, A., and Walker, M., 2014. Bank accounting conservatism and bank loan pricing. *Journal of Accounting and Public Policy*, 33, 260–278.

Lobo, G.J. and Yang, D.H., 2001. Bank managers' heterogeneous decisions on discretionary loan loss provisions. *Review of Quantitative Finance and Accounting*, 16: 223–250.

Maystadt, P. 2013. *Should IFRS Standards be more European*. European Commission.

Mishkin, F.S., 2006. How big a problem is too big to fail? A review of Gary Stern and Ron Feldman's *too big to fail: The Hazards of bank Bailouts. Journal of Economic Literature*, 44 (4), 988–1004.

Mora A. and Walker, M., 2015. The implications of research on accounting conservatism for accounting standard setting. *Accounting and Business Research*, 45 (5), 620–650.

Morris, D., Kang, H., and Jie, J., 2016. The determinants and value relevance of banks' discretionary loan loss provisions during the financial crisis. *Journal of Contemporary Accounting & Economics*, 12 (2), 176–190.

Nichols, D., Wahlen, J., and Wieland, M., 2009. Publicly traded versus privately held: implications for conditional conservatism in bank accounting. *Review of Accounting Studies*, 14, 88–122.

Nier, E. and Baumann, U., 2006. Market discipline, disclosure and moral hazard in banking. *Journal of Financial Intermediation*, 15, 332–361.

Novotny-Farkas, Z., 2016. The interaction of the IFRS 9 expected loss approach with supervisory rules and implications for financial stability. *Accounting in Europe*, 13 (2), 197–227.

O'Hanlon, J., 2013. Did loan-loss provisioning by UK banks become less timely after implementation of IAS 39? *Accounting and Business Research*, 43 (3), 225–258.

O'Hanlon, J., Hashim, N., and Li, W., 2017. *Research Briefing: Issues Arising in the Development of the FASB's and IASB's Expected-Loss Methods of Accounting for Credit Losses*. Institute of Chartered Accountants of England and Wales.

Papa, V. and Peters, S., 2014. *Financial Crisis Insights on Bank Performance Reporting (Part 1). Assessing the key Factors Influencing Price-to-Book Ratios*, CFA Institute, July. Available from: http://www.cfainstitute.org/learning/products/publications/ccb/Pages/ccb.v2014.n3.1.aspx [Accessed 4 March 2017].

Penman, S. and Zhang, X., 2002. Accounting conservatism, the quality of earnings and stock returns. *The Accounting Review*, 77 (2), 237–264.

Pérez, D., Salas-Fumás, V., and Saurina, J., 2008. Earnings and capital management in alternative loan loss provision regulatory regimes. *European Accounting Review*, 17 (3), 423–445.

Pope, P. and Walker, M., 2003. *Ex-ante and Ex-Post Accounting Conservatism, Asset Recognition and Asymmetric Earnings Timeliness*. Working Paper, Lancaster University and University of Manchester.

Poveda, R., 2000. La reforma del sistema de provisiones de insolvencia. *Boletín económico del Banco de España*, January, 79–92.

Purnanandam, A., 2011. Originate-to-distribute model and the subprime mortgage crisis. *Review of Financial Studies*, 24 (6), 1881–1915.

Rixtel A., Romo González, L., and Yang, J., 2015. *The Determinants of Long-Term Debt Issuance by European Banks: Evidence of Two Crisis*. BIS Working Papers No 513, September.

Ross, S.A., 1973. The economic theory of agency: the principal's problem. *American Economic Review*, 63 (2), 134–139.

Ryan, S.G. and Keeley, J.H., 2013. Discussion of 'Did the SEC impact banks' loan loss reserve policies and their informativeness?' *Journal of Accounting and Economics*, 56, 66–78.

Saavedra, D., 2018. Syndicate size and the choice of covenants in debt contracts. *The Accounting Review*, 93 (6), 301–329.

Securities and Exchange Commission (SEC), 2001. Staff Accounting Bulletin 102: No.102 Selected Loan Loss Allowance Methodology and Documentation Issues. July.

Shrieves, R.E. and Dahl, D., 2003. Discretionary accounting and the behavior of Japanese banks under financial duress. *Journal of Banking & Finance*, 27, 1219–1243.

Sivakumar, K. and Waymire, G., 2003. Enforceable accounting rules and income measurement by early 20th century railroads. *Journal of Accounting Research*, 41, 397–432.

Sundaresan, S.M. and Wang, Z., 2016. *Bank Liability Structure*. Kelley School of Business Research Paper no. 14–41, March 24.

Sutton, M., 1997. *Current Developments in Financial Reporting: Perspectives from the SEC*. Remarks to the AICPAs 1997 National Conference on Banks and Saving Institutions, Washington DC. Available from: https://www.sec.gov/news/speech/speecharchive/1997/spch195.txt [Accessed 4 March 2017].

Tang, P. (Rapporteur), 2016. *Working Document on Common Rules on Securitisation and Creating a European Framework for Simple, Transparent and Standardised Securitisation*. Committee on Economic and Monetary Affairs, European Parliament, 15th May. Available from: http://www.europarl.europa.eu/sides/getDoc.do?type = COMPARL&reference = PE-580.483&format = PDF&language = EN&secondRef = 01 [Accessed 18 January 2018].

Trombetta, M., Wagenhofer, A., and Wysocki, P., 2012. The usefulness of academic research in understanding the effects of accounting standards. *Accounting in Europe*, 9 (2), 127–146.

Vyas, D., 2011. The timeliness of accounting write downs by US financial institutions during the financial crisis of 2007–2008. *Journal of Accounting Research*, 49, 823–860.

Wahlen, J.M., 1994. The nature of information in commercial bank loan Lloss disclosures. *The Accounting Review*, 69 (3), 455–478.

Wall, L. and Koch, T., 2000. Bank loan-loss accounting: a review of theoretical and empirical evidence. *Economic Review*, 2, 1–19.

Watts, R.L., 2003. Conservatism in accounting part I: explanations and implications. *Accounting Horizons*, 17 (3), 207–221.

Zeff, S.A., 2012. The evolution of the IASC into the IASB, and the challenges it faces. *The Accounting Review*, 87 (3), 807–837.

Appendix

Example 1

Let's consider a loan portfolio of CU 1,000, originated at the beginning of period 1, to be returned entirely at the end of period 3, with a charged interest of 8% to be paid at the end of each period. The bank manager estimates that CU 160 (expected loss) will be unpaid at the end of period 3. Given the assumption that the expected loss can take place in the 3rd year only, total expected cash flows will be CU 80 at the end of periods 1 and 2, and CU 920 (1,000 + 80–160) at the end of period 3. The adjusted effective interest rate considering those expected cash flows would be 2.8%.

According to the economic approach (IASB 2009), the bank will recognise revenue of CU 28 in the income statement in each period. If the incurred loss model were used, revenue would have been larger in periods 1 and 2, CU 80, while in period 3 a loss of CU 80 (+80–160) would have been recognised. Under the economic approach, at origination the present value of future cash flows (including expected losses) discounted at the adjusted effective rate of interest is CU 1,000 (the so-called 'economic value'). Thus, using any amount lower than that, entails an undervaluation of the loan portfolio.

Given that the expected loss will take place in the 3rd year, the IASB model does not allow to record any loss at origination. However, following the FASB approach, the loan value at origination would be CU 840, which is lower than the economic value: CU 1000.

Example 2

Let's assume the bank originates a 2-year loan portfolio at the end of the first reporting period (period 1), which requires the repayment of the outstanding contractual amount in full at maturity (for the sake of simplicity time value of money is ignored). Its contractual par amount is CU 1,000. The bank estimates that the probability of default is 20% (no matter when it happens), and, in that case, the non-recoverable amount is on average 80% of the contractual value. In addition, the probability that the default happens in the first year is 30%.

Following the FASB model, all life expected losses at origination, which are CU 160 ($0.20 \times 0.80 \times 1,000$), should be immediately recognised, and the carrying amount of the loan portfolio at the end of period 1 will be CU 840 (contractual value CU 1,000 minus allowance CU 160). Therefore, an impairment of CU 160 will be recognised in the income statement for the first reporting period (day-1 loss). If everything happens as expected, and the CU 160 loss does occur in period 3, the carrying amount of the loan will be the same (CU 840) at the end of period 2, and will be recovered at the end of period 3. There will be no impact on the income statement in periods 2 and 3.

According to the IASB model, at the end of each reporting period, it is necessary to estimate the probability that the default happens within the next 12 months (even if there has not been a significant change in credit quality). At the end of period 1, the allowance is estimated as the probability of default in the next 12 months (30%) multiplied by the total probability of default (20%) and the non-recoverable portion in case of default (80%), which is CU 48 ($0.30 \times 0.20 \times 0.80 \times 1,000$). The carrying amount of the loan portfolio at the end of that period will be CU 952 (contractual value CU 1,000 minus allowance CU 48) and there will be a recognition of impairment of CU 48 in the income statement for the first reporting period (day-1 loss). Let's assume that at the end of period 2 there is a significant change in the credit risk of this loan portfolio, and the expected loss happens. At that moment, the allowance must increase to cover all-life expected losses: CU 160. This deterioration (change from allowance CU 48 to allowance CU 160) will be recognised in the income statement of period 2 as an impairment of CU 112. The carrying amount of the loan portfolio will be CU 840 at the end of period 2 and will be recovered by the bank at the end of period 3. Table A1 summarises the impact on the Balance Sheet and Income Statement of both models.

Table A1.   Impact of IASB and FASB expected loss models.

	Balance Sheet Income Statements	FASB	IASB
Period 1	Loan asset	1000	1000
	Minus Allowance	(160)	(48)
	Net value of the asset	840	952
	Impairment loss	−160	−48
Period 2	Loan asset	1000	1000
	Minus Allowance	(160)	(160)
	Net value of the asset	840	840
	Impairment loss	0	−112
Period 3	Net value of the asset	0	0
	Impairment loss	0	0

Example 3

Let's assume the bank originates a 5-year loan portfolio at the end of the first reporting period (period 1), which requires the repayment of the outstanding contractual amount in full at maturity (for the sake of simplicity time value of money is ignored). Its contractual par amount is CU 1,000. The bank estimates at origination that total all-life expected losses are CU 160.

Let's consider total accuracy in the estimation of the whole life expected losses (CU 160) when the portfolio is originated, and that the incurred losses (triggering events) happen at the end of the fourth year (one year before maturity date). Although we are assuming perfect accuracy for the 5-year estimations, this is private information, so investors do not know how accurate the estimations are, and ignore when the triggering events are expected to happen.

Under these circumstances, with an incurred loss model there is no impact on the profit and loss account from year 1 to 3, but in year 4 there is an impairment of CU 160. Consequently, assuming that everything happens as expected, the incurred loss model is not per se unconditionally conservative, as it always requires some news about the underperformance of the asset before recognising a loss (triggering event). Following the FASB model, however, the whole amount (CU 160) should be recognised as a loss at the date of origination. This example shows that the FASB model is entirely unconditionally conservative because the whole loss is recognised before the existence of any evidence about the underperformance of the loans. In this example, apart from the initial loss recognition of CU 160, if it is reported truthfully, the impact on the income statement in the 5 years after origination will be nil. However, annual income could be managed. As nobody can observe the accuracy of the estimate and cannot anticipate when the triggering events occur, managers can exercise their discretion to manage earnings through the following 3 years after origination, and before the loss is incurred. Thus, an impairment reversal of CU 30 (due to a change in estimations of all life expected losses) could be recognised during year 2 (perhaps because it is a recession period and the manager wants to increase reported earnings), while recognising CU 30 as a loss during year 3 (also explained as a change in estimation), and in that way achieving an allowance of CU 160 (the accumulated incurred loss) at the end of year 4. (The IASB model could be partly unconditional conservative, and allow more or less earnings management depending on the estimation at each year end of the next 12-month loss). Table A2 summarises the impact on the Balance Sheet and Income Statement of the incurred loss model and the FASB model considering two scenarios: (A) the manager reports truthfully, and (B) the manager manipulates earnings.

Table A2.   Incurred loss model vs FASB model (true vs manipulated earnings).

	Balance Sheet Income Statements	Incurred	FASB (A)	FASB (B)
Period 1	Loan asset	1000	1000	1000
	Minus Allowance	0	(160)	(160)
	Net value of the asset	1000	840	840
	Impairment loss	0	−160	−160
Period 2	Loan asset	1000	1000	1000
	Minus Allowance	0	(160)	(130)
	Net value of the asset	1000	840	870
	Impairment gain	0	-	+30
Period 3	Loan asset	1000	1000	1000
	Minus Allowance	0	(160)	(160)
	Net value of the asset	1000	840	840
	Impairment loss	0	0	−30
Period 4	Loan asset	1000	1000	1000
	Minus Allowance	(160)	(160)	(160)
	Net value of the asset	840	840	840
	Impairment loss	−160	0	0
Period 5	Net value of the asset	0	0	0
	Impairment loss	0	0	0

Index

Page numbers in *italic* denote figures and in **bold** denote tables.